Between Universalism
and Skepticism

Between Universalism and Skepticism

Ethics as Social Artifact

MICHAEL PHILIPS

New York   Oxford
OXFORD UNIVERSITY PRESS
1994

Oxford University Press

Oxford   New York   Toronto
Delhi   Bombay   Calcutta   Madras   Karachi
Kuala Lumpur   Singapore   Hong Kong   Tokyo
Nairobi   Dar es Salaam   Cape Town
Melbourne   Auckland   Madrid

and associated companies in
Berlin   Ibadan

Published by Oxford University Press, Inc.
200 Madison Avenue, New York, New York 10016

Oxford is a registered trademark of Oxford University Press

Library of Congress Cataloging-in-Publication Data
Philips, Michael, 1942-
Between universalism and skepticism : ethics as social artifact /
[Michael Philips].
p.   cm.
Includes bibliographical references and index.
ISBN 0-19-508646-5
1. Ethics.   I. Title.
BJ1012.P455   1994   171'.7 — dc20   93-24722

246897531
Printed in the United States of America
on acid-free paper

For my wife, Marion, whose amazed criticisms of my earlier moralistic tendencies forced me to rethink basic questions of ethics and whose deep appreciation of innocence, kindness, and humor helped me to understand the relation between the good and the right.

Preface

During the many years I worked on this book, I taught in three philosophy departments and was a visiting scholar at another. I am indebted to students and colleagues at all of these institutions for their comments, criticisms, and encouragement. I am especially grateful to Ramon Lemos, with whom I talked philosophy nearly every working day while we were colleagues at the University of Miami. Although our approaches to ethics are very different, I learned much from his good-natured but penetrating questions, comments, and arguments, and was buoyed by his friendship. I also benefited considerably from frequent conversations with Dick Sikora, Sam Coval, and Earl Winkler during my two years as a visiting professor at the University of British Columbia. The tenacity and intelligence with which each of them criticized my views and with which Dick argued for his own distinctive version of rule utilitarianism forced me to rethink and clarify many ideas. Neil Thomason was my main philosophical companion in Portland during his years at Reed College. His unusually high standards of rigor and argument helped constrain my tendencies to leap from peak to peak, and his tough-minded but good-natured (and often very funny) questions about my views of responsibility and blame (and many other issues) helped to improve them. Gerald Doppelt and I have been friends since graduate school and have had many memorable discussions about ethics and political philosophy over the years. His wildly comic and often deadly accurate portraits of our common philosophical opponents and of professional philosophy in general have helped me to see things more clearly and keep them in perspective. I am also indebted to Mark Okrent and

Charlotte Witt, with whom I exchanged work regularly while we were visiting scholars at U.C. Berkeley, and I am extremely grateful to the readers for Oxford University Press for their many careful and useful criticisms of the text. But I owe the most to my wife, Marion. Before we met I had no interest in writing academic philosophy. She helped convince me that it is a respectable activity and that I would find it rewarding. Our (well, yes) arguments about practical ethical issues helped to awaken me from my dogmatic Kantian slumbers. And I learned much about life and ethics from her courage to face what is real and see the good in it.

Portland, Oregon   M.P.
June 1993

Contents

Between Universalism
and Skepticism

Introduction

Since the end of World War II, much moral philosophy has been driven by the question, "What can be said in condemnation of Nazis and other moral monsters that is not merely an expression of personal preference?" Many contributors to this discussion have accepted something like the following stark assumption: either there is some set of moral standards binding on human beings (or rational agents) as such, or there is no rationally defensible objection to the behavior of Adolf Hitler, Pol Pot, and their like. Here the term "morality" is typically used as if it were the *name* of this set of universal standards (rather than a general term). Society, conscience, or religion may demand one thing. Morality may demand another. Unfortunately, all attempts to defend descriptions of these standards have faced formidable obstacles. So much so that many hearty souls—trusting philosophical argument more than their own deepest prereflective convictions—have abandoned the effort and declared the objective chimerical. Given the stark assumption, their skepticism amounts to the view that there is no more rational justification for opposing murder, torture, theft, or betrayal than there is for preferring the taste of chocolate to that of vanilla. But few are happy with this conclusion, and no one (to my knowledge) acts as if his own moral convictions were mere matters of taste.[1]

By contrast, philosophers who believe in universal morality tend to accept the fundamental convictions by which they live as evidence of deep moral truth. Their starting point is "the natural attitude"— nothing could be more certain than our beliefs that murder and torture are wrong. Their problem is to overcome the enormous set of intellectual barriers that appear to block the move from "I am certain of S" to "S is binding on rational agents as such," where S is a moral standard. Many theories have been proposed, none command consensus. Nonetheless, what keeps this particular cognitivist program alive is confidence in the reliability of our pretheoretic moral convictions (however much they may disagree with those of other times and places, and vary within our own culture).

Some philosophers now believe that there is no need to choose between these alternatives. I will argue for that position here. More specifically, I will argue that we can deny that there is such a thing as universalist morality and still maintain that one set of moral standards is better or wiser for a group of people than another. That is, "morality" should not be used as a proper name for some specific standard or set of standards. There are no such standards (i.e., there is no such thing as Morality). Instead, "morality" should be used as a general term. "Morality" (lower case) stands to moralities as "language" stands to languages. Just as there are no universally binding linguistic rules in relation to which actual languages are evaluated, there are no universally binding moral standards in relation to which actual moral codes are judged.[2] The skeptics' arguments against the universalist are sound. But they don't entail skepticism. Moralities, like languages, are human artifacts and are to be judged by how well they serve us.

As suggested, I am not the first to look for a middle ground between universalism and skepticism. Indeed, throughout the 1970s and the 1980s many philosophers influenced by John Rawls (of the Dewey Lectures) and/or by Kuhnian accounts of science have denied universalism but have argued that ethics has the same claim to rationality that science does.[3] We discover the deep structure of the moral life at our time and place by attempting to set "our" ethical intuitions and background theories in wide reflective equilibrium.[4] We recognize that our collective moral sensibilities (and social theories) will change with time, place, and circumstance; but we insist that if scientific change is no obstacle to scientific rationality, moral change should be no obstacle to moral rationality either. Moral thinkers, like scientists, must simply learn to live with the fact that their results might seem quaint, absurd, or even evil one hundred years from now.

I will argue that this attempt to find a middle ground is also mistaken. Indeed, it is subject to many of the objections that skeptics make of universalists who appeal to "our" moral intuitions. Moreover, because it tends to assume a nonexistent moral consensus—or to suppose that such a consensus can be approximated given appropriate reflection—it ignores serious moral (and empirical) differences grounded in gender, class, and culture. Accordingly, it has little or nothing to say about the role (and limits) of reason in adjudicating such conflicts. On my view, Ethics as Social Artifact (ESA), the differences must be adjudicated. We cannot assume that the wisest or most reasonable code is simply a compromise between competing and divergent moral (and empirical) visions.

Some rule utilitarians and perhaps some contractarians seek a middle ground that can be defended without appealing to intuitions. We are on the same side of one important line. Yet there are also significant differences between these views and ESA. ESA rejects the desire satisfaction theory of the good on which these sorts of theories are typically grounded (and rejects traditional hedonism as well).[5] It also rejects the view that some abstract notion of rational bargainers, indeed, any notion of bargainers at all, is relevant to the process of justifying moral codes.[6] Very roughly, ESA holds that moral standards are justified to the extent that they promote a reasonably valued way of life, and it evaluates ways of life by considering the concrete, historically specific goods and evils they promote and protect us against. Unlike standard forms of rule utilitarianism and contractarianism, then, it moves from the ground up, not the top down. We begin with a rich account of a social milieu, a set of individuals, and the wider world in which they live. And, roughly, we ask whether the relevant individuals have rational complaints against the moral standards by which they organize their mutual interactions and relationships.[7] If there are no such complaints, the standards are justified.

As this suggests, ESA is not a substantive moral theory but rather a theory about how moral standards are rationally defended and criticized. The point is to show how the argument goes when the argument goes right. Since the arguments for or against a moral standard may include appeals to controversial or uncertain empirical claims, moreover, ESA acknowledges that there is often considerable room for rational disagreement about standards. Given the limits of our knowledge, we can expect cases in which the arguments for each of two competing standards are equally strong. Moreover, since ESA regards moral standards as tools, it holds that it is in principle possible that two competing standards or codes may be equally justified.

Because ESA holds that standards of right action are justified by appealing to the evils they prevent and the goods they promote, it is a teleological rather than deontic moral theory. In addition, it is an instrumental rather than a metaphysical theory. According to metaphysical theories, moralities are evaluated by how well they conform to some supercode (Morality) which is binding on rational beings as such. Morality has and needs no point or purpose extrinsic to itself. It tells us how to do right and be good and how to evaluate the actions and characters of others. And that is the only justification it requires. According to instrumental theories, moralities are tools and are properly evaluated by how well they do their jobs. Since this is a function of cultural traditions, economic circumstances, and other variables, a moral code may be justified for one society but not another.[8]

The strategy of this book is straightforward. I begin by criticizing the main theoretical supports for universalism. Chapter 1 is a sustained attack on various versions of intuitionism. Chapter 2 argues against various forms of the respect for persons view. Since wide reflective equilibrium has an important intuitionist dimension, I discuss that view in chapter 1 as well.

I am not, of course, the first person to attack these positions. There are sound objections to each of them scattered through the literature. But the point of these chapters is to provide a sustained, systematic, detailed, and comprehensive critique of them. The criticisms in the literature tend to be insufficiently detailed, systematic, and sustained. Often, they are heavily rhetorical. For this reason, they have not been terribly effective at convincing their opponents. Appeals to intuitions and to respect for persons continue to abound in discussions of abortion, euthanasia, capital punishment, workers' rights, pornography, the distribution of resources, and other questions of applied ethics. And appeals to reflective equilibrium are still current. The arguments in chapters 1 and 2 are directed at those who make these appeals. They combine certain familiar criticisms with certain original ones. But their main virtue is that they cover the ground more carefully and comprehensively than other attacks on these positions. Philosophers who reject these approaches already may find this tedious. They are invited to skip these chapters and to begin with chapter 3.

After arguing against what I take to be the main deontological theories of justification in chapters 1 and 2, I consider the main teleological alternatives to ESA, namely, rule utilitarianism and abstract contractarianism. As I understand them, these theories depend on desire satisfaction or hedonistic theories of the good.[9] I argue against these conceptions in chapter 3, and in chapters 5 and 6, I develop an alternative that is suitable to evaluating moral standards. My claim is that standard desire satisfaction and hedonic accounts are both philosophically unsatisfying and too abstract for this purpose, and that we must appeal instead to more specific, historically situated values. But these values are open to criticism. Chapters 5 and 6 describe strategies for rationally evaluating them, and chapter 6 develops a philosophical theory of the good that supports those strategies.

Chapter 4 describes and defends the heart of the theory. Every human society has certain fundamental needs. Among other things, it must care for and socialize its young, produce and distribute material goods, heal the injured and the sick, enforce its moral standards, and protect itself from attack. In every society, moreover, there is a division of labor to meet these needs. This division of labor creates what I call "domains." Roughly, a domain is defined in terms of a set of goods and evils and a set of roles. The goods and evils define the purposes of the domain, and the roles define the social "structures" that are supposed to realize those purposes. Roughly, roles themselves are defined in relation to qualifications, rights, duties, privileges, reward schedules, virtues, and vices. Examples of domains in contemporary North American societies include the family, the realm of commerce, the health care delivery system, the educational system, the criminal justice system, and so forth. Each of these may be understood as a set of interrelated roles responsible for producing certain goods and suppressing certain evils.

According to ESA, all moral standards are domain sensitive. ESA distinguishes between three categories of standards, namely, core moral standards, domain-specific standards, and group-related standards. Core standards regulate the activities that any society must regulate to perpetuate itself and provide its members a tolerable existence. They include regulations governing homicide, property use, information exchanges, physical violence, sexual access, and so forth. Accordingly, core moral standards apply in every (or almost every) domain. Nonetheless, core standards are domain sensitive. The weight and scope of these standards differ justifiably from domain to domain depending significantly on the goods and evils at stake in those domains. Stealing, for example, involves the violation of the regulation governing property use, but what counts as stealing in one domain may not count as stealing in another, and the weight of the prohibition against stealing is domain sensitive as well.[10] I argue for this in chapter 4.

Domain-specific standards define roles and, ultimately, social structures. They establish qualifications for role occupancy; they assign rights, duties, rewards, and penalties to role occupants; and they define role-related virtues and vices. These assignments are justified to a significant extent by appealing to the reasonable justificatory goods and evils of the target domain (although the reasonable goods and evils of other domains and more general goods and evils are also relevant). As indicated, the account of goods and evils on which this theory relies is developed and defended in chapters 5 and 6.

Finally, group-specific standards assign roles to persons as members of identifiable groups. Thus, many societies have standards governing our interactions and relations as members of an age set, a gender, an ethnic group, a religious group, or a hereditary caste or class. Given the enormous waste and misery such standards have "justified" in the past, many of us are understandably hostile to them. However, ESA provides no a priori reason to reject them as such. Indeed, it provides us with a basis of accepting some and rejecting others. Thus, age-set standards of some kind are almost certainly reasonable in any society. Moreover, the significance of age will vary reasonably from domain to domain. I will discuss other cases in chapter 4.

There are two arguments for ESA in chapter 4. The first assumes that the arguments in chapters 1 and 2 have cleared the field of deontic moral theories and attempts to show that ESA is superior to its main teleological alternatives, rule utilitarianism, and abstract contractarianism. Each of those theories holds that there is a single rationally compelling principle for the aggregation/distribution (hereafter "a/distribution") of utility in general. Like many others, I argue that there is not. There is an enormous range of possibilities between the major pre-Rawlsean alternatives, namely, egalitarianism (equalize distribution first, worry about aggregation later) and utilitarianism (maximize aggregation, forget about distribution). That is, Rawls's Difference Principle is but one of many live possibilities on the continuum between these poles. And none of the possibilities is uniquely rational.

But there are reasonable principles for a/distribution at the domain level. And even where there is room for rational disagreement at this level, there is sometimes sufficient agreement to settle controversies. Michael Walzer is right in his claim that different goods are justifiably distributed in different ways.[11] But ESA provides a clearer account of how principles of a/distribution are defended than he does.

The second argument is that ESA explains an important and pervasive but generally unrecognized feature of moral reasoning. Virtually everyone recognizes that making moral decisions often requires determining the weights of competing moral considerations, but there is scandalously little theorizing about how this is properly done. Many discussions of actual moral problems assume or presuppose that moral reasons (considerations, principles) have constant weights across contexts and that we decide between conflicting considerations by choosing the set that has the most weight.[12] I argue that this is false. The weight of a moral consideration is not constant, but varies from domain to domain in systematic ways that have been generally ignored by moral philosophers (there are variations within domains as well). ESA explains these systematic variations. Moral thinking turns out to be more complicated than most philosophers acknowledge, but complicated in believable and illuminating ways (and no more complicated than, for example, the rules governing conversation).

ESA is primarily a theory about the justification of moral standards. Since moral standards govern our behavior as members of groups, we are really asking, "By what set of standards should we govern our mutual affairs?" Roughly, we are wondering what is best for a group or individuals as members of a group (I will make this more precise presently).[13] For that reason, the question must be asked from an impartial perspective. Yet obviously, we make moral choices as individuals. And I argue in chapter 7 that the fact that a standard is justified for a group does not by itself entail that an individual is obligated to act on it. If the justified standard is not currently in place, this would be wrong under certain circumstances. And even if a justified standard is in place, there are circumstances under which it is not obligatory, that is, under which principled nonconformity is justified. We have standards governing these issues as well. The first part of chapter 7 addresses these complexities.

The second part of chapter 7 is devoted to the question of moral motivation. If the violation of morality mutilates the best part of ourselves, as Socrates says in the *Crito*, we have a reason to be moral. Kant gives us a similar reason, but ESA rejects the metaphysics that underlie such noble sentiments. What substitute reasons, if any, does it offer for being moral? Indeed, what reason can *any* theory that rejects the relevant metaphysics offer? I argue that a reason can be given, but not one that will *convince* a hard-core amoralist. This does not mean that there is anything wrong with the reason. The idea that a good reason must somehow *convince* an amoralist is confused to begin with. In any case, the real challenges posed by the amoralism are social and psychological. The pressing problem is to instill the desire to be moral. I argue that a form of moral education compatible with ESA can do this job.

This overview of ESA may well provoke a variety of doubts and questions in the minds of attentive readers. I hope that the following chapters will answer most of them. But four very general doubts are worth discussing here. I will state these in the form of objections: (1) ESA entails skepticism; (2) ESA is covertly universalist; (3) ESA is not a theory about the justification of specifically *moral* standards; and (4) ESA is essentially partisan in its outlook and provides no principled basis for extending moral boundaries beyond a particular society. I will consider these in turn.

Since ESA asserts that a standard may be justified in one society but not another, it denies that moral standards are true or false. According to the first objection, this entails that moral judgments are not true or false either, and we appear to be left with a form of skepticism.

Although I have heard this objection several times in conversation, I have yet to see the force of it. According to ESA, the proper terms of evaluation for moral standards are not (strictly speaking) "true" and "false" but rather "reasonable" and "unreasonable" (or perhaps "wise" and "unwise"). But this does not lead to skepticism since the claim that a standard is reasonable or unreasonable is either true or false. Moreover, the denial that standards are true or false does not entail that judgments of acts are neither true nor false. Very roughly and incompletely, an act is wrong if it violates a justified standard currently in place. In some cases it is clearly true that an action does this. In general, the claim that an act violates a rule may be true or false without a rule's being true or false (whatever that could mean). A pawn move may violate a rule of chess, but this does not mean that the rule itself must be true or false.

According to the second objection, ESA is not skeptical but rather universalistic. After all, ESA holds that there is a criterion for evaluating moral codes that holds for *every* moral code. But this objection is sound only if that criterion is itself a moral standard. But it is not. We cannot use that criterion to evaluate actions or character. In this way the criterion ESA proposes differs from the utility principle, the categorical imperative, and the various items on the lists of rights, duties, and morally relevant considerations in the literature.

It also differs from abstract principles like "Respect persons." Although this principle rarely if ever applies directly to actions, some hold that we can *derive* action-related principles from it (by analyzing personhood or practical agency).[14] That is, action-related principles are supposed to be specifications or applications of this one. However, one cannot *derive* standards from the criterion of evaluation provided by ESA. That criterion allows us to evaluate standards as reasonable or unreasonable, but it does not entail that some set of standards is best. To arrive at standards by the ESA criterion, moreover, we cannot rely on analysis *alone*. We require a lot of information about historically specific goods and evils and about the impact of adopting various alternatives with respect to them. ESA, then, is a theory about the justification of moral standards. Other theories of justification include intuitionism, wide reflective equilibrium, rule utilitarianism, contractarianism, theological ethics (i.e., the appeal to God's will or wisdom), cultural relativism, and various forms of naturalism. All of these theories are "objectivist" in the sense that they believe that moral standards can be justified. But not all of them are universalist. Many of them acknowledge that a standard that is justified for one group may not be justified for another and that a given standard may have different weights in different groups.

Theories of moral justification are often misleadingly presented as if they were moral standards, that is, as if they told us how to act. Thus, it is said that theological ethics tells us to obey the law of God, that rule utilitarianism tells us (very roughly) to act on principles which maximize utility, and cultural relativism tells us to act in accordance with the dictates of our culture. But it is misleading to say that they thereby tell us how to act. The theories in question have no specific action-regulating or person-judging content. Indeed, people who subscribe to the same theory of justification may subscribe to very different standards for judging actions and character, and people who subscribe to different theories of justification may agree to the very same standards. It is more illuminating to think of a particular theory, say cultural relativism, as holding (a) that one ought to obey justified moral standards and (b) that moral standards are justified by virtue of being accepted by a culture.

Third, it might be objected that although ESA tells us how to justify rules governing various social interactions and relationships, it does not tell us how to justify *moral* rules. Indeed, it treats moral rules as if they were no different in principle from rules of etiquette or rules governing participation in conversations. Further, it is hard to see what resources the theory has for making a principled distinction between moral rules and rules of other kinds.[15] By demoting moral rules to the status of rules of etiquette, ESA rejects one traditional mark of the moral, namely, supremacy. By rejecting universalism it rejects another.[16] What can it, or any instrumentalist theory, offer in their place?

Before trying to answer this question, it is worth pointing out that, strictly speaking, we do not need a theory of this kind to say how moral rules are justified. For that purpose, we require only a plausible extensional account of the moral. If our theory of justification holds for every plausible candidate, that is good enough. It does not matter if it also holds for rules not usually included on that list. In fact, the more general the method, the better.

Can ESA distinguish between moral and nonmoral social rules? It is not clear what work such a distinction is supposed to do and hence by what criteria we are supposed to evaluate the candidates. We often speak as if every society and religion has a morality; for example, we refer to Homeric morality, Celtic morality, Buddhist morality, and so forth.[17] We *could* take this as our central datum and distinguish between moral and nonmoral rules on the basis of what all of these institutions have in common, treating our own particular institution as if it were just one among many. On the other hand, we could define 'morality' by declaring our own local version the paradigm and by trying to discover what is characteristic about that. In the first case we will get something very general. In the second case we will get something considerably more particular (e.g., we might conclude that rights are essential and, therefore, that not every society has a morality). In either case we might discover something interesting.

A third approach combines these strategies by looking for something fundamental to our own institution that also applies to every other or almost every other candidate as well. Here we look for something general, but give our own institution pride of place. I think that this yields the most interesting result, and this is how I will approach the problem here. To begin with, then, every society must have rules governing the interactions and relations of its members, but not every society *must* have what we regard as a morality. Whether a society has a morality depends in part on the attitudes of its members toward violations of and conformity to its standards. Suppose that the terms of evaluation are entirely prudential, for example, "intelligent" and "stupid." Violators are penalized because this is necessary to sustain the system of standards. But no one thinks any worse of violators (or better of obeyers) as such. Indeed, whether violations are intelligent or stupid depends entirely on the risks and the benefits. If obedience costs too much relative to lost opportunity, one is stupid to obey. This attitude is like the attitude athletes have toward the rules in certain organized sports, for example, basketball with referees. Fouling violates the rules of basketball, and if a player is caught fouling by the referee there is a penalty. But no one feels guilty about fouling per se, and no one is blamed for fouling per se by others. Fouling is part of the game.[18] There are smart fouls and stupid fouls.[19] A society that adopted this attitude toward rules would lack something central to *our* institution of morality, namely, the moral emotions. If feelings like guilt, blame, shame, pride, righteous indignation, forgiveness, and moral admiration are not regarded as appropriate responses to someone's rule-related performances, something essential is missing.

But the appropriate connection between these responses and the rules is at best a necessary condition of having a morality. We do not identify standards as moral standards merely because they are appropriately connected to these responses. Arguably, we might be trained to have these responses in relation to the rules of grammar or of bridge. We resist calling those standards moral because they do not govern the right kinds of actions. Moral standards regulate actions and relationships that are of fundamental importance to the survival of a society and the well-being of its members.[20] Examples of such actions include homicide, physical assaults, property use, information exchanges, and promises. Examples of such relationships include husband-wife, parent-child, doctor-patient, producer-consumer, and citizen-police. It is tempting to describe standards governing the former as moral standards, properly so-called, and standards governing the latter as ethical standards. But many philosophers use 'morality' and 'ethics' as rough synonyms, so this might be confusing. Moreover, unlike some other theories, ESA holds that standards of each kind are domain sensitive and that they are justified in roughly the same way.[21] So we mark the distinction by calling the former core standards and the latter domain-specific standards.

By appealing to these features, a defender of ESA can make a principled distinction between moral standards and social standards of other kinds that works for his society and most other societies as well. Nonetheless, there is a sense in which ESA undermines the significance of that distinction. Every society must have regulations that govern the sorts of activities governed by moral rules. But it is possible in principle that a society could promote a reasonably valued way of life by regulating these activities without the aid of the characteristically moral responses and emotions. Perhaps we would do better without guilt, blame, and other moral emotions. In that case, although we would continue to regulate what moral standards now regulate, we would not have the institution of morality as we know it.[22] We would have something better. But ESA will tell us how to justify those regulations as well. In general, the point of ESA is to provide a method for justifying rules regulating activities and relationships that must be regulated for societies to survive and for people to live tolerably good lives. If it can do that, it can do enough.

According to the final objection, ESA is parochial. It tells us how to identify standards that groups should adopt to regulate the interactions and relationships of their members, but it ignores relations between groups. In particular, it fails to provide a principled basis for denying that a society may promote the good of its members by adopting a predatory attitude toward other societies. But this is wrong and we need a theory that explains why. We also need a theory that explains why it is wrong for some members of a given group entirely to disregard the interests of other members. Why can't they simply adopt a code that promotes a reasonably valued way of life for themselves?

We can address both concerns by getting clearer about what a theory of justification for moral standards tries to achieve. Roughly, we want to find a way to justify rules governing certain important relations and interactions between members of a group. But what group? How widely do we cast the net? Roughly, we cast it widely enough to cover the actions and relations that concern us. Suppose we are interested in how members of a given society should govern their mutual interactions and relationships, for example, the French. We could simply ignore interactions and relations between the French and other groups. In that case we say nothing about the moral standards appropriate to those relations. But to the extent that we do so, and to the extent that we ignore the impact of the French-to-French code on other groups, the French-to-French code simply promotes collective French self-interest.

On the other hand, we can look for standards governing the relationships between the French and other groups, and we can evaluate French-to-French standards in part by how well they take the interests of other groups into account. In this case, we look down from our Olympian peak and ask, "Given the current facts of the matter, how should all those people organize their lives together? What standards should they adopt now and what standards should they work toward in the future?" If we are looking for standards governing the relation between groups or between individuals of different groups, that is our question.

The fact that we may ask that question of the larger group does not mean that we must ignore national and social boundaries. Almost certainly, the best set of standards will acknowledge the importance of societal boundaries and cultural traditions. As I will argue in chapter 5, what is good for us depends on our nature as historically situated beings, and this admits of considerable variation. We do not want to lose our traditions and the goods they make available to us.[23] Nonetheless, we need standards that govern the relations between societies and between individuals of different societies as well. And the main point is that when we are looking for standards we must take the interest of everyone concerned into account. Again, that is simply the nature of our question. We are wondering how *those* people should live together.[24]

Of course, there is nothing to stop a society from adopting standards that promote a reasonably valued way of life for its own members but that endorse predatory attitudes toward other societies. This is a stance of collective self-interest. That stance can also be adopted by subgroups within a society (e.g., by social classes, ethnic groups, crime syndicates, or clans). Obviously, such a stance can never be justified in relation to the wider group. But a predatory society or subgroup might ask why it should care about this. This is just the problem of egoism at the level of collectivities. I address the problem of egoism in relation to the individual in the second half of chapter 7. But what I argue there can be extended to this problem as well.

Before launching the argument, one further point is worth mentioning. Nowhere in this book do I directly address the question of moral realism. My purpose is to discuss the justification of moral standards, and I think I can say all that I need to say about that without worrying about questions of ontology. Of course, ESA is incompatible with certain moral ontologies. For example, it denies that rightness and wrongness are properties of actions in any strong sense, that is, that they stand to actions as liquidity stands to water or solidity stands to stones. But only universalists are tempted to hold that rightness and wrongness are properties in this (or any other) very strong sense, and I argue against the main attempts to justify universalism in chapters 1 and 2.

Nonetheless, it is arguable that ESA is realistic in some weak sense. For it holds that moral standards are justified in relation to certain sets of facts (roughly, facts about the consequences of adopting the standard). So the claim that a standard is justified entails that certain facts obtain. Since the rightness and wrongness of particular actions depend on whether certain standards are justified, the rightness and wrongness of actions depend on whether these facts obtain as well. It is not clear to me whether this counts as an interesting version of realism. With respect to that question I am prepared to let the chips fall where they may.

Notes

1. A rational person who took this attitude would attempt to divest himself of moral attitudes to the extent that they interfered with his general level of preference satisfaction. The degree of divestiture would depend on what else he wanted. But to the extent that his desires were Hobbesian, to the extent that he desired wealth and power, moral attitudes would seriously constrain what he could do to maximize desire satisfaction.

David Gauthier, of course, argues that one nonetheless does better as a "constrained maximizer" (*Morals by Agreement*, Oxford University Press, Oxford, 1986). So the degree of divestiture will also depend on the strength of his and other decision theoretic arguments.

2. This is compatible with the claim that there are in fact universal features of human languages, and that all human languages must have certain properties to serve us effectively. The same is true of moralities. To serve us effectively, all moralities must regulate certain types of activities, e.g., homicide, violence, property exchanges, information exchanges, etc. Societies that did not regulate these activities could not long survive (hence, neither could their moralities). Moreover, given certain facts about human biology, ecology, and social dynamics, there are limits on how an effective morality can do this. Universalism, however, holds that all such activities are properly regulated in the same way.

Stuart Hampshire makes this point in chapter 7 of *Morality and Conflict* (Harvard University Press, Cambridge, Mass., 1983, p. 142): "It is a plausible, though still unconfirmed, hypothesis that there is a deep structure of universal grammar, determined in its turn by the needs of learning to hear, to understand, and to speak, and that this natural and universal syntax limits the diversity of historical languages. So also in the morality that governs sexuality, marriage and family relationships, it is difficult to overlook the existence of two layers of moral requirement and moral prohibition, the natural and the conventional. The dependence of very young children on adult nurture, the onset of sexual maturity, the instinctual desires associated with motherhood, the comparative helplessness of the old, are all biological features of a standard outline of human life, which may be appealed to as imposing some limit on moral requirements at all times and in all places." As I read him, Hampshire is not arguing that, if Noam Chomsky is correct, actual languages must be *evaluated* in relation to the rules of some deep structure. After all, Chomsky's point is that all languages express that structure to begin with. Hampshire is suggesting an explanation of this. "Languages" that did not have this structure could not be learned *by us*. Accordingly, no human community could adopt them. On this reading, Hampshire is suggesting that no morality regulating certain activities in certain ways (e.g., sexual access) could be adopted by a human group or could survive. This is not universalist in the sense I have in mind since it does not justify the moral standards of a group in relation to some supercode (morality itself). Rather it imposes restraints on the possibilities and explains those restraints in terms of our biology. Moreover, given the barbarous ways in which various societies have in fact regulated the relevant activities, the limits on what is possible do not seem to be terribly demanding. However, as I shall argue, certain general biological, ecological, and sociological facts place much stronger limits on what can be justified.

3. A brave alternative is Baruch Brody's attempt to defend universal moral truth by comparing ethics to science ("Intuitions and Objective Moral Knowledge," *Monist*, 62, October 1979, pp. 440–56).

4. This position was first developed by Norman Daniels ("Wide Reflective Equilibrium and Theory Acceptance in Ethics," *Journal of Philosophy*, 76, 1979, pp. 256–83). Daniels, however, remained hopeful that the method could arrive at a universal morality. I discuss his views in chapter 1.

5. I say 'typically' grounded because there are exceptions. Tom Scanlon, for example, defends a contractarian account of morality that does not depend on such a theory (see, e.g., his essay "A Contractualist Alternative," in Joseph De Marco and Richard Fox, eds., *New Directions in Ethics*, Routledge and Kegan Paul, New York and London, 1986).

6. It is perhaps worth noting that, strictly speaking, Rawls's decision procedure does not involve bargaining. The original position need be occupied by only one person. The task is to solve a certain problem rather than to arrive at a negotiated settlement. For a detailed defense of this claim see Jean Hampton, "Contracts and Choices: Does Rawls Have a Social Contract Theory?" *Journal of Philosophy*, 77, June 1980, p. 315.

7. This formulation is rough because it ignores the distinction between "insiders" and "outsiders." I will discuss this problem later in the Introduction.

8. Certain views combine elements of instrumental and metaphysical theories. Gert, for example, believes that there is a universal moral code binding on all rational beings and that existing moralities must be evaluated in relation to that code. But he also holds that morality has a point or purpose extrinsic to itself (viz., preventing evil). See Bernard Gert, *The Moral Rules*, Harper and Row, New York, 1973, pp. 60–69.

9. As suggested, contractarianism may take other forms as well. Abstract contractarian theories justify moral standards in relation to desire satisfaction theories of goods and evils. As I suggest in chapter 4, one could also run a contractarian strategy in relation to more concrete sets of goods and evils. As we approach the appropriate level of concreteness, contractarian defenses and criticism of moral standards will increasingly resemble ESA defenses and criticisms. The extent to which differences remain may vary from one contractarian theory to another, depending on the details.

10. In *Spheres of Justice* (Basic Books, New York, 1983) Michael Walzer argues for a similar position in relation to principles of distribution. With Rawls as his main target, Walzer denies that there is a single principle for the distribution of social goods. He argues instead that principles of distribution differ from sphere to sphere in relation to the social meaning of the goods distributed. This is very much on the right track. As suggested, ESA claims that domain sensitivity holds not only of principles of distribution but of all moral standards. In addition, Walzer is not very clear about how spheres are individuated or how we determine the social meaning of the relevant goods. ESA has more to say about how domains are structured, and much more to say about the nature of the good.

11. Walzer, *Spheres of Justice*.

12. I discuss this position in detail in chapter 4. For references to discussions that embody this position, see chapter 4, note 22.

13. I will argue that we need to consider the interests of all affected individuals. This includes nonhuman animals. But I do not consider the degree to which we need to take the interests of nonhuman animals into account. Nor do I discuss (in any depth) the degree to which social or national boundaries are morally significant. These are extremely important questions, but they are too complicated to discuss here.

14. I discuss several such attempts in chapter 2.

15. The criticism would surely be made by Bernard Gert (*Moral Rules*, especially pp. 3–19 and pp. 60–75). Gert believes that "morality" is a proper name for a universal code and argues that philosophers who deny this cannot distinguish between moral rules and social rules of other kinds.

16. Gewirth (*Reason and Morality*, University of Chicago Press, 1978) takes supremacy to be definitive of the moral. Many philosophers take universality to be definitive, including Gert (*Moral Rules*, pp. 66–69). After reviewing various attempts to define the moral in his text on ethics, Tom Beauchamp denies that we can understand the distinction between moral and nonmoral rules in relation to necessary and sufficient conditions. But he includes universality and supremacy as elements of sets that can be jointly sufficient conditions for 'morality' (*Philosophical Ethics*, McGraw-Hill, New York, 1983, p. 15). I have argued elsewhere that the supremacy claim is ambiguous (see "Moralism and the Good," *Philosophical Studies*, 52, no. 1, July 1987). It is readily apparent that neither of the possible readings I distinguish offers a plausible basis for characterizing the moral. If we conjoin these readings, moreover, the claim that moral considerations are supreme is very implausible.

17. Gert strongly suggests that these are misuses of the term (*Moral Rules*, pp. 3–4). I think that there are several coherent ways to understand these uses. In what follows, I defend what I take to be the most illuminating of these for the purposes of justifying standards.

18. In "pick up games," of course, the attitude is different. Without referees, there is a code of honor with respect to fouling. This is the nontrivial significance to the anarchist claim that laws create criminals.

19. Some corporations appear to think this way about the law. Violations are stupid or intelligent depending on whether they are cost-effective.

20. Gert's argument against appealing to the moral emotions is primarily directed against emotivism and its relatives (*Moral Rules*, pp. 13–15). Accordingly, he does not consider the possibility that the presence of moral emotions in a society may be a necessary condition of that society's having a morality. The condition that moral standards must regulate certain categories of action, moreover, is consistent with his claim on p. 14 that "no attempt to distinguish moral from nonmoral judgments can be made without taking into account the subject matter of the judgment."

21. For example, Gert (*Moral Rules*, pp. 121–24) does not include domain-specific standards among his moral rules. Instead, he includes the general rule "Do your duty." Unfortunately, he provides no method for evaluating

standards that define these duties. He writes as if a theory of moral justification does not need to provide a method for evaluating standards that govern the relations between parent and child, doctor and patient, or employer and employee.

22. This is a matter of degree. We might dispense with some emotions but not others (e.g., guilt and blame but not admiration). In that case we would have something like what we now call morality.

23. Related problems arise within societies as well. Many societies are diverse, and the members of such a society will almost certainly be better off if the society respects diversity to some degree. But how much? If we respected diversity completely, we would permit members of subcultures to govern their mutual interactions and relations entirely by their own standards (as long as no outsiders were affected). If a group traditionally settled disputes by duelling or carved designs in the faces of their children at puberty, we would allow them to do so. Not only would we refrain from passing laws against these practices, but we would also refrain from attempting to mobilize the moral opinion of the society as a whole against it. Is that excessive? According to ESA, we cannot answer such questions in the abstract. Given different background conditions, we may get different answers.

24. Precisely what these standards should be is an enormously difficult and important question. Among other things, we need to decide whether national and social boundaries are as important as we have traditionally taken them to be. We also need to decide to what extent, under what conditions, and in what ways relatively better-off societies are required to rescue or to help transform relatively worse-off societies. Again, ESA does not offer answers to these questions. Rather, it provides us with an account of the way the argument should go.

1

Intuitionism and
Wide Reflective Equilibrium

Universalism holds that there is a set of ranked or weighted moral standards binding on rational agents as such that is sufficient for the moral life. Agreement on rankings is essential. After all, the universalist believes that there is one morality. But if we agree that killing and promise breaking are wrong, and you believe that it is worse to break a promise, but I believe it is worse to kill, there is an important moral difference between us. To the extent that we disagree on rankings and weighings, we will disagree about judgments in particular cases; and clearly, to the extent that we disagree about cases for *that* reason, we have different moral outlooks or subscribe to different moralities. In the limiting case, we might agree on all the same standards but so disagree on weights that we disagree in every case in which considerations conflict, that is, in almost every case. In this case, it is ridiculous to say that we hold the same morality. We simply believe that the same kinds of considerations are morally relevant. The universalist wants more. Roughly, she wants a morality binding on rational beings that produces uniform agreement on decidable cases.[1] This requires that rational beings accept the same standards and rank or weigh them in roughly the same way.

This, in any case, is the universalist ideal. Philosophers may subscribe to this ideal to different degrees. One might hold that only some standards are universal and that actual moral codes are rational to the extent that they assign these standards their proper weights. For reasons indicated, these weights must be the same in every rational code. Accordingly, any universal element of a rational morality must have greater weight than any elective elements. This is because the weight of a standard in any given code is relative to the weights of the other standards in that code. Thus, if some purportedly universal standard U has more weight than an elective standard E in code 1 but less weight that E in code 2, U would have different weights in these codes and could not be authentically universal.

There are several current strategies for justifying universalism. In this chapter, I consider intuitionism and its fashionable successor theory, wide reflective equilibrium. Both are moral epistemologies, that is, views about how moral standards are justified. We will begin with the intuitionist strategy.

Intuitionism: *Old Style and New*

The intuitionist strategy for universalism generalizes over purportedly successful results of the intuitionist method.[2] Our intuitions tell us that standards $S_1, S_2 \ldots S_n$ are true and knowable and have weights w_1, $w_2 \ldots w_n$ respectively. These standards are sufficient for the moral life. Therefore, there is a set of standards binding on rational agents as such that is sufficient for the moral life. The main target of my criticism is the first premiss of this argument. But I will also show that even if both premisses are true, the conclusion doesn't follow. It is worth noting that the argument against the first premiss undermines not only the intuitionist argument for universalism, but also the unsupplemented appeal to intuition to establish any moral claim. Such appeals abound in discussions of punishment, distributive justice, euthanasia, abortion, preferential hiring, and numerous other issues in applied ethics.

Intuitional arguments for universalism vary in two ways. First, the intuitions that ground the argument may be about cases or about principles or about both cases and principles. And second, these intuitions may be said to be fallible or infallible. Baruch Brody (among others) takes the first to mark a critical difference between "old-style" intuitionists such as David Ross and contemporary intuitionists like himself.[3] Old-style intuitionism, he claims, is committed to a kind of "Moral Cartesianism." Although he doesn't say precisely what Moral Cartesianism is, I presume he means the view that every moral principle is either self-evident itself or deducible from a self-evident principle. And he is right to object. In any case, there are many apparent exceptions (e.g., "Justice requires equality of welfare"; "It is morally permissible to get even"; "Sexual seduction is wrong"; etc.). These principles are not self-evidently true or false, and they don't seem to follow from principles that are. At the very least, this establishes that old-style intuitionism is incomplete. New-style intuitionism is not committed to this Cartesianism. Principles are established or rejected by appeal to cases.

Old-style intuitionism is incomplete in a second way as well. The standards it proposes hold only prima facie or ceteris paribus. And Ross and his followers provide no principled method for delimiting their range or determining their weights. Thus, we might agree on Ross's list of prima facie duties but—because we assign considerations different weights—we might also disagree on virtually every case in which considerations conflict (or fail to hold for some other reason). Ross, of course, would not have expected this result. He would have expected morally sensitive persons to decide cases in roughly the same way. But Ross's expectation seems to imply that there is some ordering principle or ordering techniques at work to get us from lists of morally relevant considerations (or prima facie duties) to all things considered outcomes. And Ross appears to believe that there is no such method or technique.

The best a Rossean can offer here is some scheme for weighing moral considerations. And if he is going to continue to insist on self-evidence in relation to principles, that scheme must describe something like self-evident rules of priority or superiority (a proposal actually adopted by Kurt Baier).[4] What alternative does he have? But such rules of priority require that the weight of moral reasons be constant across contexts (i.e., if r makes a difference of a certain magnitude in two otherwise identical cases, r will make a difference of the same magnitude in any two otherwise identical cases). I have argued against this elsewhere and develop the argument further in chapter 5.[5] In any case, few among us will claim intuitions with respect to questions like "Is lying per se worse than promise breaking per se?" or "Is stealing per se worse than causing unnecessary suffering per se (or some specific amount of unnecessary suffering)?" Indeed, we have a hard time understanding what "lying per se" is.[6] New-style intuitionism does not have this problem. It at least holds out the hope of discovering an order behind our convergent judgments. It does this by examining the judgments themselves.

New-style intuitionism also easily accommodates fallibility. As we have seen, when it comes to principles at least, Ross and his followers require certainty in matters of morals. New-style intuitionism more plausibly allows for considerable fallibility with respect to principles and cases. On Brody's view, intuitions about cases stand to principles as empirical observations stand to scientific laws. Like observations, intuitions can be mistaken. But this does not undermine their status as evidence. Judgments about principles are also fallible. Like scientific hypotheses, they explain but are underdetermined by the evidence.

For these reasons I take Brody's brand of intuitionism to be more promising than Ross's and I will focus my objections on it. Most of my objections, however, will also apply to Ross's version and to attempts to combine the two (e.g., narrow reflective equilibrium).

Three Arguments for Trusting Intuitions

Suppose that, using Brody's method, I arrive at a set of standards that explains all my intuitions about cases. Why have I done more than systematize my own responses? That is, on what ground can I claim to have discovered universal moral standards? The literature on intuitionism offers three answers here, but the first two are parasitic on the third, roughly, that ideally rational intuitions converge.

To begin with, there are appeals to our high level of confidence that some intuitions are glimpses of universal moral standards. The strategy is borrowed from G. E. Moore's famous handwaving "proof" of the external world. Roughly, the universalist confronts the skeptic with examples so compelling that no rational argument can unseat them. Baby-torturing cases are favorites here. Caligula shrieks with delight as he applies the hot brand to the bare feet of his innocent, helpless, and terrified nephews. No rational being can deny that this is monstrous. Only the most shameless skeptic can question the universality of the standard "Torturing babies for pleasure is wrong." But if the method works here, it is reasonable to believe that it works elsewhere. And if this standard is universal it is reasonable to believe that others are as well.

But appeals to our levels of confidence are not by themselves compelling. They become compelling only when (a) they converge on the same doctrines or (b) we can give the right kind of explanation of divergence, namely, an explanation that shows that all but one of a set of conflicting intuitions is irrational or irrelevant. Once we eliminate cases under (b), the move from confidence to evidence requires convergence. Where intuitions of sane persons diverge, and (b) fails, how can we simply take confidence as a mark of truth? Others may be just as confident as we are. Suppose there were widespread disagreement among otherwise rational people about torturing innocents. How could our confidence count as evidence for our conclusion? Suppose we favored it.

A second argument appeals to the supposedly obvious commonsense truth that intuitions have a better than even chance of being right. This position originates with Sidgwick and was recently developed with some care by Noah Lemos.[7] According to Lemos, we know that moral reflection (i.e., consulting intuitions) is a better method of reaching moral conclusions than mere chance. But unless intuitions have evidential weight, coin flips would serve us as well as reflection. This is absurd. Therefore intuitions must have evidential weight.

One could object to this argument in several ways.[8] But the most important point, for present purposes, is that it too presupposes convergence (or the right explanation of divergence). After all, if our intuitions differed wildly from those of others, and we could not disqualify theirs, why should we give ours a better than even chance of being right? Because they are ours? The situation becomes especially dicey as intuitions become more fine grained. Consider six possible intuitions with respect to act A: A is terribly wrong, A is wrong, A is one horn of an authentic moral dilemma, A is morally permitted, A is morally required, and A is morally heroic. And suppose that the intuitions of a population are distributed evenly over these alternatives. What reason remains for holding that any set of intuitions has a better than 50 percent chance of being right? Indeed, suppose there are just two categories of intuition—right and wrong—and the intuitions of a significant majority converge on one of them (say, three quarters). Do they have a better than 50 percent chance of being right *for that reason*?

Finally, there is the argument from convergence (and/or the right explanation of divergence). Roughly, the claim is that our intuitions, properly sifted and analyzed, will converge on a unique set of standards, and that this correspondence is explained as the response of rational beings to universal moral truth. Failures of convergence are explained in terms of irrational or irrelevant intuitions. Skeptics might call for accounts of the nature of the capacity for intuition and the nature of universal moral truth such that the one is capable of accessing the other. And some intuitionists attempt to provide one. Brody, for example, holds (roughly) that "right" and "wrong" refer to properties that supervene on empirical states of affairs.[9] On his account, our moral capacity enables us to detect such properties. And universal standards simply describe the occasions of their supervenience. M.B.E. Smith, on the other hand, understands moral competence as a kind of linguistic competence.[10] For Smith, universal moral standards are truth conditions of moral sentences. We learn them as we learn our moral vocabulary.

But if intuitions really did converge, these accounts would not be required to establish the intuitionist's case. Given convergence (and/or the right explanation of divergence), challenges to the evidential force of intuitions would be just another form of philosophical skepticism. Explaining how we do it would be interesting philosophically, but we could trust intuitions without such explanations (just as we can trust perceptions as veridical).

The Obvious Objection

Convergence, however, appears to fly in the face of the historical and anthropological record and conflict with our theories of how moral beliefs are formed and transmitted. Rational beings appear to have (and have had) a variety of moral sensibilities, and these seem correlated with cultural traditions, social structures, family background, personal experience, and so on. The fixation of moral belief is not best explained as the response of rational beings to universal moral truth, but in terms of the operation of psychological and social forces. People of similar backgrounds appear to have similar beliefs, and beliefs diverge as diversity increases.

This familiar picture challenges not only the convergence *argument* for intuitionism and the intuitionist argument for universalism, but intuitionism and universalism themselves. To the extent that human groups and the individuals have conflicting intuitions about cases (or standards), it is difficult to show that our intuitions (or anyone else's) are evidence of universal moral truths. The scope of the first premiss of the intuitionist argument for universalism shrinks accordingly (perhaps even to zero). Human beings have had rational capacities for the life of the species. To hold that our intuitions are accurate in the face of such conflicts seems arrogant in the extreme.

To answer the argument from diversity *against* intuitionism, intuitionists sometimes acknowledge diversity but try to show that it is compatible with intuitionism.[11] But as we have seen, the argument *for* intuitionism requires more than compatibility. It requires convergence and/or the right explanation of divergence. These tasks of defending intuitionism against the diversity argument and providing a positive argument in its favor are frequently confused. M.B.E. Smith, for example, wants to present a positive intuitionist case for universalism. But much of his discussion of diversity is an attempt to show that the diversity of moral intuitions is *compatible* with intuitionism.

The intuitionist can deal with this problem in two ways. First, he may deny that the range of diversity is very great. Second, he may acknowledge the range but attempt to give the right sort of explanation for it.

Replies to the Obvious Objection

Hearing Hidden Moral Harmonies

One way to arrive at convergence is to deny that apparent moral differences are authentic. There are two ways to do this. One may deny that the apparent differences are really differences. Thus, one might hold that, appearances notwithstanding, every group subscribes to largely the same set of moral standards. Or one might acknowledge that different groups subscribe to different moral standards, but deny that their differences are really moral. What seem to be moral differences are at root religious or empirical ones.

In a recent paper, William Shaw announces, without argument, that the moral differences between groups and individuals are greatly exaggerated.[12] Perhaps he and others are convinced by an early paper by W. T. Stace which represents these differences as small islands in a vaster sea of moral agreement.[13] The few authentic differences appear significant because they stand in sharp relief against a background of general agreement. In reality, it is said, all cultures share roughly the same fundamental moral beliefs: that killing is wrong, stealing is wrong, lying is wrong, and so forth. With perhaps a few unimportant exceptions there really is convergence.

With apologies to Stace, this understanding of the matter is depressingly superficial. It simply misreads the fact that all human societies must regulate certain classes of activities or perish (e.g., homicide, property exchanges, information transfers, sexual relationships, child rearing, nonlethal violence, exchanges of services). We regulate these classes of activities by requiring or forbidding certain subsets of them under certain circumstances. Thus, we regulate homicide by forbidding certain forms of killing, we regulate property transfers by forbidding some forms of taking, we regulate information transfers by requiring truthfulness under certain conditions, and so on.

This creates a misleading appearance of uniformity. But it is obvious from the historical and anthropological record that different societies regulate these activities in different ways. And clearly, their moralities differ to the extent that they do so. Like the Homeric Greeks, the Imperial Romans, and early twentieth-century Sicilians, we prohibit certain kinds of killing. And so it might misleadingly be said that we all agree that, other things being equal, killing is wrong.

But the morality of Homeric Greece permitted killing to avenge breaches of hospitality and allowed conquerors to kill all the able-bodied males of a conquered city. The Romans notoriously believed that it was morally permissible for professional gladiators to kill nonvoluntary combatants to entertain bloodlusting crowds and to roast slaves alive in brass bulls to entertain guests at private parties. Until relatively recently, Sicilian morality permitted (or required) a man to kill his wife's lover, and eighteenth-century American upper-class morality entitled one to kill someone in a duel to avenge an insult. We, of course, find all of this highly objectionable and some of it unthinkably barbaric. This list of differences could easily become a catalogue and similar catalogues could be compiled in relation to lying, promise breaking, and so forth.

It is even questionable that all societies believe one always needs a reason to kill another human being (beyond "It pleases me"). The Romans fed people to wild beasts for the amusement of spectators, and many groups have believed it all right to kill outsiders on sight. The Yanomamo of the Amazon basin go further—Yanomamo men are permitted to kill Yanomamo children captured from other villages when and as they please.[14]

Any frank look at history shows widespread and largely unprotested violations of what seem to us to be the most basic moral prohibitions. The Roman "games" were popular not only in the capital but throughout the empire for hundreds of years. Was there in these times a general moral presumption against causing unnecessary suffering? The Greeks routinely enslaved women and children of captured cities (after slaughtering all adult males). Was there a general presumption against violations of liberty (and, again, the creation of unnecessary suffering)? A Yanomamo is expected to lie whenever he thinks it is to his advantage. Is there a general presumption against truth telling? I am not arguing that these practices are defensible, only that they indicate fundamental moral differences.

One might object that all cultures nonetheless agree that murder and stealing are wrong. But understood such that it is plausible, this point is uninteresting. Stealing is usually defined as wrongful taking, murder as wrongful killing. Under these descriptions they are, of course, universally prohibited: wrongful taking and wrongful killing are wrong. And, because all societies regulate homicide and property exchanges, all believe some killing and taking are wrong. But what counts as wrongful taking and wrongful killing differs from place to place. (The specification of wrongful taking depends on what counts as property and how property rights are delineated.)

Denying the Differences Are Moral

The second and more plausible way to defend convergence against the objection is to deny that cultural and historical differences in intuitions are really moral differences. This argument originates with Stace, and has been developed more recently by Smith. And it has wide currency among moral philosophers.[15] What appear to be differences in moral intuitions are in fact differences in theological, aesthetic, or empirical beliefs. You believe that it is wrong for John and Mary to have sex because they are unmarried, and as a conservative Baptist, you think this jeopardizes their souls. I think that your religious beliefs are mistaken and believe that it's morally permissible for them to have sex if they please. According to the argument, our moral intuitions don't conflict. Our differences are merely theological. If I agreed with your theology, I might accept your judgment, and if you shared my positivism, you might accept mine.

If admissible, this move eliminates some of the sting of the argument from diversity against convergence (though it does not establish convergence). Cultures, classes, religious groups, genders, and individuals obviously differ widely in their empirical and theological beliefs. And since theologies and empirical beliefs affect our intuitions on cases, we should expect considerable disparities in intuitions about cases. If this argument is sound, disparities count as evidence against convergence of moral intuitions only if they are not grounded in differing nonmoral beliefs. (Though to establish convergence, the intuitionist must also show that if people held the same nonmoral beliefs, they would also have the same moral intuitions.)

But this move is unconvincing. And if it were sound it would prove too much. For agreement as well as differences in intuitions could then be called nonmoral. Suppose we agree that John shouldn't have sex with Mary, but your belief is theologically grounded and my belief is psychologically grounded. (Or, to move from cases to standards, suppose we agree that certain kinds of killing are wrong but for different reasons.) If the argument is acceptable, this should not count as moral agreement. But in that case it is hard to see how the intuitionist argument for convergence can succeed. In any case, claims to the effect that intuitions converge will be as difficult to establish as claims that they diverge. One can, with equal plausibility, point to some nonmoral difference as a basis for agreement or disagreement.

To reach a deeper understanding of the argument, however, we need to distinguish between two kinds of differences of nonmoral belief. The first are, roughly speaking, differences with respect to facts about the case itself. Thus, we may disagree about the morality of John's sexual adventurism because we disagree about the history or nature of his relationship with his wife, Mary. You might believe he pledged eternal fidelity while I might believe they agreed to an "open marriage." Here our different responses to John's acts should not count as differences in intuitions about "the" case. Roughly, since we are thinking about a different set of facts, we are really thinking about different cases. More precisely, we differ with respect to the facts of the case itself when our factual differences are such that we believe that different standards are relevant. That is, even if we agreed that the same set of standards was morally defensible, we would disagree about which of the standards applied. Thus, you believe that John acted wrongly because you believe the standard "Keep your promises (or keep that kind of promise)" applies. Since I don't believe that kind of promise has been made, I think that standard is irrelevant (even though I might believe it is sound). If we differ on what standard should decide the case for *this* reason, we are not necessarily at odds morally. And such differences should not count against convergence.

On the other hand, we might subscribe to different moral standards because we subscribe to different background theories (theological, empirical, etc.). In that case, our intuitions about cases will also differ even if we agree on what I am calling the facts of the case itself. Because we agree on the facts of the case itself, we agree that the same standards are appropriate to deciding it. Or more precisely, we agree on what standards would be relevant were they defensible, but we disagree on what standards are defensible. In this case, there is an important moral difference between us: we have different intuitions because we subscribe to different moral standards for evaluating actions and character. Our disagreement on standards might be grounded in different theological beliefs, but it is a moral disagreement for all that. Accordingly, it counts against convergence. Convergence, after all, holds that our intuitions converge on the same moral standards.

Still, it might be objected that if I shared the relevant background belief I would accept your standard and share your intuition. Wouldn't that show that our disagreement is not at root a moral one?

If this reply is to save convergence, every difference in intuitions (and standards) must be explicable in relation to different background beliefs of this sort. But that is not obviously so. It might be that even if we agreed on all the relevant facts we would still disagree on standards. One of us might be considerably more compassionate than the other. The Romans knew how much the unfortunates at the games suffered and knew that they were often innocents. Is the difference between them and us merely one of background empirical beliefs? One might say we differ in our value beliefs: we take suffering more seriously than they did. But in that case moral standards diverge because values do. And if this kind of divergence can't be explained in relation to further nonnormative background theories, we seem stuck with it.

But let's set this worry aside. Suppose differences in intuitions are ultimately grounded in different (nonnormative) background beliefs. There are still reasons for considering the different intuitions moral differences. Consider two analogies. Judges may have different intuitions about a case because they subscribe to different legal standards. In that case they differ legally about cases and standards. It doesn't matter that these differences can be traced to different sociological views or different understandings of history (e.g., of the Founders' intentions). Similarly, mathematicians may disagree about whether a theorem has been proved because they disagree about whether the argument for it counts as a proof. The disagreement about whether T is a theorem is mathematical even if the reasons are (ultimately) philosophical. And so forth.

Denying the Differences Are Relevant

Like many arguments that turn on linguistic usage, this last argument misses the deeper point behind the "not a *moral* difference" response. To capture this, we need to reformulate that response. It is not that the different intuitions in question are not authentic moral differences. They are. They are not, however, *relevant* moral differences, that is, they are not the sort that undermine convergence. They are not relevant because they are (as it were) judgments about actions or standards in different possible worlds. Your condemnation of John holds for the possible world in which there is a God of the relevant kind. My condemnation of John holds for worlds in which there isn't. The male supremacist's intuitions hold in possible worlds in which men and women have the characteristics he ascribes to them; various feminists' intuitions hold for the possible worlds in which men and women have the characteristics various feminists ascribe to them. And so forth. Convergence simply requires that we agree on the same standards for the same worlds. Given the facts of this, the actual world, there is a set of standards binding on rational agents as such. Or so the intuitionist might argue.

There is *something* right about this. Moral standards and intuitions do vary in relation to background beliefs and rightly so. Also, if we agreed on relevant background fact and theories for a certain world, we might also agree to a considerable extent on moral standards and intuitions. (Though, as I will argue in chapter 6, we need not agree completely.) But although this strengthens the case for objectivity in ethics, it does not help the intuitionist argument for universalism.

Strictly speaking, it is not factual beliefs that justify moral standards, but true factual beliefs (or, if you will, facts). And the relevant facts not only differ from possible world to possible world, but from society to society in the actual world. As every beginning ethics student learns, the Eskimos of yore had their reasons for putting old people and defective newborns on the ice to die. Their economy was such that they could not otherwise survive. Under those conditions, their form of infanticide and geriatricide made sense. The standards permitting such acts are justified. And, imagining ourselves in their place, our intuitions largely coincide with theirs. Under our conditions, however, these standards are not justified. We can afford to support people with missing limbs and old people who do less than half the work of people in their prime.

In general, differences in technological development, cultural traditions, personality types, resource bases, and other factors are often such that standards that make sense for one society are unreasonable for another. There is no uniquely right way to organize economic life for rational beings as such, for example, to define property rights. Accordingly, the standards defining "wrongful taking" will differ justifiably from place to place. Nor is there a single right way to organize family life. Better and worse here depend on what conditions prevail. In fact, as I will argue at some length in chapter 6, there are sufficient differences between domains within a given society that different standards are justified for different domains. Conditions for inmates in maximum security prisons are such that standards governing truth telling, promise keeping, and justice are rightly less stringent than those appropriate to communities of Franciscan monks. Revealing certain kinds of information can be highly dangerous in the first case, and there is little probability of reciprocity. Scrupulous truth tellers and promise keepers have high mortality rates.

The upshot is that even if people with the same background beliefs subscribed to the same standards (or had the same intuitions), universalism would not follow. For background beliefs true of one society are not true of every other. And as long as the relevant empirical facts differ from one society to another, different moral standards will be justified for each. If true, however, this hypothesis does establish objectivity in ethics. That is, it establishes that there is a method for justifying standards given background conditions. ESA attempts to describe that method.

Denying the Differences Are Relevant, Strategy 2: The Move to Ultimate Principles

But the truth of this hypothesis could be the basis of still another argument for universalism. For how could one explain that sort of convergence? The great philosophical temptation is to appeal to higher (more abstract) principles. These principles, in conjunction with various schedules of background beliefs, generate our standards and our intuitions. Differences in our intuitions about cases are irrelevant. They show only that we disagree about derived standards. The important point is that our intuitions converge on ultimate ones.

The problem is that no one has ever produced a convincing ultimate principle or set of ultimate principles. The major principles in the tradition—the utility principle and deontic versions of the categorical imperative—have well-known counterintuitive consequences.[16] So it would be hard to argue that intuitions converge on them. In any case, neither of them is sufficiently abstract to be ultimate since the plausibility of both depends on the truth or falsity of certain background theories. No Calvinist or Augustinian Catholic could possibly endorse either, and neither could a Platonist or an Aristotelian. More generally, if certain theories about God, human nature, the self, and the natural world are true, these principles lose their credibility. In short, they bear the same relation to background empirical and theological views as other moral standards.

The ultimate principles proposed by the present argument are supposed to explain why different standards are justified for different possible worlds (and actual societies). Accordingly, they must themselves hold for every possible world, that is, given any set of facts. It is hard to imagine what such principles could be. (Remember, they are supposed to explain why intuitions converge given identical background beliefs.)

In any case, we don't need such principles. Moral standards at every level can be justified by background beliefs in conjunction with a moral epistemology. Given different sets of background beliefs, any given moral epistemology will generate different standards. Theological ethicists will base their standards on their understanding of God's will or wisdom (and may disagree because they disagree on the nature of God, the meaning of Scripture, or theories of textual interpretation). Naturalists will base their standards on their understandings of human nature and the natural world. Rule utilitarians will base their standards on their understanding of the causes of misery and happiness. And so forth.

Moral epistemologies, moreover, are justified or refuted by appealing to an enormously wide range of primarily *philosophical* doctrines and theories. These include theories of meaning, language, knowledge, a priori truth, action, reason, nature, persons, selves, mind, objectivity, and philosophical methodology (among others). If ethics is a coherent subject matter to begin with, different constellations of doctrines in these areas will justify different moral epistemologies (including the limiting case view that there is no such thing as moral justification at all). And the truth about these matters will entail the correct one.

However, it might be objected that this is just a disguised version of universalism with respect to ultimate principles. After all, theological ethics is really just the view that one ought to obey the standards God has given us; cultural relativism is really just the view that one ought to do as one's society commands; rule utilitarianism is really the view that one ought to act on principles which, at some level of compliance, will maximize utility; and so forth.[17] And these are ultimate moral principles.

As I suggested in the introduction, this is a very misleading way of presenting a straightforward truth. The candidates for "ultimate moral principles" are not moral standards at all. They play no direct role in our evaluations of actions, or character, or in our decisions about how to act. Instead, they tell us what sets of facts or background theories are relevant to justifying the standards that serve these purposes.

The distinction between ultimate standards and derived standards is thought to be analogous to the distinction between (ultimate) axioms and (derived) theorems in logic or mathematics. But the analogy is false. Axioms are more basic than theorems because theorems are derived from axioms. But once a theorem has been proved, both theorems and axioms play the same role in theory development and in the evaluation of well-formed formulae. Both appear in proofs of further theorems and in refutations of proposed theorems. This relationship does not hold between so-called ultimate and derived standards in ethics. Arguments for or against the rightness of actions do not include so-called ultimate principles along with derived ones.[18] Furthermore, so-called derived standards are not derived from ultimate standards alone. Only someone committed to defending universalism would insist that so-called ultimate principles are of the same logical kind as prohibitions against various kinds of lying, killing, and so forth, yet are simply more basic.

Consider a legal analogy. Jurisprudence contains a number of different theories about how legal principles are properly justified. There are natural law theories, "strict constructionist" theories, social activist theories, Dworkinite theories, and others. These theories tell us what sorts of facts are relevant to arguments for and against legal principles that decide cases, but they are not themselves principles of law.

Denying the Differences Are Rational

The intuitionist argument for universalism requires a convergence of intuitions and/or the right explanation of divergence. Thus far we have examined two strategies for defending convergence against "the obvious objection" and one strategy for providing the right explanation of divergence. A second strategy for doing the latter remains. The attempt here is to show that all but one set of divergent intuitions about cases are irrational.

The earliest intuitionists did this by complacently rejecting the moral responses of the "savage" and the "uncultivated." Like Aristotle, they were interested only in what those of sound moral training had to say. But such dismissals are obviously question-begging or partisan. They are question-begging if we distinguish between the ignorant and the enlightened on the basis of their intuitions to begin with. They are partisan if we identify people of sound moral training as people like us. To make this strategy work, we need some defensible way of delineating the elect.

Some look hopefully to recent work in moral education. Lawrence Kohlberg and his followers claim to have developed nonquestion-begging standards for sorting out stages of moral development. This work has inspired an enormous critical literature that cannot be evaluated here. But even if we grant that there are stages of moral development, there is no reason to expect convergence of intuitions from those at Kohlberg's higher stages. People at his sixth level are characterized only by the fact that they employ general principles and try to apply them impartially. These criteria are merely formal; that is, they abstract entirely from content. Kohlberg apparently expects people at this level to share intuitions on a range of issues, but he offers no empirical evidence for this claim. And given widespread differences in intuitions between people who appeal to principles — indeed, between moral philosophers — it is hard to imagine why he believes it (if he does).

The more familiar route is to dismiss troublesome intuitions on the grounds that they are not "considered moral judgments." These are judgments made "in a cool hour," unaffected by partisan sentiment or self-love, and are the issue of some form of reflection.[19] The defining features of considered moral judgments are rarely clarified and the last condition is particularly in need of it. I presume that reflection is required since intuitions without reflection do not sufficiently engage our powers of reason. But what is to count as "reflection" here? And how much of it is required?

The term "reflection" suggests the sorts of things philosophers do when they compare intuitions to one another, compare intuitions to principles, and so forth. If so, a judgment can count as an intuition for someone only if he has the capacity to do this kind of thing. But many people are quite bad at it. One could say that j is an intuition for someone only if j would remain after reflection were one capable of reflecting. But in this case it is hard to know what should count. In any case, even for those capable of reflection, it is hard to know what sort of judgment qualifies as considered. We cannot rely on reflective equilibrium. Reflective equilibrium takes considered moral judgments as data. That is, the process begins after irrational responses have already been discarded (and without that provision prospects of convergence are nil). How, then, do we do it? Of course, any moral epistemology provides us with some method for evaluating particular moral judgments, including ESA. But the intuitionist cannot require that a judgment pass the test proposed by some other moral epistemology without abandoning intuitionism in favor of that alternative. So the intuitionist cannot do that. What, then, can he do?

It is hard to say. Almost everyone gives *some* thought to her judgments about cases and has *something* to say in defense of them. To disqualify enough judgments about cases to serve the intuitionist's need, however, something stronger is required. After all, these judgments typically reflect cultural traditions, moral training, personal history, and so forth. Indeed, there will be enormous diversity with respect to considered moral judgments, even with respect to members of the same culture (or the Harvard philosophy department).

Finally, the appeal to considered moral judgments helps the intuitionist argument only if considered moral judgments are more likely to be true than other kinds. But under certain conditions, they aren't. Human history is, to a large extent, a record of the domination and exploitation of the weak by the powerful. Warring tribes, nations, and city-states have routinely raided, conquered, or enslaved their neighbors. Serfdom, slavery, and the subjugation of women have been the rule. But the powerful rarely believed they were engaged in brutal, selfish, unjustified exercises of naked power. Usually they thought they were fulfilling some destiny, carrying out the will of some god, or exercising some right of nature. The considered moral judgments of the conquerors, then, permitted, even demanded, the subjugation, enslavement, or exploitation of the conquered.

The strong rarely rule by force alone. Typically, they try to convince weaker nations, classes, races, or genders that they rule by right and — since they control the major mechanisms of reward and punishment and the major means of transmitting information — they often have some success. Thus, large numbers of women have been "sold" large portions of various sexist moralities throughout the ages, and large numbers of peasants have accepted the right of the landowner to an enormous share of what they produce. In such cases, might not anger and partisan feeling among the oppressed and exploited be more likely paths to moral progress than calm reflective judgment? Calm reflective judgment, among ordinary people, tends to follow familiar and well-worn paths.

Here is a scenario. Constance, a Victorian woman raised in a thoroughly sexist household, adopts many standard moral attitudes defining the position of women in her time, for example, that wives must obey their husbands. She does this after devoting some thought to the matter (e.g., consulting the best "scientific" judgment concerning the nature and capabilities of the sexes). Her sister, Alice, to whom she is deeply devoted, is more skeptical. And when Alice's husband demands that she do something she regards as morally disgusting, she refuses. Her husband retaliates by humiliating her at a family gathering. Other males in the family help out. Constance has seen other women humiliated in this way and has been mildly disturbed by it. But seeing it happen to her sister, she is furious, and objects heatedly on moral grounds. She is moved by partisan feeling and anger (pain, sorrow, despair), but her judgment is the better for it. Shortly thereafter her husband orchestrates a campaign to "calm her down" and "make her see reason" (he enlists the family doctor, the family priest, her mother, her brothers, etc.). His campaign works. She cools off, reflects again on the nature and capabilities of the sexes, adopts "the general view," and returns (more or less) to her previous, morally myopic habits of thought. Her defense of her sister is regarded as just another episode of female hysteria and further evidence that men must rule.

These sorts of cases not only challenge the evidential status of considered moral judgments but emphasize the conservative character of intuitionism. How does it accommodate moral progress? Moral progress marks a departure from the moral status quo and the considered moral judgments associated with it. And this means that it requires a divergence—not a convergence—of intuitions about cases and standards.

The intuitionist might say that moral progress occurs when relevant background theories that support the status quo change for the better. But now it's not considered moral judgments that have evidential weight, but those considered moral judgments based on true background theories. Indeed, moral judgments that don't qualify as "considered," but are based on true background theories, will have a better claim than considered judgments based on false background theories.

Wide Reflective Equilibrium

Although unqualified appeals to intuition are commonplace in applied ethics, and although intuitionism refuses to die at the level of theory, unadorned intuitionism is no longer the cutting edge. A successor theory—wide reflective equilibrium—is still in vogue, however. The foundations of this view were laid by John Rawls, and it was developed more rigorously by Norman Daniels.[20]

Wide reflective equilibrium must be distinguished from narrow reflective equilibrium. We achieve narrow reflective equilibrium by making our intuitions about cases consistent with our intuitions about principles, but the argument of this chapter shows that we can't take narrow equilibrium to be evidence of universal moral truth. We have no reason to accept either sort of intuition as such evidence to begin with.

Wide reflective equilibrium holds more promise, for it allows us to revise intuitions about cases and intuitions about principles not only in relation to each other but also in relation to a significantly wider set of beliefs or background theories. On the basis of these background theories, Daniels says, "we advance philosophical arguments intended to bring out the relative strengths and weaknesses of the alternative sets of principles (or competing moral conceptions)."[21] How does this work?

According to Daniels (and Daniels's reading of Rawls), a moral theory has four levels. At level 1 we have a partial or narrow reflective equilibrium between principles and cases. At level 2 we have some device or apparatus for justifying the principles of this equilibrium on independent philosophical grounds (e.g., in Rawls's case, the contract apparatus; in R. M. Hare's case, the Archangel). At level 3 we have a set of background theories that independently validate the level 2 apparatus. In Rawls's case, these include the theory of the person, the theory of procedural justice, and the theory of a well-ordered society. Daniels takes these to have a normative dimension and to rest on both value intuitions and social theory. *These* value intuitions, however, are supposed to be logically independent of those invoked at level 1 (though Daniels never explains how). Finally, at level 4 we have a set of background social theories in relation to which we can test level 1 and level 3 theories for "feasibility." Daniels is not very specific about what "feasibility testing" amounts to, but the most important criterion seems to be that proposed standards can generate the support of those who must live by it.

Wide reflective equilibrium, then, differs from narrow reflective equilibrium in two important ways. First, it provides and defends an independent philosophical argument for the standards it proposes (e.g., they would be chosen by rational agents in Rawls's original position). And second, it allows what Daniels calls "extensive *theory-based* revisions" of level 1 intuitions about cases and principles. But does it provide us with a defense of universalism?

Daniels expresses a hope that it does but doesn't commit himself to this result.[22] It depends, he says, on the results we get and on the explanation of those results. Convergence of equilibria count as evidence of universal truth only if it cannot be explained in terms of some "provincial feature" of human psychology or biology. On the other hand, if different families of equilibria emerge, universalism is not defeated. For it might be that these differences can be explained in terms of some provincial feature and that by "abstracting from the source of divergence [we] can construct a modified and *idealized* 'agreement' on principles." That idealization would count as "a good candidate for containing objective moral truths, even though it is not accepted in any wide reflective equilibrium."[23]

But what realistic hope is there that we can achieve the right kind of convergence or that we will diverge for the right reasons? Daniels gives us no good reason to expect this result. And even if we get it, it does not follow that the standards we arrive at are universal moral truths. After all, wide reflective equilibrium treats beliefs at all levels of theory as if they were elements of some web of belief. It does not tell us how to adjust the various levels of theory in relation to one another. So it does not even guarantee that two persons starting with identical beliefs will achieve the same equilibrium. As D. W. Haslett has pointed out, equilibrium is nothing more than coherence, and it may be possible to achieve coherence in many different ways.[24] Since we might end up with many different sets of principles, the results can hardly be described as binding on rational agents as such.[25]

In any case, the nonmoral elements of levels 3 and 4 are subject to historical change. The social sciences, for example, have changed considerably throughout their histories and will no doubt continue to evolve. Any wide reflective equilibrium, then, will be an equilibrium of the present. Accordingly, the moral standards of that equilibrium can hardly be considered binding on rational agents as such.

One might say that universality awaits us at the end of inquiry. But this simply acknowledges that the method of reflective equilibrium will not get us to universal principles now or in the foreseeable future.

Moreover, the discussion of intuitionism in this chapter undercuts any evidential force that narrow reflective equilibrium is supposed to enjoy. Daniels acknowledges that we shouldn't take intuitions to be decisive, that is, that they are subject to "theory based revisions." But why should we give them any independent weight at all? Certainly, they deserve no weight at all if they are grounded in false factual beliefs.[26]

The weight Daniels attributes to intuitions is especially mysterious given his response to Richard Brandt's complaint that narrow reflective equilibrium amounts to no more than a "shuffling of our prejudices."[27] Brandt's point is, in effect, the one I made earlier about the move from confidence levels to truth. Without some explanation of why confidence maps on to credibility, he maintains, we have no reason to suppose that these judgments have any credibility at all. Daniels at first responds that this objection is motivated by a false comparison between considered moral judgments (i.e., intuitions) and observation reports. And most of his response is devoted to arguing against this analogy. But the objection does not depend on that analogy at all. Certainly, whenever there is a wide diversity of judgments we are compelled to ask why our high level of confidence is evidence of truth.

In the end, Daniels very briefly acknowledges the legitimacy of this question. Indeed, he confesses that although we have a story about the reliability of nonmoral observation reports,

> we lack a level of theory development in the moral case. What follows from this difference is that the "no credibility" argument succeeds in assigning a burden of proof. *Some* answer to the question about the reliability must be forthcoming. But the argument is hardly a demonstration that no plausible story is possible.[28]

Daniels is right to describe the issue as a burden of proof question. But, given the diversity of our intuitions, the burden of proof is surely on the person who grants them evidential weight, and Daniels has no way to carry that burden.

Daniels does discount intuitions grounded in what he calls merely "provincial" features of human biology and psychology. The suggestion is that intuitions grounded in nonprovincial features will do, but he never tells us what these are. The appeal to provincial features of human *biology* suggests something that transcends human genetics.[29] Daniels seems to be looking for something we might share with advanced aliens. Is it Reason? If so, we need some noncircular criteria for deciding what intuitions fit that bill.

In any case, if we eliminate level 1 narrow reflective equilibrium from the story, Daniels's position might develop in several different ways. Most plausibly, I think, he might hold that by reflecting on the nature of persons, the role of morality in our lives, and the best current social scientific theory we can arrive at some plausible method for assessing the rationality of social moralities (e.g., Rawls's original position). This is certainly an advance over intuitionism, and a large step in the direction of ESA. But this picture is incomplete and it needs more shape.

The Role of Intuitions in Moral Theory

Suppose that, given any set of identical background theories and facts, everyone's intuitions on both cases and principles converged across the board. In that case we would no doubt accept intuitions as evidence that certain sets of standards are reasonable *for* a certain group. For we would all agree that given certain facts about a group, certain standards were appropriate to it. But this is a long way from universalism since it is compatible with the claim that very different sets of standards are rational for different groups. Moreover, it is based on nothing but a brave hope. There is no evidence for this sort of convergence (or the right explanation of divergence).

But intuitions do play two legitimate roles in moral theory. To begin with, they are clues to the standards to which we subscribe. So they help to fix the targets of moral justification and criticism. In the second place, they are important background facts. Any suggestion for moral change must take transformation costs into account, and significant costs are often incurred by the fact that a proposal flies in the face of prevailing intuitions about right and justice. People are willing to fight for their beliefs about these matters. And whether they fight or not, they incur significant losses when their moral convictions are ignored or trampled underfoot.

If we are accurately to describe the prevailing moral sensibilities of our own society, however, we cannot merely rely on "our" intuitions, that is, the intuitions of the community of professional philosophers. It should go without saying that we need an account of the intuitions of the various subgroups of our society. We might expect significant differences based on class, gender, ethnicity, region, setting (e.g., urban/rural), education, religion, etc. To get an accurate picture of our own society, we need to arrive at narrow equilibria for representative individuals in these categories. Unfortunately, we won't get a reliable map of this landscape until philosophers become sociologists, or sociologists become philosophers, or the two somehow manage to collaborate.

Of course, none of this is to deny the possibility that the mainstream moral intuitions of a society reflect the morality that is best for it. In an ideal society the two will converge. There people will have moral responses constituitive of a moral code that is optimal for people living under their conditions. Until we reach this happy condition, however, our conventional moral responses are likely to be defective in various ways. If we take them to be the measure of moral truth, we will never make progress. This is why intuitionism is both a conservative and a dangerous view.

Unfinished Business: Partial Universalism

If the intuitional argument will not support the full universalist picture, might it at least support partial universalism?

Given certain features generic to the human condition, one could argue that some moral standards should hold prominent positions in any human morality: Do not inflict pain for the fun of it, do not kill on whim, do not rape, do not betray others for entertainment or toy with their affections to amuse oneself, do not deprive others of liberty for one's own profit, and so forth. These standards hold for every human group because certain things are true of human beings in general. We hate forced sex, we do not get great thrills by inflicting small amounts of pain on others, we value our liberty, and so forth. One could imagine rational beings sufficiently different from us whom and in relation to whom they do not hold.[30] (The Schmoos of Al Capp's *L'il Abner* delighted in being kicked and verbally abused to relieve the frustrations of humans.)

To the extent that he is a universalist, the intuitionist must claim that these standards hold for rational beings as such and claim to know this by intuition. But again, the problem is that the intuitions of our species have not converged on these standards and we don't seem to have the right explanation for divergence. The conquest of cities in the ancient world was routinely followed by orgies of rape, murder, and destruction (as was the conquest of Chinese cities by the Japanese during World War II). Many Indian tribes also tortured captives of tribes with whom they were at war. None of this seemed to violate the intuitions of the offenders on a wide scale.

Some of these intuitions were no doubt grounded on false background theories, but it is not clear that all of them were. Indians who tortured or enslaved captives did not always think their captives were less human than themselves, and Greeks didn't think this way about other Greeks. Slaughter and enslavement were simply permitted by the rules of war: everyone was equally vulnerable. In many cultures, torture of captives was "justified" on the ground that it avenged an outrage committed by someone in the captive's group.

It may be that every known morality contains two or more identical standards and ranks them in the same way (at least in relation to one another). For example, every culture holds that patricide is wrong and takes it to be worse than failing to rescue one's father at grievous risk to one's life. Given the degree of divergence, this is not strong evidence for intuitionism. A better explanation is that certain standards make sense for every human group and every group has come to recognize at least some of them (or, anyway, those that haven't haven't lasted).

Notes

1. It may be that some cases are not decidable. Each alternative may be supported by alternatives of equal weight. In that case, however, the universalist needs us to agree that the case is undecidable.

2. Moral philosophers appeal to intuitions in different contexts and for different reasons. Not all such appeals are meant to defend universalism or even to establish that certain standards are universal. In fact, some who appeal to intuitions in ethics explicitly disown that view (see, e.g., John Kekes, "Moral Intuitionism," *American Philosophical Quarterly*, 23, no. 1, 1986, and William Shaw, "Intuitions and Moral Philosophy," *American Philosophical Quarterly*, 17, no. 2, 1980). The main point of this chapter is not to determine whether intuitions have some legitimate place in moral theory but to criticize intuitional attempts to establish that moral standards (or some set of them) are universal.

3. Baruch Brody, "Intuitions and Objective Moral Knowledge," *Monist*, 62, October 1979.

4. Kurt Baier, *The Moral Point of View*, Cornell University Press, 1958, Ithaca, New York. This proposal is so unlikely, however, that no one besides Baier has (to my knowledge) explicitly adopted it. It is to Baier's credit that he sees that such rules of priority are necessary if an intuitionist metaethic is to produce uniform judgments in particular cases (or agreement that they are undecidable).

5. Michael Philips, "Weighing Moral Reasons," *Mind*, 96, July 1987.

6. Perhaps the best we can do is to isolate the lying element by abstracting from all other wrong-making considerations in situations where lies are told. In that case, however, lying (or any other wrong) will turn out not to be very seriously wrong at all. The wrongfulness of lying will then turn out to be the wrongfulness of the most inconsequential lie (e.g., to avoid embarrassment, someone lies to a stranger on a train in a foreign country about the year of her old car). Moreover, it will always be less weighty than the weight of the least weighty consideration that trumps it. My aunt asks my opinion of a hat that I know she loves and will continue to wear no matter what I say. To avoid hurting her feelings even a little, I lie. If I am justified, the weight of the consideration against lying is less than the weight of the consideration against hurting someone's feelings even a little (or, perhaps, less than the consideration against hurting the feelings of someone relevantly like one's aunt). In any case, the weight of the consideration against lying will not be very great. Comparable cases can easily be constructed for many other prima facie duties.

7. Noah Lemos, "Justification and Considered Moral Judgments," *Southern Journal of Philosophy*, 24, no. 4, 1986.

8. In the first place, this assumes that there is no alternative to relying on intuitions but random choice. No argument is given for this, and I would like to see one since the purpose in this book is to describe an alternative. Further, one might hold that intuitions carry evidential weight without holding that they are evidence of universal standards. There is plenty of room for non-universalist understandings of "being right." John Kekes, for example, argues (roughly) that our intuitions are evidence of our moral tradition, and that—if our traditions are reasonable—we ought to act on them. But he doesn't believe that there is a uniquely rational set of traditions and hence that intuitions are evidence of universal moral standards.

9. Brody, "Intuitions and Objective Moral Knowledge," p. 447.

10. M.B.E. Smith, "Ethical Intuitionism and Naturalism: A Reconciliation," *The Canadian Journal of Philosophy*, 9, no. 4, 1979. John Rawls recommended this article to me as the best defense of intuitionism he knew of in the literature.

11. Smith, "Ethical Intuitionism and Naturalism."

12. See, e.g., Shaw, "Intuitions and Moral Philosophy," p. 131.

13. Richard Brandt, *Ethical Theory*, Prentice-Hall, Inc., Englewood Cliffs, N.J.,1959, pp. 99–103.

14. Napoleon Chagnon, *Yanomamo: The Fierce People*, Holt Rinehart and Winston, New York, 1968.

15. Brandt, *Ethical Theory*, Chapter 5; and Smith, "Ethical Intuitionism and Naturalism." This strategy is so familiar and widespread that Shaw is comfortable making the briefest allusion to it in explanation of his belief that moral differences between cultures are much exaggerated (Shaw, "Intuitions and Moral Philosophy").

16. The categorical imperative is of course notoriously vague. But any version that gives bite to the idea that we should never treat others as means only is very counterintuitive. Act utilitarians are criticized for their willingness to punish the innocent person no matter how slight the gain in utility. The "ends-in-themselves" formula should be criticized for its unwillingness to do this no matter how great the gain. Suppose the planet would be destroyed by aliens if we refused?

17. There is also the view that one ought always to do as God commands one on any given occasion. The suggestion here is that God issues specific directives about action. This applies directly to the evaluation of action, so it is an authentic moral standard.

18. In practice, such a "principle" might be cited to justify a standard that decides a case in the same breath as the standard itself. Thus, e.g., God has outlawed adultery, therefore these adulterers are wrong. This is really just shorthand for (a) God has outlawed adultery, therefore adultery is wrong; and (b) adultery is wrong, therefore these adulterers are wrong.

19. It is now widely held that moral judgments must be made from an impartial point of view, but this kind of impartiality is characterized in terms of the question asked. Roughly, one is impartial in this way when one asks, "What would be right or best taking into account the rights or interests of everyone?" or "What set of moral standards would be best for everyone affected?" But the intuitionist requires more than this. For like our response to many other questions, our response to this one might well be influenced by self-regard or excessive regard for those we love or with whom we identify. It is a commonplace in the literature of clinical psychology that these (and various other) rationality-distorting tendencies are often extremely difficult to detect in ourselves and others. To the extent that this is true, it will be difficult to distinguish authentic intuitions from moral responses born of our tendencies to rationalize, to project, to engage in transference, and so forth.

20. John Rawls, *A Theory of Justice*, Harvard University Press, Cambridge, Mass., 1972, pp. 46–53; Norman Daniels, "Wide Reflective Equilibrium and Theory Acceptance in Ethics," *Journal of Philosophy*, 76, 1979, pp. 256–83. See also Daniels, "Reflective Equilibrium and Archimedian Points," *Canadian Journal of Philosophy*, 10, March 1980, and "On Some Methods of Ethics and Linguistics," *Philosophical Studies*, 37, January 1980.

21. Daniels, "Wide Reflective Equilibrium and Theory Acceptance," p. 258.

22. To be fair, it is not entirely clear that Daniels hopes for universalism. He says he hopes that wide reflective equilibrium can arrive at objective moral truth. ESA, of course, also aims at objective moral truth. However, a number of passages in Daniels's paper suggest that he thinks of objective

moral truth in universalist terms. For example, he compares moral truth to scientific truth as understood by scientific realists, and he discounts agreement and disagreement on moral matters grounded in "merely provincial features of human psychology and biology."

23. Daniels, "Wide Reflective Equilibrium and Theory Acceptance," pp. 266–67.

24. D. W. Haslett, "What Is Wrong with Reflective Equilibrium?" *Philosophical Quarterly*, 37, 1987.

25. As suggested, perhaps Daniels would be willing to settle for something weaker than this, e.g., the claim that moral standards are objective. If this is understood as the claim that it is objectively true that certain standards are more reasonable for a society than other standards, ESA agrees. But it is hard to see how the method of wide reflective equilibrium can establish even this. As the argument that follows shows, the fact that a standard survives narrow reflective equilibrium is not necessarily evidence that it is a superior standard.

26. Unless, of course, the beliefs are known to be false and one is using a hypothetical case to make a point.

27. Richard Brandt, *A Theory of the Good and the Right*, Oxford University Press, Oxford, 1979, chapter 1.

28. Daniels, "Wide Reflective Equilibrium and Theory Acceptance," p. 272.

29. This is well motivated. Intuitions rooted in our genes, if there are any, are not necessarily guides to moral wisdom. Many genetically grounded dispositions can be overcome by training, at least to some degree, and this is a good thing. Some of these are irrational. Consider our tendency to make hasty generalizations. This is what makes one-time learning possible, which has decided evolutionary advantages (e.g., one encounter with a hostile animal is enough to keep us away). But this tendency toward hasty generalization makes us vulnerable to error even in contexts in which it once had evolutionary advantages (e.g., a person bitten by a dog at an early age may tend to regard all dogs as dangerous, even as an adult). And with training it is possible to overcome it. The point holds also for moral tendencies. It is arguable that we have strong built-in dispositions entirely (or excessively) to discount the interests of nonhuman animals and to overvalue our own personal interests and the interests of those genetically related to us. Such tendencies make good evolutionary sense. But they are irrational, and we can do something to weaken them and to weaken their hold on our behavior (e.g., by rewarding and punishing). The fact that they are rooted in our genes should not give the judgments they generate evidential status.

30. The one possible exception to this is the prohibition against killing on whim.

2

Reason, Persons, and Contracts

If we can't arrive at universal standards by appealing to intuitions, perhaps some other method will do. Two alternatives now have considerable support: respect for persons and contractarianism. The first attempts to derive moral standards from the nature of persons. The second attempts to derive them by considering what rational agents would agree to under certain bargaining conditions. Sometimes these methods are fused. Thus, for example, Rawls and certain other contractarians design the contract situation on the basis of theories about the nature of persons, and the results are supposed to express what it is to respect persons (or treat persons as persons). Often, however, they are each presented independently of the other, and it is best to begin by considering them as such. I will begin with respect for persons. The question is, how far can this take us down the road to a universal morality?

Respect for Persons: Two Versions

"Respect for persons" is a phrase much in the air these days, but not everyone who uses it hopes to derive moral standards from an analysis of personhood. Our concern is with those who do. Everyone who has this intent owes us two things: (1) an account of the attitude of respect, and (2) an account of the nature of persons.

On some theories, moral standards are "derived" entirely from the latter account; on others they are "derived" from a conjunction of the two. In the first case, certain facts about the nature of persons are supposed to entail that persons ought to be treated in certain ways, for example, as bearers of certain rights. Here, respecting persons is merely a matter of treating persons as persons ought to be treated. Stephen Darwall calls this "moral recognition respect." To have this sort of respect for a person is "to give appropriate weight to the fact that he or she is a person by being willing to constrain one's behavior in ways required by that fact."[1] So the attitude of respect plays no role in the derivation of standards. Respect is merely a matter of observing standards once we have them.

In the second case, however, the attitude of respect is further defined and is intended to play some role in the derivation of standards. The standards, of course, can't entirely be derived from the attitude of respect. For however we characterize that attitude abstractly, the specific ways in which it manifests itself will change with its object. Thus, although one might adopt the same attitude of respect when one respects a painting, a tradition, and a person, the particular forms of behavior by which that attitude manifests itself may differ. Since it is the behavior that interests us, any respect for persons account requires some account of the nature of persons (and what makes them worthy of respect). But on this second version an account of persons by itself is not sufficient for the derivation of moral standards. The attitude of respect contributes something as well. On the second version, then, respecting a person is not merely treating a person as a person ought to be treated (where that is known already). Rather, respecting a person is adopting an attitude or stance toward her that includes or reduces to dispositions to act in certain ways. Moral standards codify this behavior. In some cases, it is not clear which version of the respect for persons view someone has adopted. Demanding that moralities respect persons is like saluting the flag in some circles, and requests for clarification are rarely made. Indeed, the atmosphere in the late seventies was such that Alan Donagan could write an entire book arguing that all morality is a specification of the principle that persons must be respected as rational agents without being clear on which version he was supporting. Rather than attempting to clarify the matter, Donagan simply claims that "the concept of respecting a human being as a rational agent is not usefully definable for our purpose."[2] So he is left without any principled way of arguing that candidate principles are or are not valid specifications. To equip himself with a principled method, he needs to say what he means by "person," what he means by "respect," and what sort of contribution he takes each to make.

Donagan believes this is unnecessary. He maintains instead that all heirs to the Judeo-Christian tradition in moral philosophy know which more specific principles express the respect for persons ideal. However, his own often idiosyncratic applications of the concept, his own efforts to derive specific standards from it, show just how desperately it stands in need of clarification. He says, for example, that "respecting a man as a rational creature includes . . . not thinking ill of him"; and that "anyone who, except to prevent a wrong, has . . . disparaged another person" shows disrespect.[3] It sounds as though the attitude of respect prohibits us from frankly discussing the character of our friends and associates unless such discussion is required to prevent some wrong (as opposed, e.g., to being required to solve some problem, to avoid some inconvenience, or merely to protect ourselves against an unpleasant evening). He also says, "Even for a good end it is impermissible for anybody in conditions of free communications between responsible persons to express an opinion he does not hold."[4] It sounds as though I fail to respect my aunt as a person if she asks me what I think of her favorite hat and I lie to protect her feelings. Finally, he says, "It is impermissible not to promote the well-being of others by actions in themselves permissible, inasmuch as one can do so without disproportionate inconvenience." He does not completely characterize "disproportionate inconvenience." He says only that we are not required to "procure a good" for someone "if that good can be procured only by relinquishing an equal or greater good for oneself."[5] The *suggestion* is that we are required to "procure a good" for others if we must give up just a little less than he gets. This sounds admirably high minded, but it is an incredibly demanding standard. It means, for example, that one should not pass a homeless person on one's way to a restaurant without giving her the price of one's intended meal (she almost certainly needs it more than you do). If Donagan doesn't mean this, it's not clear what he does mean. How much of our good does he think respect for persons requires us to give up for the sake of others?

The upshot is that because Donagan has nothing helpful to say about the nature of persons or the attitude of respect, he has no principled method for telling us what more specific principles the principle "respect persons as rational beings" entails, or which version of the "respect for persons" strategy he has adopted. As a result, his version of "respect for persons" is really just intuitionism in metaphysical dress. What, then, of philosophers who do provide analyses of the relevant concepts? Let's begin with accounts that provide some content for the attitude of respect (i.e., the second version).

Respect

In recent years, a moderately large literature has developed on the topic of respect. Most accounts, however, are not developed for the purpose of deriving moral standards. And they are much too thin and too vague to provide a basis for doing so. David Gauthier, for example, says that to respect others we must "take into account the wants, desires, commands and enterprises of others in acting."[6] But this is just to say that we cannot entirely ignore the interests of others. That is, roughly, it tells us only that we ought to adopt the moral point of view. It does not tell us how, in particular, considerations about the interests of others should enter into our decisions, or how and when these interests are supposed to constrain our actions. No standards at all follow (or are intended to follow) from it.

Bernard Williams has written that respecting others is "to be disposed to see the situation from the other's point of view."[7] Williams, of course, takes "seeing the situation from the other's point of view" to require more than merely understanding the world as he understands it (a con man does that). Rather, it is a matter of taking his concerns seriously, that is, giving them some importance. But again, no standards follow from this. We need to know how seriously to take his concerns in relation to the concerns of others. And, most importantly, we need to know when and how we must constrain our behavior to protect and promote his concerns. In effect, Williams is telling us what Gauthier did, namely, that persons ought not to be treated as mere things, that they have some moral standing.

B. J. Diggs appears to present a somewhat richer account. To respect persons, he says, is to join others "whenever feasible":

(1) in acting in ways each person together with others can reasonably and freely subscribe to as a common morality; and
(2) in treating each person in ways consistent with the person's developing and freely exercising his capacity as a rational being to govern himself.[8]

But Diggs's first condition simply enjoins us to act on rules that it makes good sense for one's group to adopt (if others are willing to do the same). It tells us nothing at all about what these standards might be. And his second condition is, in effect, a repetition of Darwall's injunction that we treat persons in a manner appropriate to their being persons with a few vague words appended about what persons are. Here, clearly, it is the analysis of persons, and not the attitude of respect, that does the work.

These accounts are typical. In general, accounts of the attitude of respect simply urge that we recognize that persons have moral standing. No standards follow, and usually none are thought to follow.

R. S. Downie and Elizabeth Telfer are exceptions. They self-consciously try to characterize the attitude of respect in a manner rich enough to generate standards. But what they say is really not so terribly different from what is usually said, and it is so vague that it is hard to see what is supposed to follow from it. They define the attitude of respect as an attitude of "active sympathy" or the attitude of making others' ends our own.[9] But they say very little to clarify this idea. Taken literally, "making others' ends our own" means treating others as if their interests were just as important to us as our own interests are. But Downie and Telfer don't seem to mean this. They don't say, for example, that we are to share our homes with the homeless or share our teaching jobs with unemployed philosophers. So what do they mean? To get a grasp on this we need to know under what circumstances, if any, active sympathy requires us to identify our good with the good of others (or to give up our good for their sake); under what circumstances it requires that we give only some weight to their good; and, in the latter cases, how much weight we should give. Without this information, we haven't a clue about what standards follow from respect.

A second problem for Downie and Telfer also plagues most versions of the respect for persons tradition. This problem concerns the range of beings to whom respect is owed. Why should we respect all and only persons? This excludes nonhuman animals and includes Hell's Angels and cigarette advertisers. Why do the latter have a claim to our active sympathy while the former do not? Indeed, in what sense are we supposed to take the ends of Hell's Angels to be our own? It might be thought that this isn't a problem since immoral people forfeit their right to respect. But it is hard to understand how a respect for persons view can take this line. After all, persons deserve respect by virtue of being persons (i.e., that they have certain person-making characteristics). And, on any account of these characteristics in the literature, they do not cease to have these characteristics by virtue of acting badly.[10]

Persons

If we can't get standards from the attitude of respect, can we get them by considering the nature of persons? On such accounts, if we understand what persons are, we will also understand how persons are appropriately treated. And respecting persons is identical with treating them appropriately.

Often, the term "person" is used to designate a moral status, for example, a holder of particular rights. Let's call this the normative sense. In the normative sense, it is trivially true that understanding the nature of persons provides us with moral standards. Here the interesting question is, "What characteristics of human beings (or other life forms) entitle them to the status of personhood?" But "person" is also used to designate a being with a certain set of capacities (e.g., consciousness, rationality, etc.). Let's call this the descriptive sense. Given this sense, it is not trivially true that persons are holders of rights or that we have certain duties toward them. However we use the term "person," the respect for persons claim is that possession of a certain set of capacities entitles one to a special status (defined in terms of certain specific rights or considerations). That is, the claim is that beings of whom the descriptive sense is true are beings of whom the normative sense is true as well.

Philosophers differ in their analyses of both the descriptive sense and the normative sense. Typically, however, the descriptive sense is said to require both consciousness and self-consciousness. There is disagreement on whether it also requires the capacity to communicate or to enter into social relations with others. But these disagreements play little role in the move from descriptive personhood to normative personhood. That move is typically based primarily on what most take to be the most important element of descriptive personhood, namely, reason. There is a long tradition according to which reason gives human beings their special worth and dignity and entitles them to special forms of treatment undeserved by cows, cats, dogs, and other nonhuman animals.

Respect for persons theorists tend to understand reason in one of two ways. Some identify it with prudential reason, that is, with practical reason as understood by economists, decision theorists, and many philosophers of action. Roughly, rationality is here the capacity to devise plans that maximize desire satisfaction. On this account, the object (content) of a desire of itself is irrelevant to assessing its rationality. All that counts is the degree to which having that desire makes it more likely that we will maximize desire satisfaction on the whole. Since this view abstracts from the content of our desires, I will call it Formal Practical Reason (FPR).

Others identify reason with moral reason.[11] Here to be rational is, roughly, to have the capacity to deliberate about what is right and to act on the conclusions of one's deliberations (or, on stronger accounts, to have the capacity to know the moral truth and be able to act on it). I will call it Moral Rationality (MR).

It is possible to hold that both sorts of reason are required for personhood. And there are hybrid conceptions of reason that synthesize these elements in various ways or try to reduce one to the other. But we don't need to worry about such complexities for our purposes.

On the richest accounts, then, to be a person is to be a conscious and self-conscious being, capable of entering into social relations and communication and capable of (or disposed to be) governed by FPR and/or MR. If we contemplate these characteristics, it is claimed, we will come to know how beings that fit this description ought to be treated in enough detail to enable us to formulate universal moral standards. But how is this derivation to proceed? Why are these particular capacities essential while other valued capacities are ignored? What is it that guides accounts of the descriptive sense? My strong suspicion is that, in practice, no one begins with an account of the descriptive sense and goes on to derive normative consequences. The movement is really in the other direction. Philosophers begin with strong intuitions about rights and so forth. And they move to descriptive personhood in order to explain why we (human beings) have the rights they suppose us to have. Standards are not derived from capacities; rather capacities are invoked to justify standards that are already held. This is true both with respect to standard content and standard scope. The possession of FPR, for example, is supposed to justify both rights that protect autonomy and the limitation of those rights to human beings.

If the descriptive sense is tailored to generate desired normative results, the fact that those normative results follow does nothing to justify them. To justify a particular set of standards (rights, duties, etc.), we must do more than show that they follow from some particular set of capacities. We need to show that those capacities are nonarbitrarily chosen. That is, we need to show why a morality should be based on these capacities rather than others. This, of course, holds whether or not I am right in my biographical suspicion that philosophers begin with intuitions about rights and gerrymander the descriptive sense to get them. If standards are justified in relation to a descriptive account of personhood, one needs to justify that descriptive account to begin with.

This is clear when one considers how many valued capacities the typical descriptive accounts of personhood leave out. There is no mention of the capacity for love, joy, enthusiasm, nurturing, and solidarity with one's fellows. There is nothing at all about spirituality, imagination, the sense of wonder, the sense of humor, and the capacities to create and appreciate music, painting, poetry, and theater. And there is nothing about the capacity to respond to natural beauty or to displays of human excellence. It might be said that all of these capacities presuppose reason in some very broad sense. But this is dubious, and it is irrelevant.[12] For whatever their relation to reason in the broadest sense, they play no role in the derivation of standards in the respect for persons tradition.

If they did, respect for persons moralities would look much different. Because they are "derived" from the narrower kinds of reason outlined above, FPR and MR, respect for persons moralities are designed to promote and protect the exercises of those capacities. Not surprisingly, they tend to equip us with rather different standards than we might get from moralities designed (among other things) to promote or protect the capacities to love, to joke, or to identify one's interest with the interest of some group or cause. This is not to say that a morality should aim directly to promote every valued capacity. It is just to say that defenders of respect for persons moralities need a principled reason for signalling out the capacities for MR and FPR.

Consider moralities grounded in FPR. There are several different versions in the literature, but they all place great emphasis on individuals and their projects (or life plans). They are typically rights based and stress individual autonomy. Paternalistic interventions are only very rarely obligatory (all things considered), and they are prima facie forbidden. Indeed, following Gerald Dworkin, they tend to be permitted only if they promote or protect the agent's long-term autonomy (here the capacity to formulate and act on a rational life plan).[13] Because autonomy is so highly prized, it is thought that obligations that go beyond respect for the basic autonomy-guaranteeing rights of others must be voluntarily assumed.[14] These include family obligations, obligations of mutual aid, care, concern, and so forth. Not surprisingly, the scope of these obligations tends to be minimized. The role of the virtues tends to be minimized as well.

Moralities based on FPR also provide meager theoretical resources for adjusting rights (or standards in general) in ways intended to promote or protect the quality of human existence. In particular, there is little to protect us against failures of the "invisible hand" to coordinate individual pursuits of "rational life plans" in collectively valuable ways. On Dworkin-inspired variants, restrictions on individual freedoms are justified on the ground that rational agents, knowing the consequences, would consent to such restrictions. But autonomy-respecting moralities can allow only so much of this without surrendering their spirit. In general, exercises of FPR reason are not to be sacrificed to promote human flourishing or even to protect against certain disasters. Literacy and the arts may atrophy, fellow feeling may wither, natural beauty may go unappreciated, and the environment may be poisoned, but rights to noninterference shall be protected.

Again, these results differ significantly from those we would get by basing our morality on other capacities, for example, the capacity to care and nurture, to identify our good with the good of a cause or group, or to seek and realize various kinds of human excellence (e.g., artistic, philosophical, athletic, etc.). The corresponding point holds with respect to moralities grounded in moral reason. Moralities in that tradition are more varied, but all contain elements meant to promote and protect the exercise of the moral capacity. Indeed, moral life has center stage. Morality protects and promotes the development and exercise of other capacities only if there is a specifically moral reason for doing so. Activities which undermine the moral capacity are forbidden. If, as Jane Austen seems to have thought, acting in certain theatricals weakened moral fiber, then acting in such plays is morally wrong.[15] Art, in general, is suspect and so is humor. Further, moral censure and punishment, properly deployed, are thought to benefit the recipient by educating him and by expressing our respect for him as a rational agent.

Again, this is not to say that a morality should aim directly to promote every valued capacity. Indeed, it seems strange to think that moral standards could directly promote our sense of humor or our sense of natural beauty. But one could imagine a society whose standards required respect for natural beauty in general and humor in the face of danger or privation. Moreover, it is clear that our own familiar standards affect a wide range of capacities. Arguably, changing the rules governing homicide to permit gladiatorial competition would seriously undermine our respect for life and weaken the bonds of solidarity and compassion. Changing the rules governing information exchanges to require a highly scrupulous commitment to truth would discourage many forms of humor and undermine many forms of emotional support. The connection between valued traits of character and moral standards is even more obvious at the level of domains. Thus, according to traditional socialist arguments at least, standards governing capitalist economic relations promote aggressive and competitive individuals and undermine our sense of mutual responsibility and concern.

I don't say that the moralities I have sketched follow necessarily from the descriptive accounts of personhood corresponding to them.

In fact, as I will argue presently, nothing decisive for morality follows necessarily from these accounts. But it is not surprising that the moralities *thought* to follow from these descriptive accounts bear the marks of their origins. And my point is that moralities originating in other valued capacities would bear different marks. So philosophers in the respect for persons tradition owe us an account of why they pick out the capacities they do.

This obligation is rarely paid. It is simply assumed by some philosophers (e.g., Alan Gewirth) that human beings are *essentially* practical agents and that we can arrive at morality by considering the structure of practical agency.[16] But why are we *essentially* that instead of essentially beings with a rich range of emotions and capacities to express them and/or beings capable of various kinds of inventions and achievements (e.g., joke makers, story tellers, cooks, etc.) and/or beings capable of internalizing values and looking for meaning in our lives. These capacities are even more widespread among humans than the capacity to formulate and execute rational life plans (if we place any weight at all on "rational"). After all, many people are relatively passive in relation to events. They don't develop overall plans for their lives. Situations develop and they do what seems best at the time. And, given their background, their psychological profiles, and so forth, it is often untrue that they have the capacity to do otherwise (or even that they can be retrained to acquire that capacity).

Of course, people like this are nonetheless practical agents. So it might be said that practical agency is what is essential and FPR is too strong a characterization of it. Perhaps all that is required, as Gewirth suggests, is acting from aims, goals, or purposes.[17] This weaker sense of practical agency, moreover, gives us a reason to say why practical agency is essential. It is essential because at least most of the other capacities mentioned presuppose it. Only practical agents can have values, look for meanings in their lives, and have certain kinds of emotions.

Of course, by itself, minimal practical agency cannot constitute our "essence." We need something stronger to distinguish us from dogs and cats. They act purposively just as we do. But perhaps self-consciousness will do. A self-conscious being has not only goals or purposes but also a sense of her own identity. Human beings, then, are essentially self-conscious practical agents. And once we recognize this about them we understand how they should be appropriately treated.

But there is a weak sense of "self-conscious" in which cats are self-conscious. They distinguish themselves from their environment; they mark their territories and realize when they have intruded upon the territory of another, and in many other ways enter into social relations with other animals and with humans. So we need something tolerably strong to distinguish ourselves from them with respect to self-consciousness, perhaps something as strong as a sense of ourselves as the same person over a significant length of time (say, a year). But if we make it this strong, we can have many of our other valued capacities without it. Certainly one can sing and dance, nurture, do math problems, make jokes, tell stories, and invent tools without being self-conscious in this sense.

Even if we could find a sense strong enough to distinguish us from cats, but weak enough to underwrite these other valued capacities, it does not follow that we are essentially self-conscious agents. One of (or some set of) our other valued characteristics may still have better title. The fact that they presuppose self-conscious agency is irrelevant. The inference to self-conscious agency is based on the following principle: if properties P_1 through P_n are candidates for the essence of X, and X's having properties P_1 through P_n presupposes that X has some other property P', then P' is really the essence of X. But this principle is obviously false. If we take it seriously, we have no reason to stop at self-conscious practical agency. Self-conscious practical agency presupposes the sort of practical agency enjoyed by dogs and cats. That sort of practical agency presupposes representational capacities and memories. Representational capacities and memories presuppose existing in time. And so forth.

The choice to structure a morality around this capacity for practical agency is a value choice. This is ironic since some philosophers are attracted to this approach because they believe it provides a basis for morality that is independent of particular conceptions of the good. If we promote and protect autonomy, it is thought, people may pursue their own goods in their own ways. But this value neutrality is an illusion. Autonomy is a value that can be traded off against other values. Indeed, some of the most interesting problems in medical ethics are generated by conflicts between the value of autonomy and the values of life and health. Moreover, anyone committed to FPR will want to trade autonomy off for preference satisfaction.

What Follows from Formal Practical Reason?

Suppose we accept some descriptive account of personhood, for example, the FPR account. What follows? Let's grant that it is possible to derive an "ought" from an "is" and attend to the particular "ought's" and "is's" at issue.

Consider "traditional" societies, for example, medieval European society. Here one's position (status), one's prospects in the world, and one's obligations were typically determined in broad outline by one's situation at birth, and one was expected to develop character traits and attitudes appropriate to one's station. Accordingly, there was not much room to "choose to live one's own life in one's own way." Still, it's difficult to see why restrictive role obligations of this sort are incompatible with the full exercise of self-conscious practical agency. Medieval Europeans were obviously self-conscious and they made all kinds of choices.

The corresponding point holds in relation to FPR. Indeed, it's not even true that medieval social arrangements failed to promote and protect this capacity. There is no reason to believe that medieval peasants aimed at maximizing preference satisfaction any less than we do. The difference is that their choices were socially constrained (and otherwise limited) in ways that ours are not. But, as long as any choices were open to them, they had the opportunity to exercise that capacity. Indeed, given the decision theoretic models in relation to which FPR is typically spelled out, they did so just as fully as we do whenever they made a decision.

This shows that there is a gap between formal practical reason and autonomy as it is usually understood in rights-based moralities. There are, of course, many accounts of autonomy in the literature, but they all attempt to give meaning to the root idea of "self-determination." And most of them take an agent's autonomy to be, at least in part, a function of the range of his unconstrained choices. That is, autonomy requires liberty.[18] FPR, on the other hand, always operates within a range of constraints (including socially imposed "costs"). And it operates fully and completely even when the options worthy of consideration are few. The limitations imposed by terrible penalties simplify its task but in no way impair its operation or its exercise.

Still, it might be said that the exercise of the capacity is developed by expanding the range of unconstrained options. If too much is constrained, we simply fall into routines. We don't really exercise the capacity unless there is room for "real choice" and conscious deliberation. Liberty is valuable because it expands the space in which authentic deliberation and real choice occur. But how far do we want to expand the realm of "real choice" and conscious deliberation? Surely no one wants life to be so option rich and so complicated that we are required actively to deliberate about everything.

What would an FPR agent want here? Presumably he would want what he wants, namely, the domain of liberty (or set of rights) that would maximize preference satisfaction over his lifetime. This brings us to another very serious problem with deriving a rights-based morality from an FPR account. The hope is to maximize autonomy (or liberty). But in fact an FPR agent must regard autonomy (and liberty) as instrumental values (if he regards them as values at all). Indeed, he should be no more or less committed to their value than a preference utilitarian is. If preference satisfaction is the goal, it is rational to prefer a morality that promotes the satisfaction of preferences to one that maximizes liberty (or, if one must choose impartially, it would be rational to prefer a morality that maximizes the preference satisfaction of some person taken at random to one that maximized his liberty). The importance of rights to noninterference and liberty will depend wholly on the circumstances, that is, on the sorts of preferences most easily satisfied under the circumstances. To the extent that it is rational to have relatively strong desires for creature comforts and consumer goods and weak desires for intellectual activity, it may be rational to sacrifice certain liberties for welfare. (Remember the chorus of the theme song from Robert Altman's film *Nashville*, "It don't worry me / It don't worry me / You can say that I ain't free / But it don't worry me.")

In fact, under the right circumstances, an agent interested in maximizing desire satisfaction should be willing to surrender not only her liberty but her very capacity for autonomy itself if that would increase her level of satisfaction. If there were a computer program that took psychological profiles and current situational variables as inputs and recommended courses of action as outputs, and that program produced better desire satisfaction results than agents could achieve by planning themselves, then it would be rational for such agents to follow the program. Furthermore, they should be willing to do this even if it meant the deterioration of their own capacity to plan (given sufficient assurance against computer viruses, etc.). Similarly, if we were visited by superior beings from another galaxy who consistently interfered with efforts to carry out personal and political decisions that were irrational from an FPR point of view, and we were FPR agents, we would have no ground for complaint. If the "parent" is benevolent and wise, we should be grateful.

These fanciful examples show that one cannot derive moral standards aimed at maximizing liberty or autonomy from the nature of formal rationality as such. Less fanciful conflicts between liberty and preference satisfaction are, of course, inevitable. In such cases, an FPR agent should prefer to be treated in ways that maximize lifetime preference satisfaction.

A final set of considerations shows that one can derive nothing at all from the capacity for FPR.

Although the formal conception of practical reason has its modern roots in Hobbesian individualism, it needn't be as self-centered a doctrine as its Hobbesian instantiation. It could be combined with a psychological theory according to which we can desire another's good for another's sake. On the other hand, it could be combined with a Hobbesian psychology. In any case it is surely possible that a desire satisfaction maximizer can have desires that are entirely self-centered and depraved. This sort of agent has FPR to the same degree as a more likeable counterpart. So, according to the current view, her nature entitles her to the same protections.

I confess I don't see why. Imagine a group of thoroughly vicious life planners with sadistic and predatory desires who enjoy nothing more than raping, pillaging, and torturing. What forms of treatment do we owe them (or they each other) by virtue of their capacity to plan their raids? Or consider an ambitious, torture-loving member of a Latin American death squad. What do we owe him by virtue of his capacity for career planning? It is certainly not obvious why anything follows from the capacity to plan.

Compare this careerist torturer to someone who suffers from a genetic disorder that affects her time sense such that she has no more sense of the "reality" of tomorrow than a four-year-old child has of the reality of ten years hence. Although incapable of formulating a rational life (or day) plan, she has all the various capacities mentioned earlier that are left out of the FPR descriptive account of personhood (e.g., a love of life, infectious enthusiasm, developed aesthetic standards, a sense of humor, a sense of solidarity with others, etc.). On the current account, she lacks what is essential to being a person, her nature does not entitle her to protection, and reflecting on her traits will tell us nothing about the kinds of moral standards we should adopt. But none of this is true of the torturer. One would like to see an argument for this.

FPR Agents with Moral Constraints

One might object that this final problem arises because an FPR agent need have no moral scruples. If we broadened the notion of reason to include moral reason, we might get a different result. Perhaps we can derive the standards of a universalist morality by considering the nature of persons conceived as rational planners constrained by moral reason.

But this won't work. To begin with, if having moral reason means knowing (or subscribing to) universal moral standards (as opposed to some morality or other), this gets us nowhere. In that case we are asked to derive a universal morality by considering the nature of someone who knows it. But we can't distinguish that person from others who are merely constrained by some morality or other unless we also already know what that universal morality asserts.

To get anywhere, we must understand "moral reason" (or having a moral capacity) in a manner that is independent of any particular morality. Let's begin with something minimal, namely, the capacity to constrain one's own good by obedience to the rules of a morality. This is clearly too weak. It is hard to see what forms of conduct are appropriate toward someone merely by virtue of the fact that she can do this. The Nazi had the capacity to make great sacrifices for the sake of Nazi morality. It is difficult to see how we can derive the whole of morality from a consideration of this aspect of human nature (even in conjunction with self-conscious practical agency).

Suppose we understand having moral reason as having the capacity to constrain one's behavior for the sake of others. This is also too weak. Caligula might well have had this capacity and exercised it on rare occasion. But again, nothing clear about what treatment people like Caligula deserve seems to follow.

If having moral reason is to get us anywhere, it needs to be understood such that it is weaker than knowing a universalist morality and stronger than a willingness to sacrifice for others. We might understand it as the capacity to take moral considerations seriously, and we might define moral considerations in a way that places some limitations on what counts without requiring that they be universal moral standards. For example, we might understand a moral consideration as a consideration which, if universally acted upon, would promote what is best for all concerned. Or we might define it as a consideration rational agents would choose to regulate their mutual interactions considering the matter from an impartial point of view.

But how does one get a universal morality out of this? Why does having a *capacity* for moral reason entitle one to special treatment? After all, one need not exercise one's capacities. One could know what's right and wrong, but just not care. One might simply be an amoral maximizer in practice (like, e.g., our torturer).

Perhaps we should replace "capacity for moral reason" with "willingness to act in accordance with moral reason." Further, suppose we grant that any being willing to do this has a right to expect that other members of his community will do the same. The most that follows is that they should not treat him like a mere thing. But how should they treat him, and how should he treat them? How should they regulate homicide? When should they require that truth be told? Under what conditions should they hold that saying "I promise" constitutes a contract? Under what conditions should they allow contracts to be broken? How should they arrange familial rights and duties or regulate sexual activity? Under what conditions should they require that people come to the aid of strangers? Clearly, we can't answer these questions by contemplating the abstract nature of formal practical reasoners who are willing to take moral considerations seriously.

This objection isn't directed at the claim that we can arrive at moral standards by asking "What standards would rational agents choose to govern their mutual interactions?" or one of its many cousins. These are contractarian questions, and I will address that tradition presently. In this section I have simply argued that no set of moral standards follows from contemplating the nature of FPR agents capable of acting (or inclined to act) morally.

The considerations in this section are not offered as arguments against an autonomy-promoting, rights-based morality. I think, in fact, that too much emphasis is placed on rights these days and that certain kinds of liberty are overvalued. But these are value claims, and I have not defended them here. Moreover, ESA defenders might well divide on this question. That is, given our traditions, social organization, and so forth, some might favor a rights-based morality designed to promote the realm of liberty. In any case, my purpose here is simply to show that one cannot derive such a morality from some descriptive account of the nature of persons.

The Contractarian Alternative

What, then, of contractarianism ? In the decade following the publication of John Rawls's *A Theory of Justice*, a great number of contractarian theories appeared in the literature. There are, of course, many differences between these theories, but all attempt to answer (at least one of) the following questions. What is a morality? That is, what makes a set of standards *moral* standards? Why is it rational to be moral? How are the principles of a rational morality justified? What are the principles of a rational morality? Different contract theorists emphasize different questions. David Gauthier, for example, devotes the lion's share of his argument in *Morals by Agreement* to answering the first and second questions. He takes morality to be a part of the theory of rational choice, and spends at least half of his book attempting to show that it is reasonable to be moral (i.e., to be a "constrained maximizer"). He has very little to say about the fourth question.[19] B. J. Diggs, on the other hand, emphasizes the third question.[20] He has very little to say about the first and the second and almost nothing to say about the fourth. In *A Theory of Justice* John Rawls tries to answer them all.

If contractarianism is to support universalism, it must answer the third and fourth questions. Moreover, it must hold that we justify moral principles by showing that they would be chosen *by* rational agents *for* rational agents taking only the fact of rationality into account. Any decision procedure that took more than this into account could not guarantee an outcome binding on *rational* beings as such. To guarantee *that* outcome, everything but rationality must be banished from the decision process. This, of course, was Kant's dream. And it is how Rawls seemed to understand the Difference Principle in *A Theory of Justice* (although he has long since changed his position).

Many contractarians, however, want nothing so ambitious. It does not particularly matter to them that a certain morality would not be chosen by, for example, rational dolphins. They are content with standards that would be chosen by rational humans. Indeed, once he gets beyond the most general form of the Difference Principle in *A Theory of Justice*, Rawls himself introduces claims about human nature to generate the standards he defends. Moreover, he doesn't take those principles to be binding even on human beings as such. The principle that liberty is to be sacrificed only for the sake of liberty, for example, is said to hold only for societies at a certain level of development.

As this suggests, contractarians proceed at various levels of abstraction. At one end of the abstract/concrete continuum the strategy yields standards binding on rational agents as such. In this case we ask agents who know only that they are rational (1) to bargain their way to a set of rules acceptable to everyone (each giving up as little preference satisfaction as he can) or (2) to look for a set of principles that is best for all from an impartial point of view (e.g., that maximizes the prospects for preference satisfaction of any individual taken at random).[21] The basis of a decision is very slim. We cannot assume even a "thin" theory of the good. A group of rational dolphins, for example, might not value all of Rawls's primary social goods, for example, wealth. The most we can hope for, as Rawls realized, is some very abstract principle that describes a tradeoff between maximizing desire satisfaction for the group as a whole and distributing desire satisfaction throughout the group. (And as the literature on the Difference Principle has established, there is no uniquely rational solution to this problem).[22]

At the other end of the continuum we ask a richly described set of historical agents to solve the same problems. These agents have the full variety of values and desires characteristic of their group. Here various groups of agents *might* be able to perform both tasks (1) and (2), but different groups of agents will almost certainly arrive at different solutions. Their answers will be based on different values and desires. So this strategy cannot support universalism.

Is there a defensible middle ground that achieves most of what universalists want? Suppose we set tasks (1) and (2) for rational human beings. Since virtually all contractarians assume a preference satisfaction theory of the good, let's do the same for the purposes of this discussion. Suppose, then, we set tasks (1) and (2) for beings with preferences that are universally human.

The first problem is that the number of preferences we have qua biological beings is rather small: food, warmth, sex, freedom from pain, and a few others.[23] Obviously, historically situated beings desire a much wider range of things than this. These wider desires are not unnatural. The capacity for them is rooted in our nature. That is, we are so constructed that given certain social and environmental conditions certain members of our species will come to have certain desires. So it seems arbitrary to leave them out. But they are clearly not desires we have merely qua biological beings.

Indeed, this alternative is especially unwelcome since actual persons are often prepared to sacrifice biologically basic desires to satisfy culturally generated ones. Thus, one might be willing to risk pain and bodily harm to satisfy a desire for honor (or abstract philosophical knowledge, Christian holiness, individualistic artistic expression, etc.). So one needs an argument for the claim that historically situated individuals should accept a morality aimed to promote only the satisfaction of biologically universal desires. That sort of morality might make it increasingly difficult for them to satisfy desires that are more important to them.

We appear, then, to have a dilemma. All contract situations set some preference maximization/distribution problem for some groups of agents. Either the preferences to be maximized/distributed belong to historically situated individuals or they don't. If they do, they will vary a good deal, and we will get different moralities for different sets of agents. If they don't, that is, if the preferences to be maximized belong to homo sapiens as such (or, worse, to rational agents as such), we *may* get a single solution but even if we do it is difficult to see why historically situated agents should accept it. After all, they might be willing to trade off satisfactions of these desires for the satisfaction of more important culturally generated ones.

It might be objected that all culturally generated desires are special cases or forms of some biologically general one and that the conflicts I have supposed to exist between the biological and the cultural are hence illusory. The desire for philosophical conversation might be said to be a special form of the desire for mental stimulation; the desire for Christian holiness a special case of the desire for a connection to something "transcendental" and so forth. I don't think that this is very plausible, but no matter. Suppose it's true. In that case we could place every culturally generated desire in some wider biologically general category. But this would still leave us a long way from a biologically based preference satisfying morality. To begin with, there is no biologically general way of ranking the various categories. Genghis Khan and his warriors, for example, did not rate mental stimulation nearly as highly as the fifth-century Athenian; nor did he rank connection with the transcendental as highly as medieval monks. Second, and more important, historically situated individuals don't want states of affairs that promote these general categories of desire; they want to satisfy the more specific desires they have. The desire for philosophical discourse is not satisfied by just any form of mental stimulation whatever (e.g., chess problems, crossword puzzles, or the interpretation of literature). Accordingly, it is possible that our moral standards promote a way of life that provides for a considerable amount of mental stimulation but discourages philosophical discourse (e.g., by encouraging uniformity of opinion as a way of promoting preference satisfaction).

As suggested earlier, it does not follow from this that the contractarian strategy is completely without merit. It is useful to ask what standards a group of rational, historically situated persons would choose for themselves with full knowledge. But in the first place, the outcome of this procedure is not a morality binding on rational beings or even human beings as such. Rather, it is a morality that is reasonable for a group of historical beings to adopt. And in the second place, the question should not be asked under the assumption that rational beings try to maximize some optimal desire satisfaction/distribution function. What they should look for, rather, is a set of standards that promotes and protects a reasonably valued way of life. I will flesh out this idea in chapters 4–6.

Notes

1. Stephen Darwall, "Two Kinds of Respect," *Ethics*, 88. no. 1, 1977, p. 45.

2. Alan Donagan, *The Theory of Morality*, University of Chicago Press, Chicago, 1977, p. 67.

3. Donagan, *Theory of Morality*, p. 88.

4. Donagan, *Theory of Morality*, p. 88.

5. Donagan, *Theory of Morality*, pp. 85–86.

6. David Gauthier, *Practical Reasoning*, Oxford University Press, Oxford, 1963, p. 119.

7. Bernard Williams, "The Ideal of Equality," in Joel Feinberg, ed., *Moral Concepts*, Oxford University Press, Oxford, 1970, pp. 158–61.

8. B. J. Diggs, "A Contractarian View of Respect for Persons," *American Philosophical Quarterly*, 18. no. 4, 1981, p. 276.

9. R. S. Downie and E. Telfer, *Respect for Persons*, Allen and Unwin, London, 1969, p. 24.

10. Downie and Telfer do not see the problem clearly. But they do expand their account of "respect" in a way that suggests an answer. Respect, they claim, does not entail condoning the actions of evil persons. For evil persons break moral rules, and we are not supposed to condone rule breakers on the ground that "to condone is to fail to respect persons in that it is to ignore one of the features essential to being a person—the ability to adopt and satisfy rules." This is very weak. To begin with, it doesn't solve the problem. Condoning an act is not the same as adopting the end at which the act aims as one's own. So even if Downie and Telfer don't have to approve of what the Hell's Angels do, they must nonetheless identify sympathetically with what the Hell's Angels want. And second, what they say about condoning is simply false. If I condone someone's breaking a rule, I don't *ignore* the fact that she has the ability to adopt and satisfy rules. On the contrary, if I tell you that it was a great thing to break a rule, I imply (or, to use Paul Grice's term, implicate) that you had the ability to obey it. Nor does condoning the acts of evil persons "ignore" their capacity to adopt and satisfy *justified* rules. In any case, on any expanded sense of "ignore" in which this would be true, condoning obedience to justified rules might be said to "ignore" our capacity to violate these rules or "ignore" our capacity to formulate and force others to obey some set of unjustified rules.

11. This, certainly, was Kant's view. For an interesting use of this argument to support moral protections for nonhuman animals see S. F. Sapontzis, "Are Animals Moral Beings?" *American Philosophical Quarterly*, 17, 1980, pp. 45–52.

12. Consider, e.g., the capacity to appreciate natural beauty, or to compose melodies (as one whistles them). Also, even supposing that there is a broad sense of "reason" on which many of these capacities presuppose having reason, it doesn't follow that they are forms or expressions of reason (consider, e.g., caring, nurturing, imagination, the capacity to construct appealing visual designs, etc.). Moreover, even if some of these capacities do presuppose

reason, it is not by virtue of their relation to reason that we value them. Consider all the expressions or forms of reason that we do not value (e.g., cheating).

13. Gerald Dworkin, "Paternalism," *Monist*, 56, no. 1, January 1972.

14. This is, of course, only a tendency. A defender of an autonomy-protecting morality could take Dworkin's idea about social insurance policies seriously ("Paternalism") and hold that there are obligations that are neither voluntarily assumed nor grounded in autonomy-protecting rights. Following Dworkin, he should do this if he believes that rational beings would want such obligations in place in any morality (i.e., that they would agree to an insurance policy that imposed such obligations). Such accounts, however, contain the seeds of their own destruction. The idea of autonomy-respecting moralities is to expand the realm of liberty. But depending on how we understand "rational beings," the appeal to what sorts of "insurance" rational beings would want for themselves threatens to justify as many incursions as appeals to "the real will" or reason do.

15. The moral hazards of acting in such theatricals are emphasized in the middle chapters of *Mansfield Park*. Those who do not recognize the hazards are condemned for their lack of moral perceptiveness.

16. Alan Gewirth, *Reason and Morality*, University of Chicago Press, Chicago, 1978, chapter 2.

17. Gewirth, *Reason and Morality*.

18. Most accounts of autonomous choice also require certain things of the agent, e.g., that his choice be based on his established values and that it reflect "effective deliberation." But the more one builds into such requirements, the more room one makes for interventions by others or by the law.

19. David Gauthier, *Morals by Agreement*, Oxford University Press, Oxford, 1986.

20. Diggs, "A Contractarian View."

21. As Rawls recognized, there are tradeoffs between maximizing preference satisfaction within a group and distributing that satisfaction for members of the group. But there is no uniquely rational solution to the tradeoff problem. It is widely noted that our choice of tradeoffs from the original position depends on our attitude toward risk and a number of such attitudes might have equal claim to rationality. Moreover, many possible solutions— including Rawls's—do not necessarily maximize the prospects of satisfaction of any member of society taken at random. Rawls's principle prohibits raising the satisfaction level of 98 percent of the population by any arbitrarily large amount if the effect of so doing is to lower the condition of the lowest 2 percent just a little. And as R. I. Sikora pointed out to me, this is surely incompatible with maximizing the prospects of a member of society taken at random.

22. Our choice of tradeoffs depends on our attitude toward risk, and a number of such attitudes might have equal claim to rationality. Moreover, the Difference Principle is arguably not among them. As indicated in note 21, the

Difference Principle prohibits raising the conditions of 98 percent of a population by any amount you like if so doing lowers the lowest 2 percent just a little. Rejecting such tradeoffs expresses a highly risk-phobic attitude (especially if the basic needs of the lowest 2 percent are met).

23. The precise form that some of these take, however, is quite influenced by culture. What counts as sexually attractive—even what gives sexual pleasure—is largely shaped this way. And what counts as food in some cultures is regarded as unfit to eat in others.

3

The Formal Conception of the Good

According to universalists, morality is a kind of supercode, and particular moralities are defensible to the extent that they resemble it. Chapters 1 and 2 argued against the most popular and plausible attempts to establish the existence of such a code and to describe its content. The failure of these efforts does not prove there is no such code, but it leaves us without a good reason to believe there is one. As we have seen, the rejection of the supercode conception (the rejection of universalism) is not a rejection of objectivity in ethics. The fact that there is no such thing as universal morality is compatible with the existence of criteria for evaluating moralities. ESA offers such a criterion. So do rule utilitarianism and contractarianism.

These theories are teleological. In the last analysis, they justify standards of right by appealing to facts about goods and evils. If we reject the supercode idea, it's hard to see how else justification can proceed. In that case, historical standards of right and wrong cannot be defended in relation to universal standards of right and wrong. At most, they can be defended in relation to standards of right and wrong appropriate to one's time and place. But the appropriateness of *those* standards needs to be justified, and there are no more abstract standards of right and wrong in relation to which this can be done. We need to appeal to something other than additional standards of right and wrong, and goods and evils seem the most plausible option. Roughly, one moral code is better for a group than another if it promotes a better balance of goods over evils and distributes them in a way that is defensible from an impartial point of view.

Biological and Sociological Accounts

The only alternatives to this teleological approach are theological, biological, and sociological theories of justification. The problems with theological ethics are well known and will not be rehearsed here.[1] But a few words might be in order about biological and sociological strategies.

Biological justifications move from "x is natural" to "x is good" or "x is right." But this move is arbitrary and implausible. "Natural" impulses and behaviors are presumably products (or survivors) of evolutionary forces, and more or less generic to the species. But why should that carry normative weight? Given our current circumstances, we might be much happier, kinder, or fairer without certain traits we inherited from our primate (and nonprimate) ancestors, and we may be able to deflect or eradicate some of these traits by socialization. If we can, it is arbitrary to deny that we should. Biological forays into ethics are best understood not as justificatory in themselves but as providing data. It may be that, like it or not, we are stuck with certain impulses or behaviors, or that we may have to pay too high a price to deflect or eradicate them. And any teleological account must take this into account.

Sociological accounts begin with the conviction that what's right in one society may be wrong in another. Properly understood, this is entirely unobjectionable, and it is quite consistent with ESA, rule utilitarianism, and other teleological theories. But some sociological accounts go on to identify right actions and justified moral standards in a particular society with whatever actions and standards are approved by that society. Most arguments for stretching the truth to this snapping point are based on the simple philosophical confusions exposed in most beginning ethics texts. Nonetheless, some version of this relativism might be defensible were there no objective grounds for evaluating moral standards. If there are no grounds, then we should either stop using terms like "right" and "wrong" entirely or try to articulate a meaning connected with as many uses as possible (that do not presuppose objectivity). That *might* get us the relevant variety of cultural relativism.

But there are objective grounds for criticizing the morality of one's society, so there is no reason to reserve the terms "right" and "wrong" for nonobjective uses. Roughly, these terms are used to refer to actions that conform or fail to conform to defensible standards. If there are such standards, we should retain those uses. Teleologists, of course, believe that there is a rational basis for evaluating standards.

Teleological Alternatives

As I see it, the only real question is, what sort of teleology should a teleologist opt for? Aristotelian accounts aim to perfect the potentials of human nature. But there are obviously many such potentials, some of which conflict with others and not all of which seem worth developing (e.g., sadists and torturers). To choose between the alternatives, and to eliminate the repulsive ones, the Aristotelian needs some metaphysics of human nature with strong normative implications. The Thomists think they have one, but their account rests on their theology. Most philosophers, including Aristotle's secular friends, are skeptical about the possibility (although, as we shall see, important aspects of an Aristotelian ethic can be incorporated by ESA).[2]

What then of contractarian and rule utilitarian accounts? There are many variants under each category distinguished in part by their accounts of goods and evils, but I cannot discuss all of them here. Instead I will focus on the most common variation, or family of variations, in each camp, namely, the view that the good is preference satisfaction. This view, or family of views, is also widespread in economics and decision theory. In this chapter I will argue against it. In chapters 5 and 6 I will defend an alternative.

The Formal Conception

Since Socrates, philosophers have claimed that many different things are ultimate or final goods: pleasure, beauty, knowledge, virtue, tranquility, health, justice, integrity, and so forth. However, they have disagreed about what belongs on this list and about how to rank its members.[3] Skeptical about appeals to intuition and convinced there is no other way to settle such disputes, many philosophers now insist that we stop making lists.[4] Rather than attempting to decide between competing substantive accounts, we should simply take as good what a rational agent seems to want: roughly, the maximum degree of satisfaction of her aims, goals, desires, values, or preferences. Despite their many differences, philosophers in this camp agree that (1) in the last analysis, what is good is good for some agent or other; (2) what is good for an agent is measured exclusively by what that agent desires (prefers, aims at, values, etc.); and (3) since an agent's good consists in desire satisfaction per se, the satisfaction of a desire contributes to an agent's good no matter what its content (barring impacts on the satisfaction of other desires). Certain views sometimes identified as desire satisfaction accounts do not straightforwardly satisfy the third condition (e.g., Richard Brandt's appeal to rational desires). But this chapter includes arguments against these views as well.

Because these accounts abstract from the content or object of our desires in this way, I call them formal conceptions of the good. According to a formal conception, the best life for anyone is one that maximizes the satisfaction of her desires over her lifetime.

Attractions of the Formal Conception

The formal conception is a kind of default view. It is born of the convictions that (1) there is no nonarbitrary way to adjudicate between competing substantive conceptions of the good; and (2) we do not need a justification for the claim that our desires are worth satisfying. Our desires are worth satisfying simply because they are our desires. We cannot say why satisfying them is a good thing, but we don't need to either. Since we can't establish that anything else is good, desire satisfaction must be the only good.

This view is supported (and entailed) by a common analysis of rational choice and practical reason. Roughly, according to this analysis, an agent is rational to the degree to which he acts to satisfy his desires or promote his values (given what he knows, etc.). If there were some good in addition to desire satisfaction, this account could not be right. In that case, an agent would be rational to the extent that he acts to promote that good too. This account of rational choice is dominant in economics and decision theory.

This account of rational action and the good goes hand in hand with internalism in the philosophy of action (a position held by Bernard Williams and Gilbert Harman, among others).[5] Roughly, internalism asserts that there is a reason for an agent P to do A if and only if doing A would satisfy at least one of his desires. That is, nothing standing outside his system of desires can count as a reason for acting. But clearly something may count as a reason for P's doing A if P's doing A is good for P. So if internalism is right, if there is a reason for P to do A if and only if doing A would satisfy a desire, nothing is good for him unless it satisfies a desire.[6] If someone does not desire knowledge, pleasure, or virtue (and they are not instrumental to something he does desire), they are not good for him.

The formal conception is also widely believed to have a number of important practical and political advantages. To begin with, traditional substantive accounts of the good are thought to invite restrictions on liberty and democracy. On most such accounts, the good diverges sharply from what most people want. Accordingly, if the state is supposed to maximize the good or to distribute it according to some principle of justice, the state will be required to restrict liberty in various ways. For if liberty is not restricted, people will try to get what they want (and not what's good for them). Moreover, since the ignorant masses will not vote for philosopher kings, no state interested in promoting or justly distributing the good can be very democratic. Formal conceptions, on the other hand, are thought to be more autonomy-respecting and democratic. Since they recognize no higher good than desire satisfaction, they do not allow us to interfere with liberty or democracy for the sake of a higher good.

The corresponding point holds in personal and professional contexts. In general, substantive theories of the good are thought to invite paternalistic interventions, and desire satisfaction accounts are supposed to limit them. If a person's good consists in satisfying his desires, we cannot justify interfering with actions aimed to promote his desires for the sake of some higher good.

Finally, the formal conception enjoys the reflected glamour of economics and "real-world" policy making. Economists and decision theorists have developed highly sophisticated logics and decision procedures designed to tell us how well off we are when various of our preference combinations are satisfied. Nobel Prizes have been won for developing these techniques, and their value is widely recognized by policy makers who use them to determine levels of personal and social welfare. If philosophers are to come down from the clouds and join "real-world" discussions of social policy issues, they must do the same. Vague and messy traditional talk about the good must be replaced by something more rigorous.

The Formal Conception: Sorting Out the Families

As suggested, "the" formal conception is actually a family of views. Some versions identify our good with the satisfaction of our desires; others speak of aims, goals, preferences, or values instead.[7] Although these differences are significant in certain contexts, I will ignore them for the most part here.[8]

The more important differences, for our purposes, cut across these categories. These differences determine what counts as satisfying, achieving, or realizing any of these "objects."

The question "What counts as preference satisfaction for the purposes of a theory of the good?" has received surprisingly little attention in the literature. Economists and decision theorists have developed elaborate and rigorous techniques and principles that get us from preference hierarchies and schedules of satisfactions to overall well-being. But they seem to take the idea of preference satisfaction itself for granted. They represent preferences by variables, and depending on the weight or rank, they derive consequences about well-being from the fact that various combinations of preferences are satisfied (or not satisfied). They don't worry very much about what it means to satisfy them; or rather, they don't worry very much about what ought to count as a satisfaction from the standpoint of a formal conception (though some acknowledge the need to do this and devote some effort to the task).[9] Philosophers, surprisingly, don't do much better. But the arguments for and against a formal conception obviously depend on what counts.

We can fix the meaning of satisfaction along five dimensions. The arguments for and against any particular account will depend on its position along these axes. If we identified a midpoint on each axis and divided members of the family entirely on the basis of whether they were on one side or the other of that midpoint, we could distinguish between at least thirty-two possible positions. But as we shall see, this is unhelpful and artificial. Nonetheless, the dimensions enable us to distinguish between a number of interestingly different positions.

The first dimension concerns the objects of preference. At one pole the objects are purely objective states of affairs, for example, being wealthy, being president of the United States, and so forth. At the other pole, the objects are entirely subjective. That is, they are preferences for states of consciousness as such. To identify these states we may need to refer to the conditions under which they are typically experienced (e.g., the pleasures of sex).[10] But the object of a preference is purely subjective so long as it is the experience itself one wants, not the experience caused in certain ways (e.g., one wants those pleasures even if they are produced by direct stimulation of the brain). Between these poles are objects that combine states of consciousness with objective conditions (e.g., being happily married, enjoying the respect of one's peers, etc.). Depending on the distribution and importance of these elements, an object approaches one pole or the other.

The second dimension distinguishes the objects of preference by their content specificity (to be distinguished shortly from temporal specificity). Roughly, objects are increasingly content specific as the ratio between states of affairs that satisfy them and states of affairs that don't satisfy them increases. Preferences approach the specificity pole to the extent that they are preferences for detailed states of affairs. My preference for a chocolate ice cream cone is closer to that pole than my preference for ice cream per se, but further from it than my preference for chocolate ice cream in a sugar cone. My preferences for health, wealth, or happiness in life are much more general. Many conditions of my body are compatible with my being healthy, and many detailed accounts of my assets are compatible with my being wealthy. This characterization is not entirely precise, but it is precise enough for our purposes here.

In the philosophical tradition, relatively specific objects are typically regarded as instrumental to very general ones. Accordingly, their satisfaction counts toward our good only to the extent that they promote our more general desires. But defenders of formal conceptions do not always make this assumption. As the economists would have it, if I prefer chocolate ice cream to vanilla and I get chocolate, that by itself contributes to my good.[11]

A third dimension is temporal specificity. Temporal specificity itself has two dimensions. Objects are temporally specific to the extent that they are indexed to particular times, and to the extent that these times decrease in duration.[12] Thus my preference for chocolate ice cream over other ice creams is less temporally specific than my preference for chocolate ice cream over other ice creams during 1990, and that preference is less specific than my preference for chocolate ice cream now. My preference for health, on the other hand, is temporally general.

The fourth dimension concerns epistemic status. This one runs from the manifest to the hidden. Roughly, desires are manifest to the degree that they are accessible to consciousness, and desires are hidden to the extent that they are difficult to recognize. Hidden desires are, of course, the stock and trade of psychotherapists. Freud famously held that many sexual and aggressive desires are deeply hidden, and non-Freudian therapists have expanded this list to other areas. In many areas, most of us are said not to know what we really want.

There is nothing exotic about hidden desires. We may not know we want something until we have an opportunity to choose it, and we sometimes discover what we want by reflecting on the choices we have made. Accordingly, our current beliefs about what we want may be mistaken. Roughly, if I believe I desire s, but I do not act to achieve s when I think I have the chance and *nothing* stands in my way, my belief was mistaken. (By "nothing" I mean not only that I have no other desires that must be sacrificed to achieve s, but also that I am not afflicted by irrational fears, weakness of will, etc.). Thus, the mere act that I believe I desire x doesn't mean that I have a manifest desire for x (I may not desire x at all).[13]

Finally, there is the modal dimension. The poles here are the actual and the hypothetical. This is the dimension most widely recognized and discussed by defenders of a formal conception. According to many of them, our good is not a matter of satisfying desires per se, but rather of satisfying rational desires. At a minimum, this is meant to exclude desires based on false beliefs or bad reasoning. Since this eliminates some of our actual desires, it is a move in the direction of the hypothetical. We move further in that direction if we expand the class of rational desires to include desires an agent would have were he fully informed and reasoning properly. Hence the economist John Harsanyi writes:

> [we must] distinguish between a person's manifest preferences and his true preferences. His manifest preferences are his actual preferences as manifested by his observed behavior, including preferences possibly based on erroneous factual beliefs or on careless logical analysis, or on strong emotions that at the moment greatly hinder rational choice. In contrast, a person's true preferences are the preferences he *would* have if he had all the relevant information, always reasoned with the greatest possible care and were in a state of mind most conducive to rational choice. Given this distinction, a person's rational wants are those consistent with his true preferences and, therefore, consistent with all the relevant factual information and with the best possible logical analysis of this information, whereas irrational wants are those that fail this test.[14]

By "manifest preferences" Harsanyi means what I have called "actual preferences"; by "true" he oddly means what I have called "hypothetical." By arguing that our good consists in satisfying our true preferences, Harsanyi has clearly moved some distance toward the hypothetical pole of the modal dimension. Suppose that the desires of a self-flagellating medieval monk are based on false theological beliefs. In that case his good is said to consist in satisfying the desires he would have were he free of them, for example, were he an atheist. What might these be? One can see that if we go too far in this direction, we will lose track of our agent entirely.

As suggested, the case for and against a particular formal conception will depend on where it stands with respect to these dimensions. Yet, once the dimensions are clear, it is also clear that there is a tension between the philosophical and political attractions attributed to this family of views. For the most part, a version is philosophically more credible to the extent that it allows desires that are general, hidden, and hypothetical. But the more it does this, the more it loses its supposed political and practical attractions. After explaining why this is so, I will argue that not even the philosophically more credible members of the family are credible.

The Conflict between the Philosophical and Political Attractions

It is a commonplace that someone may get much or all of what she wants, a BMW, world class chocolate, and so forth, and nonetheless be suicidally miserable. Here "what she wants" is clearly limited to objective states of affairs. The familiar point is that consumer satisfactions, the realization of career objectives, and so forth do not always bring happiness or even relieve depression. To earn philosophical plausibility, then, a formal account must give some special status to preferences for subjective and/or mixed states of affairs. But it's not clear precisely what special status they should have. We sometimes prefer one objective state of affairs to another even at the expense of our happiness or the quality of our experience. One might want to write a great book or be a good priest even if that meant more misery or lower-quality subjective experience on balance. The mixed state of happiness-as-a-priest beats either, but that might not be a realistic option. And where it is not, it is not entirely clear that rationality requires opting for happiness. I will have more to say about this in chapters 5 and 6. Nonetheless, the quality of experience occupies a special place.

One might fail to satisfy one's most important (actual) desires for objective states of affairs and nonetheless be happy. In at least some cases, no one could argue that these failures ruined one's life. But the reverse is not true. Who would describe a person's life as good if that person satisfied his most important preferences for objective states of affairs, but was depressed, despairing, or highly anxious almost all of the time? However, the more a formal conception gives pride of place to mixed preferences or to preferences for subjective conditions, the more it loses its practical and political advantages. To begin with, it is increasingly unable to bask in the reflected rigor and glamour of economics and decision theory, or play a role in "real-world" policy making that employs their models. These models yield interesting results only if they are provided with precise inputs. They are designed with preferences for rather specific objective states of affairs in mind. The relevant information here is at least somewhat accessible (e.g., given Jones's consumer preferences, his income, and the costs of various consumer goods, what choices among consumer goods would maximize his satisfaction?). But it's much harder to get information about preferences for subjective or mixed states of affairs and to measure their satisfaction. This is especially difficult for the more important ones, namely, the more content general (e.g., preferences for happiness, or meaning in life). Moreover, we don't need anything as elaborate as decision theory to estimate our well-being in relation to these more global preferences. If one insists on calculating, the method will be primitive.[15] But it is foolish to calculate at this level at all.[16]

"Real-world" policy makers recognize this. That is why, to the extent that they employ the economists' models, they ignore desires for peace of mind, exuberance, sense of meaning, and so forth, and their contraries when they profess to calculate well-being (or "welfare"). To the extent that they do this, however, they are not calculating well-being at all. To estimate well-being we must move beyond the limits of these models.

Further, to the extent that a formal conception gives pride of place to global experiential preferences, it loses its supposed political advantages as well. The political difficulty with substantive theories arises on the assumption that the state has a (relatively unconstrained) right or duty to maximize the good of the citizenry or to distribute the good according to some principle of justice (e.g., Rawls's Difference Principle). Without that assumption, such theories pose no threat to liberty. But given that assumption, a preference satisfaction theory that gives pride of place to general subjective or mixed preferences poses as great a threat as any substantive theory. For now the state will be justified in interfering with liberty to promote the satisfaction of general subjective (or mixed) desires (or a just distribution of them). Indeed, some substantive theories will favor liberty and democracy more than some formal ones. For a substantive theory could take autonomy, or the exercise of liberty, as a fundamental good. A formal conception can do this only if autonomy is in fact highly desired. To the extent that it is not, for example, to the extent that people prefer contentment or security to autonomy, liberty should be restricted for the sake of desire satisfaction. And if the population cannot be expected to see the need for this, democracy may need to be abridged as well.

The more room we make for desires for general subjective or mixed states of affairs, the more room we make for paternalistic interventions. For we might have good reason to believe that someone's satisfying her desires for certain specific objective states of affairs will not promote the satisfaction of these more important desires. And if we do, we have no less reason to intervene than we would given a substantive theory of the good.

Formal accounts are also philosophically more plausible if they make room for hidden as well as manifest preferences. Suppose that one of our hidden preferences conflicts with a manifest preference and the hidden preference is stronger. In these cases we will be mistaken about our preference. So it seems arbitrary to say we are better off satisfying the manifest one. But if hidden desires count when they conflict with manifest ones, they should also count when they do not so conflict. This point holds at any level of specificity.

Suppose that Jones wants a $500 jacket but she will not admit it to herself because it is against her principles to spend so much money on an article of clothing (she is an intellectual). She doesn't tell herself "I want the jacket but I don't want to buy it," but tells herself "I don't want the jacket." Suppose that her wealthy sister recognizes her hidden desire and buys Jones the jacket for her birthday. If satisfaction of consumer preferences contributes to Jones's good, it seems arbitrary to deny she is better off by this. She gets the jacket she wants and does not compromise the way she wants to think about herself. Similar examples may easily be constructed for less content specific cases.[17]

However, by making room for hidden desires, a formal account loses its supposed political advantages. Again, substantive theories threaten liberty only on the assumption that the state can restrict liberty to promote good (or to distribute it justly). But given this assumption, the state can restrict our liberty to satisfy our hidden preferences. How a particular formal conception compares to a particular substantive conception with respect to protecting liberty will depend on (1) the ratio of hidden to manifest desires acknowledged by the formal conception and (2) the weight that the substantive account places on the good of liberty, autonomy, and their relatives.

The greater the number of deeply hidden desires, moreover, the less confident we can be of "real-world" decision theoretic or economic calculations of our good, for they take as their data articulate or revealed choices. To the degree that important desires do not directly express themselves in choice, their results will be misleading. And for obvious reasons, a desire satisfaction account that stresses hidden desires provides no greater protection against paternalistic interventions than many substantive conceptions would provide.

The corresponding points hold for the final dimension. Thus, a formal account becomes more plausible philosophically as it makes allowances for hypothetical preferences (or, in any case, a subset of them, namely, the preferences we would have if we knew what it would be like to satisfy them and we knew what our prospects for satisfying them were). This is so at any level of content specificity. A hiker wants to drink from a cool mountain stream. Since the stream is contaminated, satisfying this desire will not promote his good. If he knew the stream were contaminated, he would want to drink from his canteen instead. Satisfying his actual desire is harmful. Satisfying this hypothetical preference for canteen water promotes his good. Such examples have moved Peter Railton, among others, to characterize an agent's good at least partly in relation to the satisfaction of hypothetical desires for specific states of affairs.[18] But examples can be constructed for more global desires as well.[19]

Again, a formal conception that allows hypothetical desires is likely to be practically and politically less attractive than a substantive approach that stresses autonomy, liberty, and self-development. How much less will depend on the degree to which we would retain our actual desires under improved epistemic conditions. As the number decreases, the case for infringements on liberty and democracy gets stronger, and the use of the economists' models by "real-life" policy makers becomes progressively misleading. For again, policy makers take revealed and articulate choice as their data (i.e., actual, not hypothetical desires).

The Deeper Problem

The fact that the more plausible versions of the formal conception lack the practical and political advantages often claimed for them does not, of course, refute them. Is some member of this family defensible?

The formal conception is sometimes represented as the default view. It is what remains, this side of skepticism, when we realize we have no method for deciding between competing substantive accounts. It is not just one more conception competing along with the rest. It is somehow in a league of its own. But if optimizing preference satisfaction conflicts with other accepted goods, and it is not clear why desire satisfaction should take precedence, it is also not clear that it deserves this special status.

The conflicts in question depend on the kinds of preferences we have in mind. The conflict is sharpest in relation to preferences for objective, temporally specific, content-specific states of affairs. Most of us could do better as maximizers with respect to these if we preferred small talk to serious conversation, elevator music to Mozart, and network television fare to good theater. We may have the potential to learn to appreciate both members of each pair, but the first is more readily available. We are better off having and satisfying these desires than we are having and satisfying the alternatives as long as we satisfy the former a little more often.

The problem does not disappear if we introduce preferences for subjective states of affairs. A deaf, blind, and mentally retarded person may have powerful and elaborate desires for various taste and tactile sensations, and if he belongs to a wealthy family and he is attentively cared for, these preferences might be immediately satisfied. Were he miraculously to acquire sight, hearing, and normal intelligence, he would develop many new desires he could not satisfy. Even if he did considerably better than most people with full capacities, the gap between satisfied desires and unsatisfied desires would be less favorable in his new condition. In his incapacitated condition nearly all his desires were satisfied, and although they were less varied, it is not clear that there were fewer of them (no formal account of which I'm aware includes criteria for counting desires according to which this would be true). In any case, it is clear that his *ratio* of satisfactions to dissatisfactions is higher in his incapacitated state.[20]

If we are disturbed by these consequences, we doubt that the satisfaction of temporally and content specific preferences is in a league of its own. Does preference satisfaction of any kind deserve this status?

The obvious move is to desires for global states of affairs. But the desires for wealth, fame, and power are reasonably global, and as we have seen, some people who satisfy these desires are suicidally miserable. So *these* desires for global states of affairs are not in a league of their own. Desires for more subjective global conditions are more promising. But if we restrict ourselves to the most plausible candidate, for example, happiness (subjectively understood), we have in effect abandoned a preference satisfaction account for some form of hedonism. Moreover, as suggested earlier, it is not clear that we should restrict ourselves to subjective conditions. Someone might be willing to sacrifice happiness to write great poetry or to discover a great truth. And most of us prefer to be happy in conjunction with certain objective states of affairs (e.g., we would rather be happy and accomplished than happy and unaccomplished, and we might prefer being unhappy and just to being happy but unjust).

The best option for preference satisfaction accounts is to address this problem by appealing to hypothetical preferences. Roughly, our good consists in whatever we would choose for ourselves if we had all the relevant information, if we reasoned accurately, if we were in a state of mind most conducive to rational thought, and if we vividly and accurately imagined what it would be like to realize the alternatives. Only the satisfaction of preferences that meet these conditions contributes to our well-being. From this epistemically ideal condition, different people might choose different combinations of points in our five dimensional "space." Thus, some might choose combinations of global and specific, objective and subjective conditions, and others might choose simply to maximize some global, subjective condition (say, happiness or ecstasy).

This is rough because our choices must be made against certain background conditions. Perhaps most importantly, we will get one set of results if we choose for ourselves as we are now psychologically constituted, and another if we choose for a self we would most like to be (i.e., if we can also choose new traits). But we can distinguish between these cases, and we can qualify our statements about our good accordingly. Suppose I am a believing Christian and want above all to lead a religious life. I want to go to church twice weekly, sing in the choir, perform charitable acts, and so forth. Suppose that from an epistemically ideal condition I would realize that my religious beliefs are false, and realize that if I knew the truth I would not have these preferences. Nonetheless, from that point of view, I might prefer to retain my desire to live a religious life. For I might realize that I would be utterly miserable as an atheist. My epistemically ideal self would have different reasons for this than my actual self. But, choosing for my actual self, our preferences would be the same.

Will this account do? The formal conception is forced to the hypothetical preference position by various obvious problems. It abandons desires for objective states of affairs in favor of desires for mixed or subjective ones to avoid saying that someone can be well off despite being suicidally miserable. It must move from actual desires to hypothetical ones for similar reasons (a masochist might prefer global mixes that feature degradation and humiliation because he holds some false belief, but might abandon these preferences from an epistemically ideal condition). But if we really believed that desire satisfaction is the only good, why should we flee from these consequences? Specifically, why should we prefer the satisfaction of hypothetical or rational desires to the satisfaction of desires *simpliciter*? We flee because we are trying to match desire satisfaction to something else, and misery, degradation, and so forth do not seem to be instances of what we want to match it to.

The logic of the formal conception is analogous to Euthyphro's (in Plato's dialogue of that name). Roughly, it holds that something is good because we desire it; it is not desired (or desirable) because it is good. To defend this view against obvious objections, the formal conception replaces "desire" in the first clause with "desire under optimal epistemic conditions." But this qualification is arbitrary unless desire can be well or badly directed, that is, unless it can be directed at what is or is not desirable.[21] If desire cannot be well or badly directed, what difference does it make whether we are well or badly informed (holding other satisfactions constant)? This epistemic requirement makes sense because the desirability of a state of affairs has something to do with its nature (and something to do with ours). If x is good for us, and we are in an epistemically ideal condition, we would desire x. But we would desire it because we knew something about it that makes it suitable for us. I will argue in chapter 6 that in the last analysis a being's good consists in a relation, a fit, between its nature (innate or acquired) and some condition of the world.

Moreover, many of our hypothetical desires could not possibly be actual ones. For in many cases we lack the conceptual resources actually to desire what we might desire from an epistemically ideal point of view. If I don't know what pineapples taste like, I can't desire to have that particular taste sensation (although, of course, I could desire to have whatever taste sensation I might get from that fruit). Yet that taste can certainly please me. It can contribute to my good qua sentient being. It does not satisfy me in this way because I desire it; I desire it because it pleases me. And it pleases me because there is a certain fit between what it is like and what I am like.

The same holds for more complicated cases. Given enough money and training, some Amazonian Indian might be better pleased living in New York City than in his jungle village. But if he had no comprehension of New York City—for example, if he lacks the concept of a large city (and other concepts necessary to form that concept)—he can't be said to want to live there. In general, we can't desire a state of affairs unless we can imagine or conceptualize it. If the Amazonina Indian were transparent to himself, if he could know what he desired by introspection alone, he could not know that he wanted to go to New York.

This shows, I think, that hypothetical desires are really not desires at all. In the last analysis, then, the move to hypothetical desires simply abandons the desire satisfaction account.

Concluding Remarks

Some defenders of the formal conception may be unmoved by these criticisms, especially those who are involved in decision theoretic and economic research. Among other things, these thinkers are interested in developing logics or formalisms that enable us to move from a description of a person's preference hierarchy and lists of his satisfactions to statements of his level well-being. Given these inputs, they are also interested in developing techniques to measure social well-being. Their attempts are interesting and ingenious, but in the last analysis it's not clear how they connect to traditional philosophical concerns about goods and evils. The problem is that the concept of a preference is rarely clarified in a serious way. The standard practice is simply to represent preferences by variables and get on with it. So in the end, it's not clear what the techniques in question allow us to measure.

This problem is partly responsible for numerous disputes between preference logicians on the axioms of their logics. According to Von Wright, "The intuitions of various thinkers in this field seem largely at variance with one another." Von Wright goes on to say that we need to distinguish between various concepts of preference and to develop logics for each, a point also made earlier by Nicholas Rescher.[22] To connect with the traditional philosophical problems, of course, one would need to isolate a sense of "preference satisfaction" in relation to which one could plausibly define our good. I have argued that there is no such account.

Nonetheless, I will argue in chapter 5 that the *test* of our good is, roughly, the satisfaction of those preferences we would have for ourselves from an epistemically ideal point of view. Prominent among these will be global preferences for subjective or mixed states of affairs. A logic of preference *might* improve our capacity to assess the degree to which someone satisfies these preferences, and may therefore help us to measure someone's good. But given certain formal obstacles faced by such theories, it is not clear that even this is true.[23]

Notes

1. To begin with, of course, there are problems establishing the existence of a Supreme Being who makes definite moral demands on us. In the second place, there is the problem raised by Plato in the *Euthyphro*. If God approves of an act because it is right, then "rightness" must be defined independently of God's command. So we still need to worry about what makes right actions right, and a teleological account is not excluded (perhaps that's how God decides). Finally, there is the enormously difficult problem of deciding what God commands. I recently interviewed a dozen priests and ministers representing all shades of the Christian religious spectrum to determine how they reached their conclusions on three moral issues, viz., capital punishment,

euthanasia, and the difference between child discipline and child abuse (especially in relation to corporal punishment). Only two claimed to arrive at their position by consulting Scripture alone. Others took Scripture to set very general limits but arrived at their specific views by examining the arguments on both sides. Most acknowledged that the Bible provides insufficient guidance on these issues. It says almost nothing about euthanasia and contains passages on both sides of the other issues. Moreover, what it says is entirely general. Passages in support of capital punishment do not tell us under what conditions it is acceptable (e.g., can we execute minors, can we execute under conditions in which death sentences are meted out in a discriminatory way, etc.). Even if we subscribed to a theological ethic in principle, we would have to defend our standards in other ways in practice.

2. In particular, any ESA theory justified for our society will almost certainly stress the importance of character in moral judgment and moral training.

3. Appeals to intuition to arrive at lists of intrinsic goods were not uncommon in the early third of this century. Perhaps the most influential account was provided by G. E. Moore (*Principia Ethica*, Cambridge University Press, 1903, chapter 6). The highest goods on Moore's list were personal affection and aesthetic enjoyment. Not long after, Hastings Rashdall offered a somewhat different account (*The Theory of Good and Evil*, Clarendon Press, Oxford, 1907, chapter 7). Not surprisingly, David Ross believed one could identify intrinsic good by intuition and identifies a number of such goods in *The Foundations of Ethics* (Oxford University Press, Oxford, 1930), e.g., benevolence and conscientiousness (p. 262) and knowledge (p. 267). But C. A. Campbell argues that only moral virtue is good in itself ("Moral and Non-moral Values: A Study in the First Principles of Axiology," *Mind*, 44, 1935, pp. 273–99). One could cite many other examples from this period as well. The tendency to identify intrinsic goods by appeal to intuition has diminished in recent years but has not died. Panayat Butchvarov defends Moore's approach in "That Simple, Indefinable, Nonnatural Property Good," (*Review of Metaphysics*, 36, 1982) and argues for the importance of compiling a catalogue of intrinsic goods. Bernard Gert has defined the good as that which "no rational man could avoid without a reason" and has argued that pleasure, freedom, ability, health, wealth, knowledge, and pleasure qualify although "only pleasure is unambiguously an intrinsic good." (*The Moral Rules*, Harper and Row, New York, 1973, pp. 48–49).

4. Such lists are typically justified in terms of some metaphysics (e.g., Aristotle's) or by appeals to intuitions. Most philosophers today are skeptical about the possibility of a defensible metaphysics capable of grounding claims about the good. And there is a widespread skepticism about intuitions with respect to the good as well. I think this skepticism is well founded. The argument against the prospects of a metaphysics raises too many issues to deal with here. The case against intuitions with respect to the good is parallel to the case made in chapter 1 with respect to the right. I find it odd, however,

that many philosophers who accept intuitions with respect to the right reject them with respect to the good.

5. Bernard Williams, "Internal and External Reasons," in *Moral Luck*, Cambridge University Press, Cambridge, 1981, pp. 101–113. And Gilbert Harman, "Moral Relativism Defended," *Philosophical Review*, 84, 1975, pp. 3–22. The issue of internalism is often discussed only in relation to obligation. Thus, according to William Frankena, it is the question of "[whether] it is logically possible for an agent to have or see that he has an obligation even if he has no motivation, actual or dispositional, for doing the act in question" (p. 40). ("Obligation and Motivation in Recent Moral Philosophy," in A. I. Melden, ed., *Essays in Moral Philosophy*, University of Washington Press, Seattle, 1958). But this is a specific version of the more general problem of whether one can have a reason for an act without having a motive to perform it—and having a motive presupposes having a desire.

6. A less demanding version of internalism substitutes 'P has a reason to do A' for 'there is a reason for P to do A.' Accordingly, on this version P has a reason to do A if and only if doing A satisfies one of his desires. This version does not entail that nothing is good for P unless it satisfies one of his desires. For on any normal reading of 'P has a reason,' it is not the case that P has a reason for doing A if and only if doing A is good for him. P may not know that doing A is good for him. Nonetheless, whether he knows it or not, that is a reason for P to do A.

7. Rawls uses all of these locutions. Amartya Sen takes a person's utility (good) "to stand for a person's conception of his own well being" ("Utilitarianism and Welfarism," *Journal of Philosophy*, 76, no. 9, 1979, pp. 463–89). John Harsanyi speaks of preferences and believes that values are merely preferences of a special kind ("Morality and the Theory of Rational Behavior," in Bernard Williams and Amartya Sen, eds., *Utilitarianism and Beyond*, Cambridge University Press, Cambridge, 1982). But in the same paper he also speaks of wants "in deciding what is good and what is bad for a given individual . . . the ultimate criterion can only be his own wants and his own preferences," (p. 55).

8. I see no important difference between aims, goals, and ends. But there are differences between aims, goals, and ends, on the one hand, and desires on the other. And there are also differences between preferences and desires. To begin with, since we must desire whatever our ends or goals are, we will satisfy some desire whenever we achieve a goal. However, I may have desires to which no goals or ends correspond. Some of my desires might be too unrealistic for that (e.g., the desire to be president of the United States). So if I restrict my objectives (goals, etc.) to what I have a realistic chance to achieve, I might realize most of my objectives but relatively few of my important desires (if my circumstances are unfortunate or my desires undisciplined, I will have desires I can't satisfy). In addition, preferences differ importantly from desires since preferences are necessarily two term relations—one thing is always preferred to another—while desires are not. But since preferring x to

y is simply desiring x more, our preference ordering will be logically dependent on the ordering of our desires. Nevertheless, if my options are constrained, there is a sense in which I can satisfy my system of preferences very well while satisfying my desires badly. When presented with alternatives, I might always get the one I prefer. The problem is that I might simply be choosing between evils (the hanging or the firing squad). There are also important differences between desires (and preferences), on the one hand, and values on the other. My desires may conflict with what I judge my values require of me in my situation, and if I am weak, I will act on my desires (i.e., akratically). It is interesting that so few subscribers to formal accounts characterize an agent's good in relation to his values instead of his preferences or desires. It's not obvious that one's best interests are served by settling such conflicts on the side of desire. As this suggests, anyone who believes that the formal conception is worth developing and defending owes us a more developed account of why she chooses the particular version she does than is typically provided. Most defenders of this account largely ignore the differences.

9. Harsanyi, "Morality and the Theory of Rational Behavior," devotes little more than a paragraph to the task. J. A. Mirlees ("Economic Uses of Utilitarianism," in Williams and Sen, eds., *Utilitarianism and Beyond*) makes a more robust effort but still fails to recognize the rather obvious philosophical problems that must be addressed by his account.

10. I am convinced by Bernard Gert that this is the worthwhile truth in the Private Language Argument. We refer to inner states by relating them to external conditions.

11. Philosophers talk this way too. For example, David Gauthier (*Morals by Agreement*, Oxford University Press, Oxford, 1986) takes as his example, preferring "the eating of an apple to the eating of a pear in some given environment or set of environments" (p. 22). And Peter Railton takes as his example preferring clear fluids to milk ("Moral Realism," *Philosophical Review*, 95, April 1986, pp. 173–75).

12. I resist speaking of two dimensions here for the sake of brevity. As the discussion unfolds, there is no need to keep these temporal aspects distinct.

13. According to psychotherapists, guilt, shame, loyalties, fears, etc., may prevent us from acting on a desire directly. In some cases we are said to settle for symbolic substitutes or sublimations. If defenders of a formal account have no argument against such talk, they need to say how we are to calculate such partial satisfactions.

14. Harsanyi, "Morality and the Theory of Rational Behavior," p. 55. For a very similar view see Railton, "Moral Realism," pp. 173–75.

15. Suppose we have four major global preferences—e.g., we want a sense of meaning, a sense of exuberance, a feeling of goodwill toward fellow creatures, and peace of mind. To calculate, we assign each of these desires a weight (or rank); we score our level of satisfaction on each of them; and we employ some appropriate function to get us from weighted scores to overall well-being (e.g., we multiply weight by score and add). This technique does not rest

on the shoulders of Nobel Laureates in economics. We don't need to understand Arrow's alpha property, Newcomb's problem, the prisoner's dilemma, or the foundations of game theory to employ it.

16. The advantage of calculation in any area is the precision that numbers bring. But our output can be no more precise than our input, and here that is not very precise at all. Try ranking the global desires mentioned in note 15. Is there a clear order? Now try rating your level of satisfaction with respect to each of them on a scale of 1–10. Do you think this brings you closer to an accurate measure of your well-being?

17. Suppose that Smith wants fame but will not admit this to himself. His penchant for occupying center stage at PTA Meetings and other such occasions is a standing joke among his friends. One day, by luck, Smith has the chance to be a hero and does well. Fame is thrust upon him. If desire satisfaction is a good, it is arbitrary to deny he is better off for it.

The same holds at the global level. Suppose that Brown's most important manifest global aim is to be righteous. His meticulous moralism makes him an unattractive companion. He has no friends, but he tells himself he doesn't care. In fact, he deeply desires acceptance and affection. The prospect of a social gathering always excites him. He worries a lot about pleasing others (telling himself he is just trying to avoid causing unnecessary suffering). He sulks at any sign of rejection or indifference. He laps up affection and is easily charmed by flatterers. It seems arbitrary to deny he would be better off satisfying this hidden desire.

18. Railton, "Moral Realism," pp. 174–176.

19. A student wants to be a criminal lawyer because he wants to protect the innocent. If he knew that 90 percent of the people who see criminal lawyers are guilty, he would want to be a prosecutor instead (protecting innocent victims). So he is better off satisfying that hypothetical desire. Or, to move to a more global level, a fledgling libertine wants bodily pleasures above all else. If he knew that he would be jaded and miserable by age thirty, he would prefer something more sustaining as well. And he would be better off doing that.

20. It is not clear what method of calculating desire satisfaction is most plausible as a measure of our good. The absolute number of satisfactions is clearly implausible; for desires we fail to satisfy should also be taken into account. But the difference between satisfactions and frustrations is not obviously the best measure either. Someone who has 1500 satisfactions and 1300 frustrations is not obviously as well off as someone who has 500 satisfactions and 300 frustrations or 200 satisfactions and no frustrations at all. It's hard to know what such numbers really mean when we are given no clear idea of what a desire satisfaction is. But the lives with fewer total desires seem the simpler ones (e.g., the sort of lives the Epicureans recommended). And it's not clear why a simpler life with a higher ratio of satisfactions to frustrations is not better than a more complex life with a more favorable difference. I discuss this question in relation to traditional utilitarianism in

"A Pleasure Paradox," *Australasian Journal of Philosophy*, 59, September 1981, pp. 323–31.

21. One might hold this because one believes that rationality is an independent value. But then one has abandoned the formal conception.

22. Von Wright, "The Logic of Preference Reconsidered," *Theory and Decision*, 3, 1972, pp. 140–69. Nicholas Rescher makes a similar point in *Introduction to Value Theory*, Prentice Hall, Englewood Cliffs, N. J., 1969, p. 180. See also John D. Muller, "Does Preference Logic Rest on a Mistake?" (*Metaphilosophy*, 10, July-October 1979, pp. 247–55), for an account of the considerable disagreement among major figures on basic theorems of preference logic.

23. Every preference logic needs an axiom of transitivity. Without transitivity one cannot move from a description of someone's pairwise preferences and satisfactions to an evaluation of her well-being. Consider any nontransitive ordering, e.g., A is preferred to B, B is preferred to C, but C is preferred to A. Which preference satisfaction makes one better off? It is impossible to tell, since for any state of affairs the agent realizes there will be some other state of affairs he prefers to *that*. Yet he is not indifferent between the alternatives. For given any pair, he has a definite preference. As I have argued elsewhere, however, rational preferences may be nontransitive (Michael Philips, "Must Rational Preferences Be Transitive?" *Philosophical Quarterly*, 39, no. 157, October 1989; and in a circulating manuscript, "Transitivity and the Reverse Money Machine").

4

Ethics As Social Artifact

According to universalism, the purpose of moral inquiry is to discover universal moral standards, that is, the contents of a supercode. Advocates of this view admit that consensus on results is difficult to reach: the path is littered with bad arguments, conceptual confusions, false empirical beliefs, and partisan distortions. But, they claim, there is a truth of the matter and our methods are capable of discovering it.

ESA denies that there is a such a truth. It holds that there is a rational method for evaluating existing moral codes, and that there are rational grounds for saying that one code is better than another. But it denies that there are universal moral standards. In fact, it denies that there is *necessarily* one optimal moral code for a given society. It is in principle possible that either of two (or more) codes would work out equally well.[1] And, given our epistemic limits, there will almost certainly be cases in which we cannot say *with certainty* (or even confidence) that one of two conflicting standards (or codes) is better than another. The matter may be underdetermined by the evidence available to us. ESA is a theory about how to evaluate existing moral standards and alternatives to them. It tells what counts as a justification of a standard and what counts as a valid criticism. That is, it tells us how the argument should go. But it does not provide us with a decision procedure for arriving at rationally compelling choices between standards in every case. (Because we cannot always predict the consequences of adopting a standard, no non-Aristotelian teleological theory can do this.)[2]

Many of us became interested in moral theory because we wanted to think about how to live our lives. And it is sometimes assumed that we can answer the question "How ought I to live?" by answering the question "What moral standards are justified for my society?"[3] It is even more widely assumed that by answering the latter question we can determine what is *morally* required of us.[4] For it seems obvious that one ought to act on the moral standards that are justified for one's society. But as I will argue in chapter 7, this apparently obvious truth is mistaken. The relationship between justified moral standards and the moral obligations of particular individuals is more complex than this. But ESA provides us with a method for thinking about this problem as well.

ESA: A Preliminary Sketch

Roughly, ESA holds that moralities are justified to the degree that they promote reasonably valued ways of life, and that ways of life are reasonably valued to the extent that they promote reasonable values. A morality, or some part of a morality, can fail to do this in two ways. First, it may do a relatively poor job of promoting the values it is supposed to promote, where those values are reasonable. And second, it may do a good job of promoting the values it is supposed to promote, where those values are not reasonable. We can often be certain that a moral standard fails in one of these ways, but we can't always be certain. Accordingly, ESA acknowledges that there is room for rational disagreement on certain issues.

The standard versions of rule utilitarianism and contractarianism begin with very general accounts of goods and evils and try to justify social moralities in relation to them. They move from the top down. ESA moves from the bottom up. We begin with what we value concretely and grant those values presumptive status; that is, we assume that they are reasonable unless they can be shown to be unreasonable. Until that can be shown, we evaluate moral standards in relation to those values. I will illustrate and defend this account of reasonable goods and evils in chapters 5 and 6.

As suggested, ESA distinguishes between three types of moral standards. To begin with, certain categories of action must be regulated for a society to survive at all. These include homicide, physical violence, property use, sexual access, and information exchanges (among other things). I call standards regulating these activities "core moral standards." All societies regulate these activities, so all societies have core moral standards. But as we have seen, different societies regulate these activities differently. Accordingly, core standards vary in their content from society to society. Moreover, given differences in tradition and circumstances, these variations may be justified.

According to ESA, the corresponding point holds within a society. Although the activities in question are regulated in every (or nearly every) domain of social life, they may be regulated differently in different domains. Thus, for example, both the importance and the content of the standards regulating physical assault, property exchanges, information exchanges and so forth may vary from one social domain to another. Strictly speaking, then, it is a mistake to speak of *the* standard governing assault, property exchanges, information exchanges, and so forth. Strictly speaking, for example, there are many kinds of lies and many standards against lying (e.g., perjury, slander, falsely reporting scientific results, etc.). Again, such variations are justified. They may help to promote the goods and suppress the evils specific to the relevant domains.

As suggested, core standards are distinguished from domain-specific standards. Domain-specific standards regulate activities and relationships in specific domains of social life. Individuating by roles, examples of domains include the family, the educational system, the scientific community, the criminal justice system, the medical system, the economic system, the political system, and so forth. There may be more than one taxonomy of domains for a given society, and there may be areas of vagueness. But generally the boundaries will be clear. (I will discuss the problem of locating an action in a domain toward the end of this chapter.)

The most basic domains are generated by the way a society organizes itself to meet certain fundamental needs. Among other things, every society must raise and educate its young, produce and distribute material goods, heal the sick and injured, enforce its moral standards, and protect itself from attack. In every known society, labor is divided to meet these and other needs. The division of labor can be understood in terms of sets of social roles or positions. Corresponding to any role or position are (1) a set of qualifying standards (i.e., criteria that govern who or what counts as a role occupant); (2) a set of rights, responsibilities, duties, powers, and privileges; (3) a system of remuneration and other rewards or penalties; and (4) a set of ideals or virtues and vices (i.e., characteristics that are admired and condemned in role occupants). Taken together, these elements define a role or position. And taken together, a set of roles or positions structures a domain.

Corresponding to each element, moreover, is some domain-specific moral standard. Indeed, almost every question of business and professional ethics and of the ethics of family life can be understood in relation to these elements. Most of the standard questions of medical ethics, for example, are questions about what qualifies one to be a patient (i.e., to receive various forms of treatment) or a practitioner; what rights, duties, powers, and privileges one has as an occupant of these roles; what traits we should encourage in people who occupy them; and on what basis people should be rewarded or penalized for role-related conduct. As suggested, we answer these questions in relation to the purposes specific to a domain. Thus, for example, assuming that domain-related goods and evils of medicine withstand rational scrutiny, we answer such questions by considering whether some particular distribution of rights, powers, ideals, and so forth in that domain delivers the goods (constrained by impacts on other domains).[5]

Although all societies are organized to meet certain fundamental needs, they are organized in different ways. The ancient Spartans raised their young without benefit of anything resembling what we call families. In certain tribal societies, the primary medical figure is also an important religious figure. As this suggests, domains cannot be individuated by reference to goals or purposes alone. Indeed, any given goal or purpose may be distributed among several domains (as, e.g., we distribute education between the family and various formal institutions). Domains, rather, are sets of roles organized to achieve certain purposes.

Goals and purposes also differ significantly from society to society. Although there is a level of description at which all societies have the same basic needs, they meet these needs by pursuing particular goals. Thus, although every society must educate its young, the goals of education differ from society to society. The particular goals of education in a society define education-related domain-specific goods and evils. When we evaluate the distribution of educational responsibilities in a society, we take these goods and evils as our starting point. In addition, societies may adopt goals or purposes that are not merely specifications of more general purposes. In some cases these may be consequences of how a society organizes itself to meet its basic needs. These forms of organization may generate possibilities which may themselves become target values. In our society, the primary institution for raising children is the nuclear family. But the structure of contemporary family life creates the possibility for emotional bonds between marriage partners and between parents and children that are rare or nonexistent in societies that are highly segregated along gender lines. We now value these bonds for their own sake and evaluate the ethics of family life in relation to them. For example, we now value intimacy between partners and criticize partners for excessive distance or formality. Of course, we permit considerable variability here, but the outer limits have clearly shifted in the last hundred years.

As the mention of sexual segregation suggests, the division of labor in a society is defined not only in relation to tasks but also in relation to identifiable groups. Indeed, most societies assign roles based on age and gender, and many assign roles based on ethnicity, religion, and caste or class origin. The rights, duties, powers, and privileges constitutive of these roles belong to the third category of moral standards. To some extent, these standards overlap domain-specific role standards. Indeed, domain-specific qualifying standards may be group based. Thus, for example, certain kinds of jobs may be reserved for or denied to men, women, Untouchables, people of peasant origins, or members of certain ethnic groups. There may also be strong prohibitions against intercaste, interfaith, or interracial marriages (and even friendships). But not all group-related standards can be reduced to domain-specific standards in this way. Indeed, a moral code may assign rights and duties to members of certain groups as such and define virtues and vices in group terms. It may also regulate the relations between members of groups as such, requiring various forms of subservience and obedience.

Group-specific standards have been used to "justify" many of the greatest moral catastrophes in human history, and we have reason to be suspicious of them. ESA, however, provides us with no a priori basis for rejecting group-related standards as such. Indeed, ESA arguments can be used to justify some such standards. Thus, for example, all societies have certain age-related standards and with good reason. Under a variety of conditions, moreover, gender-related standards may be justified as well. In certain environments, at certain levels of technology, it makes sense to assign dangerous jobs to men. This is the case, for example, where it is difficult to maintain an adequate population level.[6] Furthermore, under some circumstances at least, ESA arguments could be used to defend the temporary adoption of group-related standards in certain domains to compensate people for past injustices or simply to give people a decent chance in life (e.g., race- or gender-based affirmative action programs, and special rights for the handicapped). And finally, ESA arguments could be developed in favor of the claim that members of unjustly treated groups have special obligations in relation to each other (e.g., that, for the present, at least, African-American employers should preferentially hire African-Americans). Whether these arguments are compelling, of course, will depend on the merits of the particular cases.

As suggested, however, group-based standards have often been "justified" in relation to false beliefs about the nature and capacities of the relevant groups. Moreover, given the vast misery and enormous waste of talent historically associated with such standards, few of them could have been adopted from an impartial, epistemically advantaged point of view. Influenced by an understanding of this history, some philosophers seem deeply hostile to group-related standards in general. But these problems were generated by standards that could not be justified in ESA terms. And as the examples in the previous paragraph suggest, group-related standards can make good sense. Obviously, the rights and duties of children reasonably differ from those of adults, and the rights of the blind reasonably differ (in more limited ways) from the rights of the sighted.

To the extent that a society is divided along class, gender, ethnic, or religious lines, moreover, we can expect disputes about domain-specific goods and evils. Nonetheless, in most contemporary industrial societies there is considerable consensus about certain basic matters. For example, according to the mainstream English and American views, the nuclear family is supposed to meet the basic physical and emotional needs of children and to educate them in certain ways. It is also supposed to provide emotional support, love, and intimacy between marriage partners. The scientific community is supposed to deliver truths about nature in general, with an emphasis on truths that help to improve our lives in various ways (e.g., medical and energy research). The criminal justice system is supposed to deter crime and otherwise protect our rights as citizens. We may disagree on how more specifically these goals are to be understood, and to the extent that we do, we may disagree on the wisdom of certain domain-specific standards. As we shall see, some such disputes can be settled by rational argument, but some are matters on which reasonable people may reasonably agree.

Before the development of applied ethics, philosophers paid little attention to domain-specific moral standards. To the extent that they were interested in normative questions at all, as opposed to questions about moral language, they focused their attention on standards that were supposed to be binding on persons or rational beings as such. It was widely assumed that we could generate role-related standards by applying these basic or core precepts to specific circumstances (much as we apply basic principles of physics to solve problems of engineering). Few writers in applied and professional ethics now accept this engineering model. It has not worked in practice. But ESA rejects it in a particularly radical way. For it holds that there is no important difference in kind between core standards and role-specific standards. Both sorts of standards are domain sensitive. And, roughly speaking, both are justified in the same way.

Core standards seem to be more fundamental than domain-specific standards in part because they seem to be perfectly general. But as suggested, both their importance and, in some cases, our criteria for applying them vary from domain to domain as well. For these reasons it is, strictly speaking, misleading to speak of *the* prohibition against lying (stealing, killing, etc.). There seems to be a single prohibition here because a single category of action is regulated, for example, in the case of lying, information exchanges. But as I will argue, these activities are regulated differently in different domains and for good reasons. Strictly speaking, then, there is no perfectly general standard "don't lie." Instead, there is a cluster of regulations governing information exchanges in various domains. Moreover, we justify these domain-related variations in the ethics of lying in the same that way we justify role-defined standards (e.g., "Don't neglect your children").

Nonetheless, core standards differ from role-defined standards in that core standards regulate types of action that occur and need to be regulated in almost every domain. Moreover, although they regulate those activities differently in different domains, we can expect some justified constancies. For example, we are permitted to kill in self-defense in every domain, and we are nowhere permitted to kill other people merely for sport.[7] These constancies are not explained in relation to domain-specific goods. They are explained in relation to the more general set of goods that transcends domain boundaries. Obviously, the primary objection to killing is that it deprives others of life.[8] I will have more to say about general goods and evils in chapters 5 and 6.

I have said enough about ESA to begin developing the argument in its favor. Additional features of the account will emerge as that argument progresses. In this chapter I will argue for ESA in relation to core moral standards. In chapter 5 I focus on domain-specific standards.

Arguments for ESA

ESA and Its Instrumentalist Alternatives

In chapters 1 and 2, I argued against the main deontic alternatives to ESA. If those argument are sound, the field is left to the teleologists, or, rather, to the instrumentalists. Instrumentalists are teleologists who reject the metaphysical conception of morality.[9]

The first argument for ESA is indirect. The point is to show that it avoids certain problems that afflict its main instrumentalist rivals, namely, the standard version of rule utilitarianism and abstract contractarianism. Although ESA attempts to improve on these views, it springs from the same deep impulse. All three approaches hold that, in some sense or other, the point of moralities is to promote the well-being of those affected by them.[10] They disagree on how, more precisely, to develop this idea.

As I understand them, both standard rule utilitarianism and abstract contractarianism hold (roughly) that a moral code is justified for a society if and only if it produces the most favorable balance (aggregation/distribution) of goods and evils for that society (at expected levels of compliance).[11] They differ on how to understand "most favorable balance." The usual versions of rule utilitarianism identify the "most favorable balance" as the one which creates the highest total good over evil (aggregate good). Abstract contractarians identify the "most favorable balance" as that which satisfies some principle for tradeoffs between aggregation and distribution: a principle to be selected behind a veil of ignorance. (I call abstract contractarians "abstract" because they look for a single abstract principle to govern distribution.) My claim is that neither way of understanding this goal constitutes a sound basis for justifying moral standards.

Construed instrumentally, rule utilitarians and abstract contractarians agree on a good deal. Each holds that moralities are social instruments, and each holds that they should be evaluated from an impartial point of view. Abstract contractarians rely on Rawls's veil of ignorance to capture the idea of impartiality. We choose impartially for a society if we imagine we must live in that society but we don't know which member of that society we will be. Moreover, we choose with the intent to maximize the life prospects of whatever person we turn out to be.[12] Rule utilitarians can accept this as well. In any case, the main point of difference concerns the principle that each believes one is rationally compelled to choose from an impartial perspective. And each has sound objections to the other.

The argument against the rule utilitarian account is familiar enough. We are not rationally compelled to choose a society that optimizes aggregation. One can optimize aggregation by assigning enormous amounts of good to ten individuals for vast periods of time while millions lived short, barely tolerable existences. In the limiting case, one individual experiences the greatest possible good forever while the rest of us endure long, miserable, but finite spans.

This Rawlsean objection suggests that "most favorable balance" requires some distributive constraint. But what constraint? Rawls notwithstanding, no particular distributive constraint is rationally compelling either. That is, there is no single, uniquely rational principle for trading off aggregation against distribution. The plausibility of Rawls's own candidate, the Difference Principle, clearly depends on our attitude toward risk. And, as many have argued, that principle is extremely risk aversive. Moreover, it is implausible on other grounds as well. For example, it would prohibit enormous increases in the well-being for the upper 95 percent of a population unless the well-being of the remaining 5 percent were also improved (and this even if everyone's basic needs were met).[13]

Rawls's argument for the Difference Principle identifies egalitarianism and utilitarianism as its main competitors. But these positions are simply opposite poles on a continuum for the aggregation/distribution tradeoff (hereafter, "a/distribution"). There are numerous (if not unlimited) positions between these poles, and there are alternatives that do not fall *neatly* between them, namely, those that make essential reference to "absolute" thresholds (e.g., that restrict depriving people of necessities or reducing them to misery). Consider the following alternative positions:

1. Inequalities are justified if and only if they increase the aggregate, and they improve the position of most people below the mean (or the lowest third, fourth, etc.)
2. Inequalities are justified if and only if (a) they increase the aggregate; (b) they close the gap between a relatively better off group (X) and a relatively worse off group (Y); and (c) they do not significantly reduce the position of the least well off. (Note that this will decrease the inequality between two groups, X and Y, but will increase the inequality between Y and the least well off, unless Y is identical to the least well off.)
3. Inequalities are justified if and only if (a) they increase total aggregation; (b) they increase the good of those who benefit by an average of N; and (c) they reduce the good of those below the mean by no more than N/50 (or N/25, N/10, etc.).
4. Inequalities are justified if and only if (a) they increase the aggregate; and (b) they reduce no one to misery (e.g., they deprive no one of culturally identified necessities).

As this list suggests, there are many candidates for the a/distribution tradeoff and some are quite baroque. And as it is meant to illustrate, none of the competing principles seems rationally compelling. Again, our choice from an impartial position depends on our attitude toward risk, and perfectly rational people may have different attitudes. Like the rule utilitarian, then, the abstract contractarian can offer no perfectly general account of "most favorable balance." As we shall see, ESA finesses this problem by developing Michael Walzer's suggestion that principles of a/distribution are relative to domains.[14] (Why should we assume that such disparate goods as knowledge, voting rights, medical care, parental attention, and musical training are rightly distributed in the same way?)[15]

This brings us to a second problem. Suppose we had an abstract principle for a/distribution. We would still not be in a position to apply it. For given any remotely plausible account of goods and evils, we lack the capacity to measure the aggregate amount of goods and evils for a society at large. On the most plausible account, the test of whether P is better off under condition S than under condition S' is whether P would choose S' over S given perfect knowledge and imagination.[16] In a wide range of cases we cannot determine this even for those we know best. So how can we hope to get a reliable measure for society as a whole? The epistemic problems make both rule utilitarianism and abstract contractarianism impossible to implement in any useful way.

One way to deal with this problem is to restrict the range of goods over which the principle operates to something that is measurable. Thus, Rawls limits the scope of the Difference Principle to primary social goods. But he is primarily interested in defending a principle of justice, not an entire morality, and there is no reason to suppose that we can extend that method to justifying moralities per se. Imagine attempting to justify an ethic for the family or the criminal justice system *solely* on the ground that it promotes the appropriate a/distributions for some general set of goods like liberty, income, powers, positions, and opportunities.[17] In any case, this sort of justification requires some uniquely rational general principle for a/distribution. And as we have seen, there is no uniquely rational principle.

This problem of ignorance is mitigated by the bottom-up approach of ESA. It is easier to assess the effects of changing an ethical standard in a domain than to assess those effects for society at large. For example, it is obvious that a strong prohibition against lying on the witness stand helps to protect the innocent and to convict the guilty. But it is not as obvious to what degree this promotes a more favorable balance of pleasure over pain for society at large, or to what extent it increases the satisfaction of rational desires. Of course, rule utilitarians and abstract contractarians can solve this problem. They can hold that domain-related goods and evils are the best measures or indices of the more abstract goods and evils their theories recognize. But the further they move in this direction, the shorter the distance that separates them from ESA.

Of course, ESA does not eliminate the problem of ignorance. In many cases we will be unable to decide with confidence how, for example, redefinitions of roles or positions will affect goods and evils at the domain level (e.g., how changed sex roles affect family goods). But where rational people can't tell, they are free to disagree. Again, this uncertainty will disturb advocates of the metaphysical conception. But it is just what we should expect if morality is a social tool. We cannot accurately predict the consequences of many technological or social innovations. Roughly, our capacity to evaluate proposals for new moral standards will be comparable to our capacity to evaluate new social policies. The general methods of evaluation will be the same.

The third problem with the standard formulations of rule utilitarianism and with abstract contractarianism is that they are not sufficiently anchored. This problem can be remedied, but only by bringing these views closer to ESA. The problem is that whatever abstract principle we adopt, we cannot decide what set of standards produces the "most favorable balance" in the abstract. We must always consider the question given a set of background conditions. So we need to decide what conditions are to be regarded as given. One might take the minimal givens for human moralities to be facts about the following: human nature, human social organization, nonhuman animals, and physical laws. But this is too thin. If these are our only givens, our task is to arrive at a morality that produces "the most favorable balance" whatever else happens to be the case (e.g., whatever the level of technology, economic system, religious tradition, or political arrangements are in place). It is doubtful that there is any such morality.[18]

Unfortunately, the question of what should be added to these minimal constraints is rarely addressed. The result is some confusion about what is fixed and what is subject to evaluation. Is the nuclear family a given for the abstract contractarian or the rule utilitarian? What about the level of technology, the organization of the scientific community, the religious tradition, or the criminal justice system? Some of these questions are complicated since they are about institutional structures, and institutional structures embody social moralities (e.g., they are partly constituted by distributions of rights and duties). Accordingly, if we take them as givens, we take certain moral standards as givens as well.

In general, the constraints we select depend on the questions we want to answer. The ESA theorist wants to know what is best for a society given its current situation, the possibilities latent in its current situation, and the costs of realizing those possibilities. Accordingly,

ESA replaces the top-down approach of rule utilitarianism and abstract contractarianism with one that moves from the bottom up. We begin with the concrete, the actual. Our "given" is a richly described way of life. And we ask how the ethics of the relevant society can be changed to improve that way of life, taking into account the costs of change.

As we have seen, concretizing the problem this way helps solve the first two problems as well. The problem of finding principles for a/distribution tradeoffs is relativized to domains, and the problem of ignorance is mitigated by looking at impacts we can assess.[19]

Weighing Moral Reasons

The Constancy Assumption

The second argument for ESA is more direct. ESA successfully explains a feature of moral reasoning that other theories cannot explain, namely, the systematic variation in the weight of core moral standards (e.g., don't kill, don't steal, don't lie, etc.). Deontic theorists either deny that these reasons vary in their weight or admit that they vary but can offer no explanation of how or why they do.[20] Rule utilitarians and abstract contractarians can consistently admit that they vary, but they must try to explain these variations in a manner that is excessively top down.[21] ESA offers a very simple explanation.

A good many discussions in ethics and applied ethics presuppose that moral standards have constant weights or rankings across contexts.[22] Let's call this the constancy assumption. Formulated in relation to weights, the constancy assumption holds that if a moral standard has a weight of a given magnitude in a given case, it has a weight of that magnitude in every case. Formulated in relation to rankings, it holds that if consideration A is more significant than consideration B in a given case, then A is more significant than B in every case. Some argue that moralities cannot be more complicated than this since moralities must be widely learned, and nothing more complicated than this could be widely learned.

As suggested, ESA maintains that constancy is an illusion. The illusion arises because certain kinds of activities must be regulated in nearly every domain in a society, for example, homicide, property exchanges, and physical violence. For this reason, there seem to be rules against certain classes of actions across the board, for example, assault, stealing, lying, and murder. However, a more careful look reveals a more complex picture. What counts as assault, murder, and stealing in any society may differ from domain to domain; and the strength of the prohibitions in question may vary as well. That is, although homicide, property exchanges, and physical violence are regulated everywhere, they are regulated differently in different domains (although, as I mentioned earlier, there are overlaps as well).

The rejection of the constancy assumption is a surprising result. The constancy assumption seems quite sensible. Moral standards are reasons and, as Jonathan Bennett says, "Once a reason, always a reason." It seems natural to add "always a reason of the same weight." Indeed, if we do not add this, the claim that we should make moral decisions by "weighing moral reasons" is about as helpful as Aquinas's dictum that we should do good and avoid evil. If reasons have different weights in different domains, we cannot implement this scale-of-justice model until we know how to assign weights to them in various domains. The unqualified advice that we should decide moral questions by assembling the considerations on each side and determining which set of considerations has more weight pragmatically presupposes constancy.[23]

The constancy assumption is presupposed by two very popular styles of moral argument, namely, the (unqualified) appeal to counterexamples and the comparative case argument.[24] Thus, if the constancy assumption is false, the fact that a moral precept fails to hold in one domain does not entail that it holds in no domains at all. Similarly, the fact that it is relatively unimportant in a given domain does not entail that it is never a serious consideration. So what appear to be counterexamples to a standard are not necessarily decisive.

Nor can we determine the relative weights of two moral considerations by determining the "bare difference" between them in a set of two otherwise identical cases. According to the constancy assumption, we should be able to do this. For if the difference in weight or relative ranking between two precepts is of a given magnitude or order in two otherwise identical cases, that difference should be the same in every set of otherwise identical cases. Several influential moral philosophers have relied on this assumption to arrive at conclusions about the relative weight of various moral considerations.[25] But if the weight of moral reasons is domain sensitive, this parallel case technique is unreliable.

To some, the rejection of these techniques threatens the project of moral philosophy in general and applied ethics in particular.[26] If we cannot appeal to counterexamples and parallel cases, what can we do? In fact, the rejection of constancy is not damaging to moral philosophy at all. On the contrary, appeals to counterexamples and comparative cases that rely on constancy are usually just so much intuition mongering. Philosophers persist in this method because they don't know what else to do. Thus, most of us are embarrassed when we have to explain this "method" to mathematicians or physicists.

ESA offers an alternative. Very roughly, the weight of moral reasons varies from domain to domain, but varies in systematic ways depending on the effects of the sort of act in question on reasonable goods and evils. This is rough (in part) because it suggests that there is a single standard corresponding to each category action named by a core standard, and that that standard varies in its weight (e.g., that there is a single standard with respect to lying, "other things being equal, don't lie," and that that standard varies in its weight). But matters are more complicated than this. To begin with, what counts as an instance of a category may differ from domain to domain (e.g., what counts as stealing in one domain might not count as stealing in another). In addition, there may be more than one standard regulating instances of a category in a given domain. Thus, for example, in family contexts (medical contexts, legal contexts, scientific contexts, and so forth) we distinguish between several different categories of lying, some more seriously wrong than others.

Still, we can assign temporary and contingent weights to moral standards. As long as the relevant conditions remain the same, we can assign them the same weight over time, and, hence, rank them (relative to those conditions). Lying about experimental results obviously does more damage to the goals of science than lying about one's contribution to a large project. Thus, other things being equal, from the standpoint of a social morality, lies of the former sort should be more seriously wrong in science than lies of the latter sort (i.e., we are justified in taking a stronger stand against them).[27]

But this is just an exposition of the ESA alternative. What are the arguments against constancy?

The Case against Constancy

Let's begin with a famous application. In his widely anthologized paper "Active and Passive Euthanasia," James Rachels attempts to establish that there is no morally relevant difference between killing and letting die. He employs a comparative case argument.[28]

> Is killing, in itself, worse than letting die? To investigate this issue, two cases may be considered that are exactly alike except that one involves killing whereas the other is a case of letting someone die. Then it can be asked whether this difference makes any difference to the moral assessments. It is important that the cases be exactly alike, except for this one difference, since otherwise one cannot be

confident that it is this difference and not some other that accounts for any variation in the assessment of the two cases.

Notice that Rachels is not assuming that every act of killing is either morally inferior, superior, or equal to every act of letting someone die. That would be quite implausible. Rather he is trying to determine whether the "bare difference" between killing and letting die is morally relevant at all. His assumption is that if one consideration is more important than the other in one set of two otherwise identical cases, it will be more important than the other in every set of two otherwise identical cases. That is, he assumes the ordinal version of the constancy thesis. Rachels goes on to describe a set of two otherwise identical cases. In the first case, Smith stands to gain a large inheritance if something lethal should befall his six-year-old cousin. One evening, while the child is bathing, Smith sneaks into the bathroom and drowns him and then arranges things to look like an accident. The second case is the same except that when Smith enters the bathroom with murder in his heart he sees the child slip and hit his head. Rather than rescue his cousin, Smith watches gleefully as the child drowns. Rachels sees no morally relevant difference between what Smith does in these cases, and concludes that there is no morally relevant difference between killing and letting die in general.

For what it's worth, my intuitions happen to match Rachels's here. But consider two other sets of cases.

1. (a) Dirty Harry, the avenging police officer, discovers that Scarface is responsible for raping and disfiguring a number of young women. He has discovered this illegally, and his evidence will not stand up in court. So Dirty Harry drives to Scarface's country retreat, and when Scarface opens the door, Dirty Harry shoots him in the head. (b) The same as (a) except that when Scarface opens the door and sees Dirty Harry, he chokes on the sandwich he is chewing. Dirty Harry, who knows the Heimlich maneuver, smiles delightedly while Scarface unsuccessfully fights for breath and dies.

2. (a) Wasserman, a former concentration camp inmate, spots a former brutal guard, Hinckle, on the street. Wasserman follows Hinckle home and strangles him. (b) The same as (a) except that Hinckle collapses from heart failure when he sees the expression on Wasserman's face and Wasserman, who knows CPR, does nothing to save him.

Although I agree with Rachels about his case, I think that killing is considerably worse than letting die in these. The difference has mostly to do with the relative strengths of the obligation to rescue. That obligation is very strong in Rachels's case and much weaker in these.

The reasons clearly have to do with the relations between the relevant parties. In most cases, we have an obligation to rescue anyone we can rescue without undue risk or sacrifice. What counts as undue risk and sacrifice varies from domain to domain. Families are supposed to provide love, intimacy, and protection. Accordingly, family members are justifiably expected to risk and sacrifice more to rescue each other than to rescue strangers. And it is more seriously wrong to fail to rescue a family member than to fail to rescue a stranger.

Similarly, we are expected to do more for people specifically entrusted to our care. Caretaking relationships occur in many domains, and strengthen the obligation to rescue in almost all cases. But they are especially strong in family contexts and perhaps strongest of all in relation to children. The consequences of negligent or abusive "care" are disastrous.

These considerations make the uncle's actions especially monstrous in Rachels's case. But the parties stand in much different relations in the cases I describe, and the difference in their relations reduces the obligation to rescue. In the first case the parties do not meet as family members or even (merely) as fellow human beings, but rather as police officer and suspect. For obvious reasons, we do not want police officers taking it upon themselves simply to kill people they think we are better off without. But we think it is less seriously wrong for an officer to fail to rescue someone he is morally certain to be a rapist or a murderer (especially if that person is somehow protected against legal sanctions, or the officer must put himself at serious risk). For one thing, there is much less potential for abuse (e.g., we do not need to live in fear of unofficial police hit squads).

In the second case, the parties meet not as family members, but as former victim and victimizer. This relationship obtains in many domains, and the ethics governing it are domain sensitive.[29] But certain psychological facts are constant across domains and influence the shape of the ethic as well. In a word, victims hate victimizers. These feelings are powerful, and if they can be eliminated at all, it requires great effort to eliminate them. Often, victims are better off without these feelings. But in most domains, it is unreasonable to regard someone as morally defective for retaining them. For one thing, the hate response serves a useful social purpose. If victims didn't feel this way about victimizers, if they routinely forgot or forgave, victimizers could act with far less fear of reprisal. Obviously, however, these feelings must be regulated. So we are left with two questions: (1) when, if ever, should we require people to strive to overcome or minimize these feelings? and (2) when and in what ways should we be permitted to act on them? The answers are domain related since the consequences of alternative policies will differ from domain to domain.[30]

It seems to me that we can't reasonably condemn people in Wasserman's position for hating. It is hard to imagine that they could do otherwise without taking extraordinary measures, and we have no special reason to insist that they try. We can and should demand that they control their actions, and that they control their feelings to the extent necessary to do *that*. Otherwise we risk a world of vendettas. But obviously one can hate without killing.

Wasserman wants to kill. We might sympathize with this impulse, and even feel some pleasure at the thought that he acted on it, but we can't *morally* approve his acting on it. Again, moral approval of such actions invites vendetta. So, however much we sympathize, we must take a hard line here. As they say in countless western movies, no one can be allowed to act as his own judge, jury, and executioner. That threatens the existence of society itself (and hence almost all reasonable values).

Letting die is another matter. It is one thing to ask Wasserman to keep his hatred from becoming homicidal. It's another to ask him to act in direct opposition to it by rescuing his victimizer. Some might claim that he has an obligation to do this. But barring further domain-related considerations, few would argue that that obligation is as strong as his obligation not to kill. Letting die in these cases does not threaten the existence of society. It's important that here Wasserman and Hinckle have no further relationshp. The weight of the obligation to rescue is stronger where victims and victimizers are members of the same family, or are fighting for the same just cause, or where the victim has a professional responsibility toward his victimizers (e.g., where he is a medical doctor).

It might be objected that these arguments against constancy appeal to intuitions, and that they are vulnerable to the arguments made against such appeals in chapter 1. But this is to mistake their purpose. The present argument is no less strong if our intuitions differ in the cases I describe. The point is not to show that a standard is a universal truth (or any sort of truth at all), but rather to show that moral thinking has a certain structure. What is important is that our differences in judgments correlate with certain other differences (e.g., the value we assign to certain goods, and the consequences we expect from adopting certain standards). These correlations are evidence for the claim that we do in fact assign weights to moral standards on the basis of the sort of domain-related considerations I have described (at least, when we are not doing moral philosophy). This is as it should be. After all, it improves the quality of our collective existence.

One could acknowledge this but object that this practice is a mistake, that is, that moral reasoning *should* have some other structure. But one needs an argument for this that is grounded in some alternative picture of morality. I have argued against the main candidates in chapters 1 and 2.[31]

It must be acknowledged, however, that the previous argument against constancy is not completely compelling. A defender of constancy could just bite the bullet and insist that the "bare difference" between killing and letting die is the same in each pair of parallel cases. It is hard to see how one could defend this without appealing to an unusual set of intuitions. But suppose one insists anyway. In that case he will insist that the all-things-considered wrong is identical for each pair of parallel cases. He can acknowledge that there are differences between the sets of parallel cases (e.g., that the wrong in each of Rachels's cases is greater than the wrong in each of Wasserman's cases). He can insist that these differences can be determined by adding up the constantly weighted moral considerations. Still, he must tell us how to assign weights to these considerations.

There is a serious problem here even if we grant the evidential status of intuitions. Consider the following examples of lying:

1. lying to one's aunt about how well one liked the hat she wore to the Christmas party to avoid hurting her feelings (the hat was destroyed so there is no danger that she will wear it again);
2. lying to a stranger on a train it is highly unlikely one will see again about one's intention to live according to one's horoscope for the next week (to end a tiresome conversation about astrology);
3. lying to a braggart in the steamroom about one's vast wealth to get "one up" on him;
4. lying to a friend about something unimportant to him to embellish a good story;
5. lying to an athlete one coaches about her prospects in a tournament to give her the confidence she needs to perform well;
6. lying to a competent patient about a cancer prognosis so that he will not be depressed (intending to inform him soon);
7. lying in a news story about what happened during a political demonstration to create more interesting "news";

8. lying to one's spouse about one's intention to be monogamous in the future to calm him down;
9. lying on the witness stand about what one saw at the scene of a crime to help a friend;
10. lying in a scientific paper about the results of an experiment to advance one's career.

We all agree that some of these lies are more seriously wrong than others. Since the weight or order of the obligation not to lie is constant according to the constancy assumption, these variations must be explained in terms of the presence and absence of other morally relevant considerations, also constantly weighted or ordered. How do we determine these weights or this ordering? There is only one plausible suggestion. First, we fill out the cases (as they stand they are mere case sketches). Second, we devise a ranking of the acts on the basis of their wrongfulness. Third, we try to explain our ranking by assigning weights or an ordering to all relevant standards. The process is analogous to solving a set of equations by assigning values to variables such that every equation comes out true. But in this case we are trying to preserve rankings, not equivalences. Our goal is to arrive at an assignment of weights to all standards such that our rankings are preserved. We test our conclusions by amending the cases or by introducing new ones (e.g., cases involving killing or stealing).

Again, let's grant for the sake of argument that intuitions have the evidential status required by this approach. Still, the prospects of arriving at such a ranking seem dim. With all the talk about weighing moral reasons over the past thirty years, no one has ever produced an account of this kind. Moreover, attempts to do so often require "reducing" wholes to alleged parts in artificial ways. Thus one is forced to represent "stealing $50 from one's mother" as a compound of the several constantly weighted considerations. One might choose (a) stealing; (b) lowering one's mother's net worth by $50; (c) causing someone a specific amount of suffering; and (perhaps) (d) doing something wrong to one's mother. But this seems arbitrary. Returning to the mathematical analogy, it seems more plausible to represent roles as operators on the weight of moral standard rather than artificially to reduce them to standard among standards.[32]

There is a still stronger argument against getting the desired results from this procedure. Again, according to the stronger version of the constancy assumption we can nonarbitrarily assign fixed and invariant weights to moral standards. This means that we can say for all times and places whether stealing in itself is worse than lying or promise breaking, in themselves, and by how much. This "how much" is extremely important since ordinal rankings are insufficient to settle all but the simplest cases. Indeed, whenever there are more than two considerations, the most important of which favors an act and the two less important of which oppose it, we still need to determine whether the weight of the more important obligation is greater than the combined weights of the other two. But since each act of killing, theft, and so forth is done to a particular person and from a particular motive, and since each act has a particular set of expected consequences, no *actual* killing or stealing is an act of killing or stealing per se. How, then, could we isolate the per se case to determine just how seriously wrong stealing per se is?

The only plausible suggestion is that the per se case can be reached by a method of approximation. We look for acts of stealing or killing such that other considerations against the act are minimized, and there are no considerations in its favor. These would necessarily be the least serious of the cases, or rather, the least serious of the cases in which there are no moral reasons favoring the act. But identifying such cases is not always an easy matter. What would the least serious cases of killing or letting die be? Are they the acts performed from the least serious motives with the least serious consequences? It is difficult to produce clear and convincing examples here. But if we can't do this, how do we know what weight to give to the considerations against killing or letting die per se?

We are not much better off when we can imagine the least serious cases. For the wrongs at issue here are often so small that it is difficult to see how the obligation in question could be a serious one. Consider lying or promise breaking. Suppose again that I promise a stranger on a train that I will read my horoscope when I get home and I don't; or suppose I lie to him about my intention to do so. I do both to change a tiresome topic, that is, to save myself a few minutes of boredom. These seem very small wrongs indeed, so small they are nearly (if not entirely) nullified by the fact that I save myself a few minutes of boredom. The same holds, for example, for harmlessly embellishing the truth for the sake of a good laugh. If the weights of the standards against lying and promise breaking are reduced to these minute dimensions, then the all-things-considered wrong of more serious lies and broken promises will have almost nothing to do with the fact that they are lies and broken promises, and almost everything to do with other matters. And since the same sort of argument applies to at least most "other matters," few acts will turn out to be seriously wrong at all.

The ESA Alternative

The general approach of ESA with respect to these matters should now be reasonably clear. Nonetheless, it might help fill out the picture to discuss in further detail how certain considerations vary in their weights. The question that concerns us is how the weight of a moral consideration is justified in a social morality. To get clear about this we need to distinguish between social moralities and personal moral codes. One subscribes to a moral standard if one's moral judgments are governed by it. But one may subscribe to a standard without believing that one's society should include it as part of its public moral code. One might believe, for example, that it is better to allow a person's decision in the relevant area to be a matter of personal conscience, unpressured by social opinion. Some people feel this way about abortion. In that case one would want others to conform to one's standard. But one would not want people in general to endorse the standard in public or to publicize judgments made on the basis of it. To the extent that one adopts this attitude toward S, S is a personal moral standard. On the other hand, one believes that S should be part of one's social morality to the extent that one believes it should be publicly endorsed and defended and used to justify public moral judgments.[33]

ESA tells us how to assign weights to considerations in a public morality. Roughly, the weight of a consideration C in domain D varies in relation to the importance of a society's taking a strong moral stand in relation to C-type acts in D. This in turn is a function of (1) the importance of the reasonable goods and evils C-type acts protect or suppress in D (and in general); (2) the extent to which mobilizing public moral opinion in relation to those acts promotes those goods or protects us from those evils; and (3) the costs and benefits of mobilizing public moral opinion in relation to those acts in relation to a wider class of goods and evils.

Let's begin with lying. Truth telling promotes a reliable flow of information. Successful lying promotes misinformation, but not all information is reasonably valued for its own sake. If it were, one could profitably spend one's time randomly memorizing tables of weather statistics and the like. Very roughly, most information is reasonably valued by virtue of its relation to other goods and evils.[34] But the importance of these values and the degree to which they would be endangered by a socially neutral attitude toward lying differ from domain to domain, and within domains as well. So then does the wrongfulness of lying. (The corresponding point holds for misinformation.)

Consider a few examples from the lying list. Let's begin with lying between strangers unlikely to meet again (case 2). To change a boring topic, I lie by announcing my intention to read my horoscope when I get home. Nothing is endangered by this sort of lie. No one will be hurt by this kind of misinformation. Trust between strangers will not be jeopardized. And there is no reason to believe that my character will be damaged such that I am more likely to tell serious lies in the future. (If you disagree about the wrongfulness of such lies because you disagree with me about these considerations, ESA describes the structure of your thinking.)

Lying in scientific papers (case 10)—for example, faking experimental results—is another matter altogether. Virtually all the goods associated with scientific activity depend on an accurate flow of this kind of information. False experimental reports undermine the entire enterprise. Moreover, the career demands on scientists are such that there is pressure to fake results. In the absence of a strong negative moral attitude toward lying, there would be a great deal of it. So we need a strong standard.

Let's move to the family. There are many interesting categories of lying here, but I will discuss just one, namely, supportive lying (case 1). My wife is competing in a tennis tournament, and she must believe she has a good chance to win in order to play well. I tell her she has a good chance, believing she has only a small one. My aunt has just given a disastrous speech at a toastmasters club, quaking and stammering her way through the delivery. She is very upset about it, and petrified at the thought of speaking again next week (and she can't be talked out of doing *that*). "The speech was nothing to write home about," I say. "You were a little off your form and you need to work on relaxation and focus, but it wasn't nearly as bad as you think." These lies seem perfectly acceptable. Family members are supposed to provide emotional support and to help each other during tough times. Of course, one must be convincing, and this is not always easy if people expect one to lie supportively. But many people want to believe and are buoyed by good news even if they have reason to be suspicious. Of course, it is pointless to lie to people who will not believe one and who will resent the effort. And one must be careful not to undermine one's future credibility. But these are just matters of lying intelligently. The only plausible argument against a permissive moral attitude in these cases is the risk of abuse.[35] Under the banner of taking care of someone, one might manipulate information such that the person is harmed or deprived of choices. The weight we attribute to supportive lying depends in part on the degree to which we assess this danger. I believe that the good accomplished by supportive lies outweighs the evils of their potential abuse. Again, if you disagree with my view of supportive lies because you disagree with *this*, you accept the ESA account of how the argument goes.

Finally, consider lying in medical contexts (case 6). Before the emergence of medical ethics as a discipline, most doctors routinely lied to patients about unfavorable cancer diagnoses when they thought the truth would have a bad impact on the patient's health. Now most doctors believe that typically the patient should be told the truth. The earlier view was defended on the ground that the goals of medicine are to combat disease, promote health, and prolong life. The current view is defended on the ground that the patient has a right to autonomy. To assert this right is tantamount to rejecting the traditional goals of medicine as paramount. The conception of the morality of lying has changed because these goals have been either rejected outright or demoted.

According to ESA, the right to autonomy must be defended on the ground that autonomy is intrinsically valued (rationally) or on the ground that it is instrumental to some other good (e.g., desire satisfaction). In either case, the scope of that right depends on how we understand autonomy. Almost everyone agrees that not all lying about diagnoses and prognoses violates autonomy, and there is a considerable literature discussing which sorts of lies do.[36] If this discussion is to rise above mere linguistic intuition mongering about the use of the term "autonomy," the concept must be understood to have a normative dimension.[37] That is, the boundaries of autonomy must be set by the kind of freedom it is reasonable for us to value (or value in medicine). Where the right to autonomy is grounded on the claim that autonomy is intrinsically valued, we need to specify the kind of freedom that is reasonably intrinsically valued and do so precisely enough to help with hard choices in medicine. And where the right to autonomy is defended in relation to other goods, the boundaries of the concept should be tailored to promote those goods. In either case, the ethics of lying in medicine depends on values it is reasonable to pursue in the medical context. The weight of the right, of course, depends on the importance of those goods.

Similar analyses hold for the remaining examples, but to avoid excessive tedium I will move now from lying to stealing. Like lying, the weight of the consideration against stealing varies from domain to domain (and within domains). But unlike lying, the criteria for identifying an act as an act of stealing vary as well. (I believe this is also true of coercion, physical assault, bribery, extortion, false promising, insults, promise breaking, and even killing, but I will not argue for this here.)[38]

Roughly, stealing is taking something that belongs to someone else without permission.[39] What counts as stealing depends on what counts as belonging and what counts as permission. What counts as belonging depends on how we assign property rights. We have already seen that cultures differ considerably here. But there are domain-related differences within a culture as well. Thus, we can't know whether Paul steals by taking something from Janet's house without her permission unless we know how Paul is related to Janet. And the relevant relations are domain related. Suppose Paul takes food from Janet's refrigerator without asking and eats it. If Paul is Janet's child, husband, or best friend, he does not steal. If Paul is a stranger (e.g., a refrigerator repairman), he does.

In some domains, it matters what Paul does with what he takes, and in others it does not. If Paul takes food from his mother's refrigerator, sells it to his friends, and keeps the money, he has stolen. If he simply eats the food, he has not. But if Paul and Janet are strangers, it doesn't matter what Paul does with the food. If Janet owns a food store, and Paul is a stranger, Paul steals whether he eats the food or sells it to someone else. Similarly, in many organizations employees may appropriate supplies from a storeroom for their own job-related purposes without asking anyone's permission, but they can't sell these supplies (even if they are particularly thrifty in their use of them and sell only what they save the organization by their thriftiness).

We can understand these differences as differences in what counts as belonging, or differences in what counts as implied permissions. But however we understand them, we must recognize that they change from domain to domain, and so therefore does the extension of "stealing." According to ESA, this is as it should be. What counts as belonging and/or the range of implicit permissions is justified on a domain-by-domain basis in the same way as the weight of the obligation not to steal. For example, it is hard to imagine how we could realize the goods of family life if property rights between family members were the same as property rights between strangers. Family relationships, and to a lesser extent friendships, are relationships of mutual reliance sustained (ideally) by affection and concern. The blurring of the line between mine and thine is an expression of this relationship and reinforces the feelings that sustain it.

Let's now turn to the weight of the consideration against stealing. Plato's remark that friends have all things in common notwithstanding, there is such a thing as stealing from friends, and it is more seriously wrong than stealing from strangers. Friendship involves trust, and trust creates many opportunities for theft. If we had to worry about friends taking advantage of these opportunities, if we could not trust them, we could not have true friendship. In addition, stealing destroys the emotional bonds constitutive of friendship. The thief becomes a false friend and feels like it (if he is capable of bonds of friendship to begin with). And if the victim discovers his act, the victim can no longer regard him as a friend. These are, at least, typical reactions. Finally, perhaps most importantly, friendship requires that friends be special to one another. A friend is not just another person, but a person toward whom one has special care and concern. Part of what it is to have special care and concern is to regard harms and wrongs to friends as a more serious matter than harms and wrongs to strangers. If we do not understand a relationship in this way, we might have bonds of mutual affection with someone, but we would not have a friendship. Accordingly, we rightly attach considerable blame to theft against friends. And, for obvious reasons, we attach still greater blame to theft against family members.

Finally, when domains become sufficiently pathological, the obligation not to steal has no weight at all, at least in relation to certain people. In that case the presumptive goods and evils in relation to which the relevant institutions are "justified" are unreasonable or simply not served. Thus, for example, the inmates of concentration camps, gulags, and other horrors of modern history are not morally prohibited from stealing from the kitchens of these institutions. Other things being equal, they may also lie to their guards, break promises to their commandants, and so forth. Indeed, they may have no obligations at all that are justified in relation to the defensible purposes of these institutions. Prisoners nonetheless have a moral life. There are standards governing their interactions with each other and standards governing their interaction with various officials as well (e.g., other things being equal, prisoners should not report guards who break the rules to do them kindnesses). But these standards cannot be justified in relation to the goals of the institutions. Rather, they are ground rules for making the best of a bad situation. And they permit prisoners to steal from, lie to, cheat, and even kill their captors in an unusually wide range of circumstances.[40]

Again, the reader may disagree with these judgments without rejecting ESA. As long as we agree that the wrongfulness of stealing varies from domain to domain in relation to the goods and evils at stake in them, we agree on what is important at the level of theory.

Multiple Considerations and Conflicts

As suggested, responsibility for certain goods and evils may be distributed among several different domains. In our society, for example, educational and health care responsibilities are divided between the family and a class of professionals. But this does not create a serious problem with respect to defining domains or assigning actions to them. As suggested, domains are sets of related roles organized to promote certain goods. Typically, we have no difficulty determining which roles go together in this way. Although parents are responsible for certain health care needs of their children, we have no difficulty distinguishing between the role of parent and the role of health care professional or between the family and the health care delivery system. Nor is there usually a problem deciding whether the standards of a given role are relevant to judging an act.

Because we all occupy many different roles, there will be cases in which standards related to more than one role will be relevant to judging our actions. For this reason, it is misleading to speak of "locating" an action in a domain. Rather, we need to determine which domain-related considerations are relevant to judging an act. But in most cases, this is reasonably clear. Typically, we have no difficulty determining when we have obligations as a teacher, as a doctor, as a parent, and so forth.

Difficulties may arise when considerations conflict. But an effective social morality tries to minimize conflicts by building appropriate exceptions into role definitions. I am an elementary school teacher and a single parent. My child develops a bad case of flu, and I need to decide whether to stay home from work to care for her. Whatever I do, I do as both a teacher and a parent. But there is now general agreement that my responsibilities as a parent take precedence. Indeed, in general, barring special circumstances, we believe that moderate to serious family health obligations override the obligation to show up to work. This understanding is now explicit in many labor contracts. It was achieved by negotiation, but it reflects a moral stance. We can defend it or criticize it in ESA terms.[41] We defuse many conflicts, or what would otherwise be conflicts, by building exceptions into role definitions in this way.

We also defuse them by explicitly prohibiting certain exceptions. Police officers are required to investigate friends as thoroughly as strangers. Scientists are required to report results that may be harmful to a family business (e.g., the dangers of a pesticide). Judges and juries in criminal cases are supposed to ignore everything but legally legitimate arguments for or against the guilt of the defendant in reaching a verdict, and so on.[42] These choices may also be defended or criticized in ESA terms. In general, defenses are based on the importance of the relevant requirement to the domains in question. As the examples suggest, there are cases in which permitting the relevant exception would seriously undermine the central good of an important domain while prohibiting it would not. For example, allowing police to play favorites would entirely undermine the goal of criminal justice, and allowing scientists to suppress results for personal reasons would seriously hamper the goal of truth in science (or its nonrealist substitute). On the other hand, the goods of family life and friendship in general are not seriously jeopardized by our refusal to allow special consideration to families and friends in these areas.

But matters are not always this clear. We confront conflicts between domains when considerations from more than one domain are relevant to a decision and we cannot settle the matter by appealing to exceptions or prohibitions. In these cases, we try to simplify the conflict and arrive at a reasonable strategy for dealing with conflicts of that kind. We begin by identifying and clarifying the standards in conflict. We then try to reduce the number of standards involved by looking for defensible exceptions or prohibitions of the sort discussed above. To do this, we try to determine the importance of the competing considerations to their respective domains. We do not try to assign cardinal values or ordinal rankings to these standards (hoping perhaps to manufacture some pseudorigorous, mathematical-looking solution). Rather, we try to get a sense of what is at stake with the hope of simplifying the problem. Once this is done, we compare the relative importance of the considerations from an impartial point of view. That is, we try to decide how to decide cases of *this* kind, impartially considering the interests of everyone affected.

This is not simply an appeal to intuitions. We are thinking about the general consequences of deciding cases of *this* kind in *that* way. Accordingly, empirical arguments may be relevant. And so may various kinds of arguments used to evaluate candidate goods and evils that I discuss in chapters 5 and 6.

Moreover, ESA provides a principled way to deal with certain familiar problems that face appeals to generalization. First, one cannot simply gerrymander solutions to suit one's interest by ignoring morally relevant considerations. Those considerations come with the problem. That is, they generate the dilemma we are trying to resolve in the first place. One can eliminate a consideration only by appealing to a prohibition or an exception. Second, although there may be more than one way to describe a "case of this kind" ESA provides us with a principled way of choosing between formulations. In general, we can criticize a characterization by showing that there is some other characterization which generates superior results in ESA terms.

This is not a decision procedure. It may not even deserve to be called a method. But it is an approach, and I think it gives us as much as we can hope for here.

Consider an example. A middle-level executive of a bottle cap company is ordered by a superior to falsify a report on the characteristics of a childproof bottle cap in order to help his company keep a contract. The act is illegal. Moreover, if the cap reaches the market, many people are likely to be annoyed and frustrated (the cap is childproof but harder to remove than it should be), and the drug company that contracted for the cap is likely to suffer. On the other hand, if the contract is lost, the executive's company will fail and many people will lose their jobs, including him (and times are hard). By refusing to lie, the executive will incur the enduring anger of his coworkers (including many friends) and the anger of his superiors (and may therefore have a difficult time getting another executive position). Thus, on the one hand, he appears to have obligations as an employee, a coworker, a friend, a spouse, and a parent. On the other hand, he appears to have obligations as a businessman (not to misrepresent his product), as a citizen (to uphold the law), and as a member of society (not to subject others to unnecessary frustration and annoyance). Which should he honor? Or do we need a still more detailed account of the case?

Although there has been a good deal of recent discussion concerning the possibility of authentic moral dilemmas, I know of no plausible ethical theory that yields a clear and convincing answer in questions of this kind.[43] The ESA approach offers no obvious solution either. But it may do something both to simplify the problem and to show what is so difficult about it. As suggested, after listing the obligations apparently involved in the conflict we try to simplify by looking for defensible exceptions and prohibitions. In this case, we can immediately eliminate the executive's obligation to his employer qua employee. His obligation to his employer does not include violating reasonable laws governing business practices, or reasonable standards of business ethics. These are justified and mandatory exceptions to one's obligation to obey one's superior. Other things being equal, employees are and should be morally required to conform to reasonable laws and standards of business ethics (imagine what the economic domain would be like if there were a moral consensus permitting or requiring the opposite). If nothing else were at stake here, that would settle the matter. In simplified cases of *that* kind—in cases where nothing else *is* at stake—the executive is morally required to refuse.

It is less clear how things stand with respect to obligations to coworkers. Part of the problem is that the stakes are so high. If the stakes were lower, the case would be less difficult. Suppose that only a single coworker and friend were involved. In this case, the manager is asked falsely to report the effectiveness of the bottle cap to save the job of that person. Again, I think, there is a strong ESA argument for refusal. Other things being equal, one is not morally entitled to break reasonable laws governing business practices or to violate principles of business ethics to protect the job of a coworker (even a coworker who is also a friend). A moral consensus to this effect would have terrible consequences. So would a consensus allowing business executives to violate reasonable laws or reasonable principles of business ethics to protect their jobs. Of course, losing one's job reduces one's capacity to support one's family. But if we made that an exception, we might as well not have business ethics at all.[44] In any case, no one is morally obligated to support a family with an executive's salary. So again, if this were all that is at stake we have our answer.

If this is correct, then, other things being equal, the executive's obligations to his employer and to his family are irrelevant to deciding the case. Moreover, if his obligations to his friends and coworkers are relevant, they are relevant because the futures of so many people are at stake.[45] In effect, then, we need to weigh these obligations against the obligations on the other side. How do we do this?

To get a sense of this, we might raise the stakes on the other side. Imagine that it is too late to lie to the representative of the pharmaceutical company. He has discovered the truth about the bottle cap and he is planning to report it to his company. Now, instead of being ordered to lie to him, our executive is ordered to kill him. Clearly this is intolerable. We cannot permit people to murder to save a company. When the stakes are this high, moreover, one's obligations to one's friends and coworkers are also overridden. They cannot expect us to murder someone to save their jobs.

Nor could they reasonably ask us to help cause the death of strangers to save their job. Suppose that the product in question were not a bottle cap but rather an exploding gas tank.[46] To approve of lying in this case is to approve of helping to cause death and injury to strangers to save the jobs of friends and coworkers. A moral consensus in support of this could be disastrous.[47]

This analysis tells us why the case in question is difficult. It is difficult because (a) the consequences to the lives of friends and coworkers of honoring one's obligations as a business person and a citizen are so serious; (b) the damage done by violating those obligations is relatively minor; and (c) comparatively speaking, the violation of the law and the principle of business ethics is also minor (compared, e.g., to dumping toxic waste, falsifying reports about the safety of airplane brakes, bilking retired people of their savings, and so forth). As we have seen, were we significantly to alter any of these variables in the right way, the case would be easier.

Reasonable people might disagree about how to decide cases of this kind. And everyone might have trouble in relation to certain more detailed accounts of (a) (suppose that the plant employs hundreds of people, the livelihood of an entire town depends on it, including the livelihood of one's parents, siblings, and childhood friends). Again, the most that ESA can do in these cases is tell us how the argument should go.

Still, ESA has certain advantages over appeals to intuition. It tells us how to determine the importance of the conflicting considerations in their respective domains and, in many cases, how to simplify the problem. It also tells us what empirical considerations are relevant. Again, this may be the most we can reasonably expect. Fortunately, real dilemmas do not often arise (how many does one actually face in one's life?). Generally, the standards that govern our action are reasonably clear. And, again, ESA tells us how to determine their importance in their respective domains.

The Complexity Objection

It might be objected that moralities must be teachable and that ESA is too complex for that. Most people simply do not understand enough about domains and their goods to do the sort of thinking ESA requires.

But this objection confuses two kinds of thinking. Roughly, there is thinking about whether an action is right and thinking about whether a standard is justified. As I argue in chapter 7, the relation between these questions is complicated. In any case, as developed thus far, ESA addresses only the latter question. That is, it tells us how to evaluate moral standards. And, as anyone who has taught ethics knows, few techniques for evaluating moral standards are easily teachable to everyone.

A more plausible objection in the same spirit is that an acceptable theory for evaluating standards must generate teachable standards (i.e., standards that can be easily learned by anyone of normal intelligence). But this requirement is excessive. Not every person of normal intelligence can easily learn the principles of medical ethics, business ethics, legal ethics, journalistic ethics, and so forth. Of course, very generally speaking, we want people to learn enough to promote the reasonable values of the domains in which they participate. But we should expect that some people will be able to do this better than others. Certain complexities, for example, certain distinctions between cases, may be too difficult for some people to grasp. But this is not an argument for reducing everything to the lowest common denominator. Levels of complexity should be decided in ESA terms. We want the level that serves us best.

Some may favor a morality that everyone can master equally well because they believe that morality should be an equal opportunity institution (i.e., that everyone should have the same chance to be moral). Given a metaphysical conception of morality, this makes some sense.[48] But there is no a priori reason to require it on an instrumental account of morality. On such accounts, the degree of allowable variation is obviously decided on instrumental grounds. And we may do better if our standards are too complex for some to grasp. This does not mean we ought leave them without a clue. We can offer, for example, Ross's list of prima facie duties as rough guidelines for those unable to comprehend anything more sophisticated (relatively few, I think). Moreover, we need not be harsh with people unable to understand the more fine-grained distinctions. There are good instrumental reasons against blaming people for failing to understand complexities that exceed their capacities.

But the strongest response to the complexity objection is that it simply underestimates how complicated moral thinking actually is and needs to be. The simpler normative theories, for example, Ross's prima facie duties or Gert's ten moral rules, provide only minimal guidance. Moral decisions often require us to choose between Ross's prima facie duties or Gert's ten moral rules, and neither Ross nor Gert tells us how to do this. In addition, they both nearly completely ignore role-specific standards. But these are obviously central to moral thinking. Clearly, we have different obligations to family members (clients, colleagues, etc.) than we do to strangers.

The complexity objection may also be motivated by a mistaken belief that moral thinking is typically a matter of conscious deliberation (i.e., of consciously and explicitly applying standards to cases). But more often it is not. Most moral decisions are made "on our feet." A situation presents itself and we do or say what seems right. Without thinking about it, most of us are continually passing up opportunities to get our way by lying or otherwise manipulating others.

Much of what we do is rule governed but does not involve the conscious and explicit application of rules. Consider driving a car or participating in a conversation. The rules governing these activities are quite complex. Few of us can state them with any accuracy at all. To participate in conversations, for example, we must know when it is appropriate to speak, in what tone of voice, on what topic, and so forth. And all of this varies with the context. But although we cannot hope to state the rules, few of us have trouble participating in conversations. Perhaps inspired by the Ten Commandments, many moral philosophers have tried to uncover a handful of simple, highly general standards that are supposed to govern our moral lives. But this effort has not gotten us very far. At best, we can articulate a rough set of incomplete general guidelines riddled with exceptions. ESA has an explanation: moral thinking is indeed more complicated than that.

Notes

1. A partial universalist theory could acknowledge this as well. As long as the alternative codes included the universal elements, a partial universalist might regard them as equally adequate.

2. By "Aristotelian teleological theory," I mean a moral theory that (a) justifies standards of conduct in relation to goods of character and (b) justifies these goods in relation to some metaphysics of human nature. The goods in question here are obviously the virtues, and the standards in question direct us simply to promote them. Since Aristotelian teleological theories do not justify standards in relation to consequences, they are of course free from the uncertainties to which this subjects us.

3. For example, Kant represented almost every decision as a moral decision (or in any case, as having a moral dimension). So do act utilitarians.

4. Thus, e.g., rule utilitarianism is often described as the view that one ought to act on that set of standards which, if adopted, would maximize utility.

5. There are, of course, disputes about what precisely these goods are. We will discuss the logic of these disputes in chapters 6 and 7. Also, as the parenthetical qualification suggests, no domain can be evaluated exclusively in relation to the goods and evils specific to it. The organization of one domain very often has important impacts on the organization of another domain (e.g., economic structures importantly affect political structures and family life). And the fact that the structure of one domain has adverse impacts on the reasonable values of another counts as an argument against it. I will discuss this further in chapters 6 and 7.

6. From a reproductive point of view, men are obviously more expendable than women. Theoretically, at least, one can remove many men from a population without losing any reproductive potential (within limits, the remainder can impregnate all the women). But whenever a woman is lost, the

society loses all the offspring she might yet produce. The point about the males is theoretical since a society may not be able to change rapidly enough to allow the surviving males to impregnate all the women.

7. The weights may still differ. Other things being equal, it is worse to kill one's mother for sport than to kill a stranger. Also, it is not perfectly clear that one has a right to kill in self-defense in every domain. If one believes that the death penalty is justified, it is not obvious that someone who deserves that penalty has a right to defend himself by killing a guard or an executioner.

8. This is rough because people may not always want to live (and that desire can be rational). There are also terrible cases in which people are incapable of telling us whether they want to live, but it is clear that no reasonable creature would want that under their circumstances (e.g., severely retarded, badly compromised newborns who face very short lives of severe pain).

9. Teleologists embrace the metaphysical conception to the extent that they accept the picture sketched in the introduction. The contrast to "metaphysical" is "instrumental." Roughly, instrumental theories hold that moralities are tools that are justified by how well they serve certain goals or realize certain ends. Accordingly, the distinction between the metaphysical and the instrumental is not isomorphic to the distinction between the deontic and the teleological. Depending on her views about the nature and purpose of morality, for example, an act utilitarian could be a metaphysical moralist or an instrumentalist (although, since so few philosophers hold this view and there is such a strong case against it, I do not consider it a major instrumentalist rival to ESA). Still, no deontic picture of ethics could be instrumental. For as I understand them, at least, deontic theories hold that the right is logically prior to the good, i.e., that we can justify standards of right action without appealing to goods or evils at all. And instrumental theories hold that standards of right action are justified by how well they serve certain goals or purposes (i.e., promote certain goods).

10. Thomas Scanlon's version of contractarianism is an exception. Roughly, on his view the point of morality is to enable us to justify our actions to other rational beings on grounds that they cannot reasonably reject (see "Contractarianism and Utilitarianism," in Bernard Williams and Amartya Sen, eds., *Utilitarianism and Beyond*, Cambridge University Press, Cambridge, 1982). Scanlon's account of the point of morality leads him to understand questions of justification somewhat differently than Rawls and rule utilitarians do, but his account also involves evaluating standards by comparing how well people do under various alternatives codes or standards. That is, with respect to justification, he differs from Rawls and rule utilitarians primarily on the question of which global patterns of gains and losses constitute a defense of or objection to a moral code. For this reason, his discussion *suggests* a view of justification that is as abstract and domain insensitive as standard versions of the views he opposes. But what he says is also compatible with a domain-sensitive account of justification. Moreover, given the level of abstraction and generality at which he expresses his views, it is hard to know

exactly what disagreements with an ESA account of justification his views entail. One could argue that ESA tells us how to arrive at standards for justifying actions that other rational agents in our society, with an interest in agreeing on such standards, could not reject (at least where it is possible to arrive at such standards). Of course, Scanlon's account of the point of having a morality does differ from the account I have defended here. ESA says that the point is to protect and promote a reasonably valued way of life. Scanlon says (roughly) that it is to enable us to justify our actions on grounds other rational agents cannot reject. But if it turns out that we justify our actions to other rational beings by appealing to standards that promote and protect a reasonably valued way of life, his account of the point of morality is compatible with the ESA of the justification of moral standards. In that case it does not seem necessary to address our difference concerning the point of morality here.

11. This may seem a little strange in relation to Rawls, but I think it is accurate. Rawls wants a principle that governs the aggregation/distribution of primary social goods. He takes these as his targets because he thinks they correlate best with the successful completion of rational life plans. Roughly, a rational life plan is a plan which provides the best chance to maximally satisfy one's system of desires over one's lifetime. I don't think Rawls is entirely clear about the relationship between rational life plans and the good. But the most plausible interpretation is that the plan itself has merely instrumental value. In the end, one's good consists (roughly) in the satisfaction of one's desires. Roughly, then, Rawls is concerned with the aggregation/distribution of desire satisfaction in the population.

12. Strictly speaking, this is weaker than Rawls's since it does not require one to be ignorant of one's own values, etc.

13. This was pointed out to me by R. I. Sikora.

14. Michael Walzer, *Spheres of Justice*, Basic Books, New York, 1983.

15. It might be objected that there is an impartial procedure for selecting a principle in the face of such disagreement. The procedure would enable us to choose between principles given the rates at which those principles would be endorsed from an impartial point of view or to synthesize elements of principles in a manner that reflected the rates of endorsement. We might be able to rule out some procedures in this way, but many possibilities will remain. Social choice theory offers no compelling candidate for such a procedure, and it is hard to believe that there is one. Do we opt for the principle that most people would choose from an epistemically advantaged point of view? Or do we choose a principle that expresses some compromise or average position among those choices or some range of those choices? Do we rank principles or merely vote for our first choice? And if we try to compromise or synthesize, how do we do that? In any case, the search for such a procedure is at best theoretically interesting, for even if we had a procedure we could not apply it. We have no reliable method for discovering at what rates people would choose principles from an impartial and epistemically ideal point of view. We do not know this even about ourselves or our spouses.

16. Because of the impossibility of measuring pleasures and pains in relation to a single metric, hedonists must rely on preferences to make tradeoffs between pleasure/pain packages. Thus, hedonism is really a preference satisfaction view where the objects of preference are feeling states and the basis of choice is restricted to how those feeling states feel.

17. There is also the problem that our choice of primary social goods is not indifferent between conceptions of the good. Indeed, by identifying a good as primary in this way, by measuring justice in relation to how it is distributed, we encourage people to measure their well-being in relation to that good. Children raised in a Rawlsean society are likely to grow up placing a good deal of value on liberty, money, and power (as opposed, e.g., to familial love, job satisfaction, free time, artistic creativity, and enjoyment of nature). After all, social institutions are evaluated by the degree to which they promote and distribute primary goods (where "more" is always better, whatever the collective impact of pursuing "more" on other goods turns out to be).

18. In another way of understanding givens, one is free to add anything to these conditions one wishes, e.g., the best economic system, the best political system, and the best religious tradition. The result is a utopian vision constrained by facts about human nature, human social organization, and so forth (e.g., the sort of thing Plato attempts in *The Republic*). But interesting as they are, utopian visions are not necessarily useful guides to moral thinking. The problem is that often we can't get there from here or even move significantly in that direction.

19. Rule utilitarianism and abstract contractarianism could also begin with a richly described way of life and do moral evaluation on a domain-by-domain basis. In that case rule utilitarianism would look for rules that maximize preference satisfaction, domain by domain. And an abstract contractarian might look for rules yielding the proper a/distribution of primary social goods. The latter might also relativize principles of a/distribution to domains (although the former could not). If each then indexed its relevant goods and evils to domain-specific goods and evils, there would be little to separate them in practice from ESA. I would be very happy with this convergence of the major teleological alternatives. If ESA is sound, it would mean that more people are thinking sensibly about ethics.

20. Ross holds that where considerations conflict we must decide by "flair." In *The Moral Point of View* (Cornell University Press, Ithaca, N.Y., 1958), Kurt Baier holds that there are rules of superiority (pp. 101, 171–72).

21. Although as suggested, a rule utilitarian or abstract contractarian could simply adopt the more concrete ESA account as the best approximation of what he is after. In that case the only real difference between ESA and these views is that they hold that one and the same principle for a/distribution holds in every domain. But a contractarian could amend this as well.

22. I will discuss James Rachels's use of this presently (in "Active and Passive Euthanasia," *New England Journal of Medicine*, 292, January 9, 1975, pp. 78–80). In addition to Rachels one finds examples of such arguments in

Michael Tooley, "Abortion and Infanticide," *Philosophy and Public Affairs*, 2, 1972, pp. 58–60; Richard Trammell, "Saving Life and Taking Life," *Journal of Philosophy*, 72, 1975, pp. 131–33; Peter Singer, *Practical Ethics*, Cambridge University Press, Cambridge, 1981, pp. 149–52, and many other papers.

23. I take this to be a matter of Gricean implicature. The advice is incomplete with respect to the purpose it is supposed to serve unless there is constancy.

24. See Shelly Kagan's "The Additive Fallacy," *Ethics*, 99, October 1988. Kagan is the only other philosopher I know who has attacked the constancy assumption. Although he published this article after I published my criticism ("Weighing Moral Reasons," *Mind*, 96, July 1987), he arrived at his conclusion independently.

25. See note 22 for references.

26. Shelly Kagan ("The Additive Fallacy") is not so pessimistic. He concludes that the possibility of effective moral reasoning depends on further advances in moral theory.

27. We also need to consider the strength of the temptation to perform acts of that type and the degree to which adopting a standard of a certain strength will discourage acts of that type.

28. Rachels, "Active and Passive Euthanasia," p. 79.

29. It may also occur in families, but where that is the case there are good moral reasons for expecting victims to attempt to get over their feelings of resentment. But there are limits to this as well. Victims cannot be expected to endure a continuation of the victim role, and some forms of victimization are so severe that one may not be able to normalize relations at a later age (e.g., child sexual abuse).

30. Certain victim-victimizer relations are structured along group lines, e.g., ethnic, gender, or religious. These relations generate a number of complicated ethical issues, including issues of forgiveness. Thus, Howard McGary has argued that under certain conditions, victims of racial injustice have strong self-interested reasons to forgive ("Forgiveness," *American Philosophical Quarterly*, 26, 1989, pp. 243–51). But in these cases too the ethics of forgiveness is domain sensitive. An African American has more reason to forgo hating an Anglo American who has married his sister than he does to forgo hating any anonymous Anglo American.

31. In fact, roughly, any such argument must show that we should adopt an alternative structure even if that diminishes the quality of our collective existence. This is rough because advocates of the alternatives will claim that any losses in the nonmoral dimensions of our existence will be exceeded by gains in the moral dimension. The idea here is that it is intrinsically valuable that people and states of affairs have certain characteristics (e.g., that people are of goodwill and that states of affairs are just). I will argue in chapter 6 that although we may value these moral states of affairs intrinsically, they do not have intrinsic value. We are justified in treating them as good in themselves, but only because of certain contingent features of our nature. ESA accounts

must take these valuings into account, but only as goods among goods. As this suggests, we can value them too much.

32. Kagan, in "The Additive Fallacy," also suggests that certain considerations are best treated as operators, but not in relation to roles.

33. According to ESA, personal moral standards are properly justified in a manner similar to that in which social moral standards are justified. Roughly, we consider what the world would be like were people to act that way. In the case of personal standards, however, we can consider the consequences of everyone acting that way, as opposed to the consequences of people acting at expected levels of compliance. And we are free to ignore transition costs and the social costs of enforcement.

34. I mean intrinsically as well as instrumentally. As we have already seen, it is possible to intrinsically value something for a reason. Information is reasonably valued intrinsically in a domain if so valuing it promotes certain other values.

35. Some might argue that these lies are disrespectful because they treat their victims as if they were incapable of facing the truth and had to be manipulated. I am not moved by this. There are times at which most of us are incapable of facing the truth and would prefer to be lied to. Our small plane is forced to land in the mountains. The only way out is through a pass where there is a significant danger of avalanche. You are an experienced mountaineer, I am a very anxious novice. Although you know that I am generally agile (we play basketball together), you notice that my anxiety is adversely affecting my agility and that I am climbing clumsily. You also know that I am terribly afraid of avalanches (I do not cross-country ski in the mountains for that reason), and that I suffer from occasional panic attacks. I ask you nervously whether you think there is an avalanche danger. You lie, thinking that if I knew the truth I might refuse to go on or climb so badly that I will fall. It seems forced to evaluate your behavior in relation to categories like respect and disrespect here, but if we must I don't think you can be accused of the latter. To tell the truth in that situation would be to show a complete lack of care or concern, a complete disregard of my interests. As suggested, this sort of thinking can be abused. Disrespectful forms of manipulation can be justified by appealing to one's love of one's victim. But that is the only plausible argument against permissive standards here.

36. The best paper I am familiar with in this area is Bruce Miller's "Autonomy and the Refusal of Lifesaving Treatment," *Hastings Center Report*, August 1981. Miller distinguishes between four senses of autonomy. These are perhaps better described as four autonomy-related reasons for lying to patients (or overriding the patient's expressed wishes with regard to treatment). According to ESA, we decide which reasons have what force in what range of cases by considering the advantages and disadvantages of a policy that permits lying to patients or overriding their judgments for *that* reason in *that* range of cases. It does not help matters to appeal to the intrinsic value of autonomy per se. As the argument in chapter 2 suggests, it is not at all clear

what autonomy per se is. And when we assign clear meanings to it, it is not at all clear that it has intrinsic value.

37. Philosophers use "intuition" to refer to a great many different sorts of things. Philosophers in many areas could profit from a systematic account of the various categories of intuition there are and evaluation of the uses to which these intuitions are put in philosophical argument.

38. Killing might appear to be the least variable. But there are domain-related differences. If a doctor removes a terminally ill patient from life support at her request, he is said to let her die. But if a family member pulls the plug at her request, he will be charged with killing. Also, certain acts will count as killing if done by ordinary people, but not if done by police officers (e.g., certain accidental deaths caused by driving at high speeds during a car chase).

39. The usual account, wrongful taking, is mistaken. I may wrongly take something someone is willing to give me. I may even wrongly take something to which I have a right (e.g., rent from a tenant who desperately needs the money).

40. The ethics of this situation are complicated. Certain constraints on a prisoner's behavior can be justified in relation to a wider set of goods. Because life is valuable, one ought not to kill a guard without good reason. But one may be entitled to do so to escape or to prevent some other prisoner from being killed or tortured. Other constraints may be justified in relation to valued traits of character. I argue in chapter 7 that we reasonably value certain character traits for their own sake. These valuings are domain sensitive. But traits like kindness, compassion, and gratitude can be especially prized in harsh and brutalizing settings. They remind us of the best in ourselves and help to protect us against the total deterioration of our character.

41. I think it is defensible. The world would seem a harsher and colder place if we could not take care of the health needs of family members (and they could not take care of ours). And family bonds would suffer. On the other hand, the amount of absenteeism involved does not seem seriously to jeopardize prosperity.

42. From a logical point of view, prohibitions may be equivalent to built-in exceptions. That is, it may be possible to say everything that needs to be said in the language of prohibitions or exceptions alone. After all, if police are prohibited from treating friends with special consideration in the line of duty, there is some corresponding exception with respect to the obligations friends have to one another. But the use of both locutions is more illuminating since it helps us to focus on the relevant issues.

43. For discussions of the possibility of dilemmas see Christopher W. Gowans, ed., *Moral Dilemmas*, Oxford University Press, Oxford, 1987.

44. It is arguable that cases in which one is faced with this choice are relatively rare, and that we could do better with a consensus that prohibited such violations of the relevant laws and ethics to advance one's career, raise one's salary, and so forth but permitted violations to protect one's job. However, given the competitive nature of the corporate world, it is often difficult

to distinguish between these considerations in practice. Moreover, a standard permitting these exceptions would obviously be subject to widespread abuse.

45. If the numbers get high enough, there is a dilemma even if the executive is not employed by the company threatened with bankruptcy. Suppose one is called as a consultant to evaluate the bottle cap. One knows that a negative evaluation will close the plant and put several hundred people out of work in a recession. One believes that if he lies about the cap, the company will be able to survive its temporary difficulties and get other business.

46. Obviously, this would be disputed by some business leaders. The decision to use the Pinto gas tank was not a desperate measure to keep Ford afloat but rather an attempt to improve profits. The relatively low level of general moral outrage at that decision shows how ridiculously weak our standards governing business conduct are.

47. Our society is much too lenient about such matters, and we suffer for it. In fact, relatively few people seem outraged by the terrible damage some corporations do merely to increase profits (and that executives approve merely to advance up the corporate ladder). We pay a high price for this.

48. On this account, morality is the ultimate measure of human worth. From this perspective, it might seem unfair that some people have a greater opportunity to be moral than others. Our democratic sentiments are such that we want the uneducated and slow-witted to have the same chance as the educated and intelligent. Of course, in many ways they do. Intelligence has little to do with moral courage, compassion, or many of the other virtues. However, it does put one in a better position to understand complex moral situations. Only someone blinded by ideology could deny this truism.

5

Evaluating Standards

In chapter 4, I argued for ESA in relation to core moral standards. In this chapter I will further develop that account in relation to domain-specific standards. I will also discuss the problem of evaluating goods and evils. Before beginning, it is worth repeating that the fact that a standard is justified for a society does not entail that every member of that society is obligated to act on that standard. The relation between justifying moral standards and evaluating individual conduct or character is more complicated than is ordinarily supposed. I will discuss that relationship in some detail in chapter 7.

According to ESA, moral standards are justified on the ground that they adequately promote reasonable values (where "adequately promote" has a distributive dimension). A standard, or set of standards, can fail to do this in two ways. First, the values in relation to which it is justified may be reasonable, but it may fail adequately to promote them. And second, the values in relation to which they are justified may be unreasonable to begin with. I call arguments aimed to establish the first "consequential arguments" and arguments aimed to establish the second "axiological arguments." Many criticisms of domain structures employ both kinds of arguments.

The point of this chapter is to explore these argument strategies, with an emphasis on domain-specific standards. The strategies are familiar enough. They are the standard techniques of social and moral criticism from Plato to the present, and they occur in popular as well as philosophical writing. This chapter simply collects the most important instances of them and organizes them in ESA terms. Among other things, these arguments enable us to settle many moral disputes before we reach the level of abstraction at which standard versions of rule utilitarianism and abstract contractarianism begin.

Consequential Arguments

Consequential arguments are empirical. But what at first appears to be a consequential argument for or against a standard may turn out to be axiological. Thus, we may disagree about whether certain standards promote education, mental health, intimacy, and so forth because we disagree about the nature of those goals or because we disagree about what more specific versions of them are valuable (e.g., we disagree about the sort of education that should be our goal). In that case, of course, we are really committed to different goals and our dispute about standards is not consequential. Accordingly, disputes about moral standards should begin with conceptual analysis to determine the extent to which the issues are consequential and the extent to which they are axiological. As suggested, to the extent that the dispute is consequential, the arguments are empirical. The point is to determine whether a given standard, or set of standards, at the expected level of compliance, adequately promotes a set of values.

Assuming that relevant domain-specific goods and evils are reasonable, then, other things being equal, a standard is justified only if the benefits of adopting it exceed the costs with respect to those goals. (As we will see, whether or not other things are equal depends on how adopting the relevant standard affects a wider set of values.) But this is only a necessary condition. Consequential arguments are implicitly comparative. A standard adequately promotes a given set of values only if it does so at least as well as any realizable alternative (counting the transition costs of each). Assuming the relevant values are not in question, we justify a standard by showing that it satisfies these two conditions.

Let's consider this account in relation to domain-specific standards. Criticisms of domain-specific standards may be more or less fundamental depending on how much they ask us to change. The most fundamental criticisms call for completely reorganizing the roles constitutive of a domain structure (i.e., providing new qualifications for role occupants, assigning them new rights and duties, devising new bases of payment and penalty, and evaluating them in relation to new virtues and vices). Arguments for moving from private to socialized medicine (or socialized to private medicine) call for changes in all of these areas.[1] Less fundamental criticisms call for changes in fewer roles or fewer role dimensions. Thus, for example, arguments for a more expanded conception of child abuse restrict the rights of parents without fundamentally redefining their role. And arguments for less restrictive requirements of confidentiality in medicine do the same for doctors.

In the case of fundamental criticisms, the role of consequential arguments is generally obvious. Many of the arguments for and against socialized medicine are grounded on empirical premises about the cost and quality of medical care available under that system. And many disputes about the relative merits of capitalism and socialism in general are grounded in disputes about how effectively each system provides the material basis of a good life and promotes decent working conditions. These are not the only issues, but they can be decisive. If everyone's chances for a decent standard of living and a decent job are significantly enhanced by either system, the issue is settled.[2]

The relevance of empirical arguments is obvious to everyone when we are considering fundamental redistributions of rights, duties, and responsibilities in a domain. Ironically, it is often less obvious when we are considering less fundamental changes. In that case the point at issue is often the scope and importance of some particular right. Accordingly, many philosophers are tempted to consult their intuitions. ESA, of course, treats questions of particular rights the same way it treats other moral standards. The appeal is to reasonable goods and evils, and the arguments are importantly empirical. I will illustrate the plausibility of this approach in relation to two examples.

Consider the requirement of confidentiality in relations between professionals and their clients. One could understand this in relation to a client's right to privacy and attempt to fix the scope and importance of that right by appealing to intuitions or to the nature of persons. But that will not get one very far. ESA justifies the professional's obligation and the client's right in relation to domain-specific goods and evils. In general, without guarantees of confidentiality clients would be reluctant to provide professionals with the information the professionals need to do their jobs. Accordingly, professionals would not be able as effectively to utilize their expertise to suppress the relevant evils and promote the relevant goods. In addition, breaches of confidentiality can be harmful to clients in various ways. But all of this will vary from domain to domain. Accordingly, the limits and importance of "the" right to privacy should vary in this way as well. Indeed, "the" right to privacy may vary within a domain in relation to certain domain-related variables.

Consider an example from medicine. It is now generally agreed that HIV test results should be confidential in the normal run of cases. The main argument is empirical. If the results were publicized, many people would refuse to be tested. In that case, the disease would spread faster and would be treated less effectively than it would be were results private. But it has been argued that an exception should be made in relation to health care professionals themselves, especially doctors and dentists. Because many people fear being infected by doctors and dentists, the argument goes, they are reluctant to seek medical treatment. Accordingly, the population at large is becoming less healthy. The issues here are obviously empirical. Among other things, we need to decide (1) how many doctors and dentists would refrain from taking HIV tests if they knew that positive results would be publicized; (2) to what extent this would delay the treatment of infected doctors and dentists and increase the number of patients infected by them; (3) were test results confidential, how many infected doctors and dentists who knew they were infected would practice in ways that put patients at risk; (4) how many patients currently avoid doctors and dentists because they are afraid of HIV infections; and (5) to what extent this avoidance results in a deterioration of public health. Agreement on these factual scenarios does not guarantee agreement on a policy. We might disagree in our choices between packages. But agreement on the facts will often generate widespread and reasonable agreement. If publicizing positive results did not reduce the number of doctors or dentists seeking tests but visits to dentists and doctors fell 20 percent per annum because of fear of HIV contamination, the results should not be confidential. If publicizing positive results reduced the number of doctors and dentists seeking tests by 10 percent but did not significantly increase the number of people seeking medical and dental attention, the results should be confidential. Some factual scenarios might produce tougher choices. But the limit and importance of the right to privacy clearly depend on the facts here.

Or consider an example from the criminal justice system. How strong should our safeguards against false conviction be? That is, what sorts of rights should we grant criminal suspects against the state? Metaphysical moralists appeal to intuitions here. Since it is never right to punish the innocent, presumably our safeguards should be as strong as we can make them. (Or perhaps the intuition is, "better ten guilty people go free than one innocent person is convicted.") ESA appeals to impacts on reasonable goods and evils. Safeguards against false prosecution promote a form of justice that almost everyone values intrinsically and reasonably, and it relieves us all of the anxiety that we might be victims of false convictions. On the other hand, the stronger the safeguards, the more difficult it is to convict the guilty. That the guilty go unpunished violates the very same ideal of justice, and it undermines the deterrent force of the criminal law (i.e., it results in greater numbers of rapes, murders, thefts, etc.).

An ideal criminal justice system will protect us against injustices and harms at the hands of the state and at the hands of our fellow citizen. So, according to ESA, we should opt for the distribution of rights and duties that provides us with the best overall protection package from an impartial point of view. That package takes into account the magnitude and the probability of the harms we risk from each source.[3] The specifics of that package clearly depend on social conditions. Roughly, conservatives are right if conditions are now such that it is reasonable to risk additional abuse from the authorities to reduce risk at the hands of criminals. And civil libertarians are right if conditions are otherwise. The issues here are nearly entirely empirical.[4]

Evaluating the Goods

As the considerations in the last section suggest, many disputes about moral standards could be settled if the disputants agreed sufficiently on the relevant empirical facts. But many other disputes would remain.[5] According to ESA, these are disputes about goods and evils themselves, namely, what goods and evils (or distributions of goods and evils) are reasonable, or what packages are preferable to their alternatives.

To understand these disputes we must distinguish between four types of goods and evils. The boundaries between these categories are not precise. But since this taxonomy does not describe a value hierarchy, since there are no "trumping" relations between categories, they don't need to be. To begin with, then, there are the justificatory goods and evils that are specific to domains (e.g., criminal justice, health, and familial bonds). Second, there are cultural values that are not domain specific (e.g., in our case, leisure time and social equality). Third, there are goods and evils we enjoy or suffer us qua human beings, that is, goods and evils that are specifically related to characteristic human capacities and open to human beings of any culture (e.g., goods and evils associated with conceptual abilities, linguistic abilities, aesthetic capacities, and distinctively human social relationships). And fourth, there are goods and evils we have qua mammals, organisms, and sentient beings (e.g., vitality, and enjoyable sensations and their opposites).[6] In chapter 6 I will develop the abstract theory of goods and evils that motivates these distinctions.

As suggested, the justificatory goods and evils of a domain have presumptive status. That is, they count as reasonable unless we have a reason to reject them. The fact that our pursuit of one presumptive good conflicts with another presumptive good can be such a reason. So can the fact that our pursuit of it sufficiently suppresses a good or sufficiently promotes an evil of another kind. As we shall see, we can also reject presumptive goods and evils on the ground that they are illusory. The arguments here are conceptual (e.g., it is sometimes argued that the goal of retributive justice is illusory since it presupposes free will and there is no free will).

Where our pursuit of one goal conflicts with our pursuit of others, we must choose between packages. The critic of existing standards must show that we would be better off pursuing another set of goods and/or suppressing another set of evils. Philosophers, religious leaders, and other social critics have often made such arguments. In the more interesting cases, they do not simply appeal to intuitions to support their choice of packages. Instead, they try to show that the prevailing choice is based on ignorance, confusion, impoverished imagination, or false belief. Were these epistemic defects eliminated, the critic holds, others would share the critic's choice of packages. The core of this strategy was developed by Plato in *The Republic* and by John Stuart Mill in *Utilitarianism*.[7] Despite differences in detail, both Plato and Mill evaluate competing goods and evils by appealing to how they would be rated by someone who had experienced them all. The idea is to eliminate misconceptions based on ignorance and false belief.

ESA adopts this strategy as well. In any case, it accepts a version of this strategy that places the burden of proof on the critic. If our society now justifies a set of standards by appealing to package B, we can criticize those standards by showing that people favor B over some alternative package A because they suffer from some epistemic defect (and that pursuing A requires different standards). ESA adds to this that the choice must be made from an impartial point of view. Since the point of morality is to promote a reasonably valued way of life for a group, the values in question must be reasonable for that group. This rules out goods that are essentially predatory and antisocial (e.g., the pleasures of the torturer). And it demotes in importance goods accessible to limited numbers of people by virtue of their special capacities. For this reason it might generate different results than Mill's method or Plato's.[8]

As we will see in chapter 6, some cases of this kind will be undecidable. There may be no unique solution from the relevant point of view, or there may be a solution that we are not in a position to know. But life is uncertain in this way. Indeed, since the possibilities for personal change far exceed the possibilities of social change, we are confronted with even greater uncertainty in our own lives, but this does not preclude the possibility of reasonable choice. For example, one could disown the world and become a Buddhist monk. Perhaps, if one really knew what that was like, one would prefer it. Or perhaps one would prefer a simple existence devoted to simple pleasures and good works in beautiful natural surroundings (e.g., the life of a park ranger). It is difficult to be certain about what would be best, but we try to make informed comparisons. In any case, we believe that we should face the issues as squarely and as knowledgeably as we can and that it is possible to make progress. Although we fall short of certainty, there is such a thing as the best we can do at the time. Here, as in the case of social values, we are better off acknowledging these limits than pretending we have access to some universal ordering of values that holds for rational beings as such. Still, here and in the case of social values, one may have good reason to believe one more closely approaches the epistemic ideal than someone else. Sometimes we can be reasonably certain that our disputant's choice between values is based on a partisan perspective, grounded in simple ignorance or supported by a wildly inaccurate or severely impoverished imagination. With respect to evaluating goods, then, argument can get us somewhere.

In the remainder of this chapter I will illustrate the relevant argument strategies.

Illusory Values

Some goals are unreasonable because they are impossible to realize. Arguments to this effect are conceptual. Typically, they try to show that the goals in question presuppose background conditions that do not obtain. The most obvious examples are atheistic attack on the specifically religious goods of religious life (e.g., sanctity, holiness, saintliness, etc.). Religious institutions and practices cannot promote these goods, atheists argue, because we cannot realize them to begin with. Insofar as the social moralities of religiously dominated societies are "justified" by appealing to such goods, those justifications are invalid. In some cases these goods may be justified on other grounds (e.g., they provide life with meaning and promote goodwill toward others). But in other cases they may conflict with other important values. Recall Nathaniel Hawthorne's grim portraits of Puritan life.

Closer to home, impossibility arguments are employed by Rawls and others to attack a certain ideal of justice according to which people should be rewarded and punished in relation to some very robust idea of desert. On such accounts, one's desert is based on some nonrelational feature of oneself that is within one's control, that is, not merely a matter of luck. Rawls's objection is that nothing qualifies or could qualify as this sort of desert. We begin with certain hereditary traits and potentials, and our character emerges as a result of the effects of our environment on these traits and potentials. Our choices simply reflect the way we are shaped by these determinants, and these determinants are matters of luck. It doesn't matter that our current choices may shape our future character, for in the last analysis the path leads back to conditions beyond our control. Or so Rawls's argument goes. The conclusion is that we cannot possibly deserve anything in the robust sense of "desert" at issue.

R. I. Sikora develops an ingenious argument for the same conclusion in relation to the supposed good of retributive justice (i.e., inflicting on guilty parties the suffering they "deserve").[9] He argues that retributive justice cannot be justified on a merely compatibilist account of freedom since we would be free in the compatibilist sense even if we were created as adults with fully developed characters (as, e.g., Aphrodite was created by Zeus). But surely no newly created adult would deserve to suffer for his misdeeds in any robust sense of "deserve." Retributive desert requires what Sikora calls Kantian freedom. And he argues that Kantian freedom is incoherent. Accordingly, retributive justice should not be a goal of the criminal justice system.

Arguments of this kind have also been used by egoists against the possibility of altruism (and the goods of character dependent on altruism). And they have been used by materialists against even non-theistic appeals to spiritual values. In some cases the objects valued are not rejected entirely, but are reduced to something else (e.g., to certain patterns of behavior or brain states). But often it is hard to see why, so reduced, anyone would take these objects to be valuable.

Poor Prospects

As these examples suggest, pure impossibility arguments depend heavily on philosophical argument and analysis. But one can also argue that certain goods are impossible to achieve, or to achieve on a significant scale, for other reasons. These arguments are based on very general facts about human beings or human social organizations. I call values that are impossible to achieve on a wide scale "poor prospects." Obviously, a society should not structure its domains with the intention of widely realizing poor prospects.

However, it does not follow from the fact that a value is a poor prospect that no one should pursue it. Indeed, it does not follow that a society should discourage its pursuit. Certain goals that are not achievable on a wide scale may nonetheless be achievable by some people and with good results for themselves and/or for others. Obviously, a society should encourage the pursuit of such goals. It's just that one cannot justify a standard on the ground that that standard promotes such goals widely. I will return to this at the conclusion of this section.

Poor prospect arguments may be employed to oppose restructuring social institutions in an attempt to promote a goal dear to the heart of some philosophers, the flowering of the moral personality. According to these champions of Enlightenment ideals, the best society is one whose members engage in serious moral reflection and live according to principles that survive rational criticism. One might describe this as the good of self-legislating moral agency (a somewhat diluted version of Kant's goodwill). Self-legislating moral agents are contrasted with bureaucratic personalities. Roughly, the latter act according to rules that are not authentically their own. They are content to remain mere reflections of organizational arrangements. And they will exist in large numbers as long as organizations continue to be structured as they are. Self-legislating moral agents are thought to flourish in the absence of hierarchical forms of decision making. To promote this good, hierarchical forms of decision making must be abolished. This is said to hold not only in the political realm, but also in the workplace, the schools, the family, and so forth.

Opponents of such reforms argue that the flowering of the moral personality is a poor prospect. Most people do not want to engage in the arduous forms of reflection it requires, and many people are simply not up to it. Eliminating hierarchical organizations will not change matters. Rather than generating a new sort of person, it will simply create new contexts for *politics* as usual. Opposing parties will arise and rely on manipulation rather than rational persuasion, and partisan considerations will trump the general good. This pessimistic assessment might be grounded in a general view of human nature, or in a view of the sort of people we have now become. In either case, critics argue, the goal is a poor prospect. No social transformations available to us will realize it on a significantly wider scale than it is currently realized.

Finally, consider the goods supposedly promoted by open marriages (roughly, marriages with few or no restrictions on outside
sexual relations). Open marriages were said to offer not only more
sexual excitement, but also opportunities for personal growth that
are stifled by monogamous restrictions. The result was to be the
flourishing of important human potentials. This required, and partly
consisted in, transcending envy, jealousy, possessiveness, and competitiveness.

Again, critics argued that these goals are poor prospects. Envy,
jealousy, competitiveness, and possessiveness cannot be transcended
by human beings; in any case, they cannot be transcended by people
with our cultural background and training. The critics granted that
these feelings might be eliminated were everyone raised in the right
way. But given how we are raised, they claim, we can't get there from
here. The most we can do is place limits on the intensity of these
responses, the situations in which they are acceptable, and the actions
that may be justified in relation to them.

Arguments of this kind are not meant to show that the goods and
evils in question are not authentic. Roughly, they are meant to show
that they are not sufficiently viable to serve as domain-specific goals
for the purposes of justifying moral standards. I say "roughly" because
the pursuit of such goals may be encouraged as ideals. Although few
people may be capable of approaching the goal of self-legislating
moral agency, those who do are arguably better off for this, and on the
whole, we are all better off for having them around. The same arguably holds for people who are capable of overcoming jealousy and
competitiveness. If arguments to these effects are sound, the pursuit
of these goals should be encouraged. We should praise people who
achieve them, but we should not regard failures to realize them as
moral defects (within the limits indicated above). That is, we should
not regard "appropriate" jealousy as a violation of duty or regard the
disposition to "appropriate" jealousy as a vice. But we should regard
the transcendence of these responses as a very good thing. Since I
think it is misleading to call them virtues, I will call them ideals.[10]
Ideals are very important to us. Indeed, in at least some cases we
rightly excuse the violation of what would otherwise be moral obligations in their pursuit. Thus, if we recognize that someone is
passionately committed to truth and honesty in social life, we are
willing to praise some behavior we might otherwise regard as incon-
siderate or insensitive.

In sum, to the extent that a goal is a poor prospect, it is unreasonable to defend a moral standard on the ground that it maximizes the

realization of that goal (except for standards governing ideals). No reasonable person would argue that her society should design its morality to pursue poor prospects.[11] On the other hand, if people who can realize such goals are better off for doing it (and the rest of us are not sufficiently worse off), or if the rest of us are better off because they do it (and they are not sufficiently worse off), such goals are reasonable moral ideals.

Estimating Costs and Benefits

As suggested, we can also argue against candidate goods and evils by showing that people choose them because they wrongly estimate the costs or benefits of realizing them. Such arguments are not decisive. If they succeed, one may still argue for the candidates by showing that people would choose them even if they knew the truth. But the burden of proof is now on their defenders.

Examples are common. Consider the goods of family life. According to some psychotherapists (sociologists, novelists, and playwrights), harmony is now a widely accepted good of family life. Family events are considered successful if people behave amiably and there is an absence of disputation, explicit disagreement, raised voices, or other signs of conflict. Parent-child relationships and relationships between siblings are also judged favorably if these conditions are met. Psychologists do not doubt it is possible to approach these goals, but many of them claim the price is too high. Disagreements, anger, resentment, and hostility are inevitable in families, and the consequences of suppressing them for the sake of harmony can be dire. Relationships become phoney or ritualized. Love is more difficult to give and receive. Indirect or passive aggressive expressions of hostility sabotage important occasions, and when hostilities become overt the results can be catastrophic. All of this can be very painful and have a terrible impact on the general level of happiness among family members. Most people would be far better off were there freedom to express differences in direct, nondisruptive ways. Or so the familiar argument goes.

Of course, the fact that we tend to underestimate the cost of harmony does not necessarily settle the matter. Once this is pointed out, some people might continue to favor harmony as a dominant goal for *their* families. The thought of open conflict between family members might be terrifying or distasteful to them, and they might be incapable of changing their habitual responses. So they might be willing to pay the price of continued harmony in the family, even from an epistemically advantaged point of view. However, occupying that point of view, they also realize they are willing to make this choice only because they have an unusually strong attachment to harmony and that they would be better off without that attachment. They also realize that very few people would have that attachment were harmony less highly valued, and that we would better off under that condition. So, considering the matter impartially, they should reject harmony as a central value of family life in general. Among other things, this means that they should not justify standards for family conduct in general by appealing to harmony. And they should stop criticizing the conduct of family members by appealing to *general* standards—about how children ought to behave toward parents, how siblings ought to behave toward one another, and so forth—that are justified by appealing to harmony. If they insist on harmony in their own family, they should justify their insistence by appealing to their own psychological needs. These criticisms of the presumptive value "harmony" appeal both to other family values and to values of a more general kind. As the earlier taxonomy of values suggests, more general values are more general in the sense that they are associated with more general dimensions of our being (e.g., some things are valuable to us qua members of a particular culture, and others qua human beings). But there is no hierarchy of values or value types such that "higher" values always and necessarily trump "lower" values. Indeed, as we shall see in chapter 6, the weight attached to more general values is domain sensitive. In the end we must choose between competing packages of goods and evils for specific contexts or domains. The full argument for this must await the abstract analysis of good developed in chapter 6. But the point is worth developing and illustrating here.

To say there is a value heirarchy is to say that pleasure, pain, knowledge, beauty, courage, integrity, and so forth take constant values or admit of constant rankings. If they do, the total value or disvalue of a state of affairs would be a simple function of the degree to which these particular values are realized within it. Thus, every state of affairs that realizes the same particular values to the same degree would have the same rating, and every state of affairs into which a given particular value were introduced would be improved (or degraded) according to the weight of that value.

But none of these consequences hold. Consider pleasure and pain. In general, we suppose that pleasure is a good and that pain is an evil. So on the constancy account, the net value of a state of affairs is reduced to the extent that it is painful and increased to the extent that it is pleasurable. But suppose one is forced to witness the torture of someone one loves. It is not better, all things considered, that the event brings pleasure. In general, we think it better that we are made to suffer rather than enjoy ourselves by witnessing or thinking about calamities that befall people we love. We also think it better that immoral people do not enjoy the fruit of their immoral acts. The addition of pleasure does not always improve a state of affairs.[12]

Moreover, the presence of pain and suffering might improve matters. Thus, pain might make an otherwise impressive achievement an act of heroism. Acts of heroism often involve enduring great suffering or overcoming powerful impulses. So if we value heroic acts for their own sake, we might value a state of affairs more than we otherwise would precisely because it included pain.[13]

This could be explained by saying that we value character traits more highly than hedonic goods. But this is not always the case. To begin with, there are limits to what we expect people to suffer for the sake of virtue. Showing up on time to a lunch date is an expression of punctuality, reliability, and honesty, but if one must endure great pain to do so, it may be better on the whole if one does not. Thus, hedonic considerations sometimes trump the good of expressing valued character traits. And this is what one would expect. For we criticize certain ideals of character on the ground that the realization of those traits increases misery in the world or interferes with our capacities for pleasure. Puritan versions of diligence, thrift, self-control, and seriousness of purpose have these difficulties. Thus, Hawthorne consistently attacks the grim Puritan ideal as the enemy of mirth and enjoyment.

Similar considerations hold in relation to other goods, for example, social equality. If we believed that people were in general much happier with strongly marked social hierarchies and elaborate rituals of respect in various domains, we should be much less favorably inclined toward North American ideals of social equality in those domains (and the virtues and vices that go with them). And we should be more favorably inclined to the sort of social relations characteristic of nineteenth-century England or present-day Japan.[14] We favor social equality partly because we believe it has positive psychological effects.[15]

The point is that we cannot apply the epistemic defect test directly to categories of goods or even to particular goods within those categories to establish constant weights. Different goods assume different weights in different domains. This recognition frees us from certain unfortunate consequences of Plato's and Mill's use of the test. Both attempted to establish the place of sensual pleasure among the general hierarchy of goods by asking us to make a categorical choice between sensual pleasure and goods of other kinds. Sensual pleasure did badly and was therefore regarded as an unimportant component of the good life (or worse in Plato's case). This devaluation of sensual pleasure is unconvincing to most people. Indeed, some who are familiar with both the "higher" goods and the "lower" goods might choose a life of sensual pleasures if they had to make a categorical choice. In any case, almost everyone would prefer a mosaic that included a helping of sensual pleasure. If the mosaic is preferable to a diet restricted to "higher" goods, the Plato/Mill application of the method is unreasonable. It assumes constancy and constancy fails.

We will discuss these issues further in chapter 6. Let us now turn to evaluations of distributive patterns.

Patterns of A/Distribution

A good deal of philosophical work has been devoted to justifying principles of distribution. As we have seen, however, the principles in question do not govern distribution per se, but the pattern of a/distribution.

ESA holds that different patterns of a/distribution are justified in different domains. In no domain are we allowed to make arbitrary distinctions between persons, but what counts as arbitrary differs from domain to domain. Thus, in most domains it is arbitrary to discriminate on the basis of race, gender, religion, national origin, and sexual orientation. But in some domains this is permissible. Religious offices and honors rightly require religious affiliation. So it is not arbitrary to require that the pope be Catholic. Nor is it arbitrary to restrict participation in certain athletic competitions to women, or to restrict certain privately conferred awards to members of certain ethnic groups (e.g., the Chicano Businessperson of the Year, the NAACP Image Award, etc.). It is not always clear precisely how to draw these lines, but they are obviously domain sensitive.

Historically, many criteria for a/distribution were based on arbitrary distinctions between groups. Of course, the distinctions were rarely thought to be arbitrary. Rather, exclusions and restrictions were defended on the basis of false beliefs about the capabilities, needs, desires, and so forth of various groups. Thus, for example, blacks and women were denied voting rights because they were thought to be incapable of effective self-government.

The arguments against the arbitrariness of these distinctions are, of course, empirical. Accordingly, some of the most important and dramatic moral debates of the last 200 years turned largely on factual questions about the nature of women, Jews, blacks, Catholics, and so forth. Often, the parties to these debates agreed on principles for a/distribution. But they disagreed on the facts, so they disagreed on the sorts of distinctions between persons and groups of persons that are justified by these principles. Over the last few decades the range of disagreement on these factual questions has narrowed. In any case, the highly unflattering and limiting pictures employed to justify the full range of earlier exclusions now prevail only on the fringes. As a result, most of us now understand these exclusions as arbitrary. Partly because so many factual issues have been resolved, disputes about justice now more often focus on principles of a/distribution themselves. As suggested, ESA holds that such principles are domain sensitive.

Since the justificatory goods of a domain are often distributed indirectly—that is, by supplying goods instrumental to them—there are typically two kinds of principles of distribution in a domain; one for evaluating the a/distribution of the instrumental goods, and another for evaluating the a/distribution of the target good. Thus, for example, the target goods of education are various kinds of knowledge and skills. But we bring about this a/distribution by a/distributing other things (money, teacher time, special programs, etc.). These a/distributions may be governed by criteria as well (admissions criteria to special programs, demands for equal funding of districts, etc.). We evaluate criteria for distributing instrumental goods on the basis of how well they promote the desired a/distribution of target goods. Assuming that prevailing principles for target goods are reasonable, the arguments for and against the instrumental principles are straightforwardly empirical. If our criteria for the a/distribution of educational dollars does not effectively bring about the desired a/distribution of the relevant kinds of knowledge and skills, we should change the criteria. (This is an obvious point but one often neglected in actual disputes about the distribution of teacher time and educational dollars.)

Many disputes about principles for the a/distribution of target goods turn on the effects of adopting these principles either in relation to the good they govern or in relation to other goods. In the first case, one might argue that such a principle is unreasonable because (a) it cannot be effectively implemented; or (b) it cannot be implemented without undue costs to the target good in question. Argument (a) amounts to the complaint that a principle is utopian. This might be said of strongly egalitarian principles for distributing knowledge and intellectual skills, love, health, political power, aesthetic sensitivity, and other goods. We simply cannot achieve anything resembling equality in these areas. Moreover, given the impossibility of raising the conditions of the least well-off beyond a certain threshold in these areas, we could maximize equality only by severely reducing the condition of the better-off.

Similar criticisms can be made of proposals to raise the position of the least well-off as much as we can. In the case of education, this would require eliminating special programs for brighter students and concentrating almost all of our efforts on students with lower achievement scores. With respect to health, this would demand that we devote all our resources to improving the condition of the very sick. With respect to interpersonal relations, it would require that we all make special efforts to befriend the loneliest or most isolated people.

We object to such allocations in the name of the target goods. They deprive too many of too much without helping others enough to compensate for the deprivation. Roughly, they excessively sacrifice aggregation for the sake of maximizing equality. Obviously, everything here hinges on "excessively." One might reasonably favor an a/distributive principle that sacrifices *some* aggregation for the sake of distribution. For example, we do not want simply to maximize the sum total of knowledge and skill acquisition among our students. We might do *that* by concentrating most of our resources on the more intelligent students and largely ignoring the slower ones. After a certain point, at least, it takes more time and money to raise the level of a slower student by a given magnitude than to raise the level of a quicker student by that magnitude. So if we are interested only in aggregation, we should ignore the less intelligent after that point is reached. And it is not obvious that this is right either.

How do we decide what tradeoffs are reasonable for what classes of goods? One approach is to begin with the sort of abstract principles for making tradeoffs we discussed in chapter 4, namely, the alternatives on the continuum between egalitarianism and traditional utilitarianism. Instead of considering these principles in relation to goods and evils in general, or in relation to some class of primary social goods, we consider them in relation to particular domain-related goods with the understanding that different principles might apply in different domains. But if this approach is to rely on more than intuitions, we will need to say why a particular principle is relevant to a given domain. That is, we need to say something about the nature of the goods and evils in question. In the last analysis, we need to

consider the impact of these goods and evils on the life prospects of
the relevant individuals.

Many philosophers will insist that to do this we need some
general abstract principle for evaluating a/distributions of life prospects. If they are right, we are in trouble. For as I argued in chapter 4,
there is no uniquely rational way to do this. But I will now argue that
we do not need a general principle of this kind to make progress. We
can settle a good many disputes about a/distributions of target goods
by moving from the bottom up. As we shall see, this will involve
considering the impact of a/distributions of target goods on goods of
other kinds.

Moving from the bottom up has heuristic advantages as well. If we
begin with the concrete we might consider principles overlooked by
selecting candidates from the continuum between egalitarianism and
traditional utilitarianism. With some ingenuity, most principles can
be formulated such that they can be situated on that continuum. But
there are an indefinite number of possibilities there, and as the following examples suggest, we might well miss the relevant ones.

Consider education. According to one often cited principle, all
students should have an equal opportunity to realize their potentials
for learning, where these potentials are understood in relation to
the sorts of knowledge and skills we take to be goals of the educational process. Let's call this the principle of "equal opportunity."
To clarify this principle we need to say what counts as "opportunity"
in this context, and we need some way to measure the degree to which
a potential is actualized. But the spirit of the principle is clear
enough. It calls for special programs for students with special needs.
Gifted children are not to be sentenced to boring and stultifying
classroom experiences. Learning-disabled children are not to be left to
sink or swim.

But given limited funding, this equal opportunity principle may
conflict with another principle for distributing the target goods.
According to that principle, all students should be raised to a certain
acceptable minimum. It is also hard to say what counts as an acceptable minimum. Very roughly, we might identify that minimum with
the range of knowledge and skills required to live a normal adult life
(e.g., one should be literate enough to read a newspaper, have enough
arithmetic skill to balance a budget, understand enough practical
medicine to avoid recklessly endangering one's health, and know
enough about history and government to understand simple political
issues). Yet given the deplorable state of American education, a basic
minimum principle with any teeth at all might require that we

concentrate virtually all of our resources at the lower end of the scale. Thus, we might not be able to afford special programs for brighter students. Moreover, if we are trying to maximize the numbers of students who reach the acceptable minimum, we might not be able to afford special programs for retarded children either (the time and money required to bring a retarded student to the minimum could be used to educate several nonretarded students).

More generally, the tradeoffs are as follows. If we adopt the acceptable minimum standard, some people will acquire basic skills who would not otherwise have them, but others will be educated well below their potential. If we adopt the equal opportunity principle, some people will make great progress who would otherwise languish, but others will lack basic skills they would otherwise have.

How should we decide between principles? Instead of simply announcing our intuitions, we should try to settle the question by considering what more is at stake. The point of education is to enable people to live better lives. This suggests that we should consider the impact of our choices on the life prospects of the people affected. In addition, we should consider the general social consequences of adopting the competing principles. These arguments become quite complex, and I will only be able to sketch them very roughly here.

The impacts in question obviously depend on the social environment. Suppose that the principal of an inner-city school must choose between hiring someone to teach college preparatory courses for her talented students or hiring someone to teach remedial courses for her least well-off. Based on past performance, the principal believes that another remedial course might help ten additional students graduate with an acceptable minimum skill level each year. And she believes that introducing college preparatory courses will help an additional ten students eventually graduate from college. Her choice should be based importantly on her understanding of how the benefits in question will impact on the life prospects of her students. The prospects of the college graduates would obviously be dramatically improved. The prospects of the remedial students would also be improved, but it is unclear by how much. We need to know to what degree an inner-city graduate at the acceptable minimum level has better employment opportunities than an inner-city graduate below that level (remembering that the latter can subsequently acquire basic skills in adult education courses). We need also to consider the general impact on society at large. Suppose that we eliminate programs for talented students so that a greater number of slower students can acquire minimum skills. The improved prospects of those at the bottom are helpful not only to the individuals directly affected, but also to society at large. Because they will be more employable and have greater self-respect, they will be less likely to turn to drugs and crime. And we will all be better off as a result.

On the other hand, eliminating special programs for talented students is also individually and socially harmful. Some may lose interest in school and drop out. Those who do go on will be less well prepared. Precisely how costly this would be depends largely on three factors: (1) the number of talented people who are lost to the system; (2) the extent to which talented people are handicapped by inferior primary and secondary educations (i.e., the extent to which skills will be degraded); and (3) the extent to which a general reduction of skills is socially damaging.

The issues here are obviously empirical. Once we get our answers we are still left with a choice between packages. But given certain empirical scenarios, our answers will be clear. Suppose that eliminating programs for talented students reduces the pool of talent at the top so that the economy becomes noncompetitive to the point of permanent recession. In that case everyone suffers, and those at the bottom suffer most. Obviously, other empirical scenarios present tougher choices. But again, some cases will be clear.

Another possibility is worth mentioning. We might decide between patterns of a/distribution without appealing to principles at all. Instead of trying to defend the alternative principles by appealing to social and individual outcomes, we might directly assess the alternatives in relation to the outcomes. Suppose that we divide students into three groups on the basis of their educational potential (e.g., their intelligence and imagination as measured independently of educational achievement). Let the groups be above average, average, and below average. Now suppose the pattern of educational achievement, as measured by test scores, looks like this:

	Above Average	Average	Below Average
Case 1	1400	800	400

The head of the gifted children's program argues that devoting educational resources to the above average is more efficient (dollar for dollar). So we could increase aggregate learning by moving funds for average and remedial students to his budget. The results might be

	Above Average	Average	Below Average
Case 2	1800	600	400; or
Case 3	1800	800	200

Instead of evaluating these alternatives by citing a principle, we might defend them directly in relation to their social and individual consequences. We can do this by considering how the numbers translate into knowledge and skills, and how knowledge and skills impact on individuals, and on society in general (or, more precisely, on the collectivity of individuals affected). Roughly, we want to know to what extent the lives of individuals are enriched or impoverished by changes in their numbers, and to what degree all of our lives are enriched or impoverished by the social consequences produced by the set of such changes. Both will vary in relation to the actual skill levels represented by the numbers and in relation to prevailing social conditions. We need this information to determine which increases or decreases in the numbers are important.

Suppose that the difference between 1400 and 1800 is roughly equivalent to a full year of calculus, a science, and a foreign language. And suppose that the difference between 200 and 400 is the difference between functional illiteracy and literacy. In that case, other things being equal, the move from 400 to 200 may have a much more significant impact on the life prospects of those immediately affected than the move from 1400 to 1800. Those at the 200 level may be restricted to menial, low-paying jobs, and they will almost certainly suffer from a sense of inadequacy or inferiority as a result of their ignorance and poverty. Those at the 1400 level may have wasted some time, but may not suffer lifelong damage (especially if they can compensate for the deficits in college).

Again, it is arguable that better high school preparation translates into better university training, and that better university training produces important social benefits. Furthermore, these benefits do trickle down to those at the bottom. But even if this is so, it must be weighed against the general social deficits of widespread illiteracy and arithmetic incapacity. On a variety of factual scenarios, then, the choice between case 1 and case 2 seems reasonably clear. The move from 1400 to 1800 might provide significant but not decisive individual and social benefits. The move from 400 to 200 might be socially and individually catastrophic.

The comparison between cases 1 and 3 clearly depends on the significance of the move from 800 to 600 for average students. Suppose that this represents a loss of high school geometry and second year science. Again, whether this loss outweighs the benefits of moving the higher third from 1400 to 1800 depends on its individual and social consequences. If those affected directly have little or no need of the relevant skills or knowledge—for example, if they typically lose the skills and forget the information within five years anyway—we should prefer case 3 (assuming that the skills and knowledge responsible for the move from 1400 to 1800 are typically retained and built upon). On a variety of realistic factual assumptions, then, the choice between packages seems relatively straightforward in these cases. We can make this choice without having to defend or choose between conflicting abstract principles governing a/distribution. Many cases are like this. Indeed, it seems to me that many of the difficulties we face evaluating moral standards arise because we describe the candidate packages at so high a level of abstraction that we are unclear about precisely what goes into the various choices. Often, we agree on enough to settle the issue given a sufficiently concrete and detailed account of the matter.[16] Numbers may mislead us. Where this is the case, it may be better to avoid appealing to principles.

In this chapter we have summarized certain basic strategies for evaluating moral standards from an ESA point of view. As we have seen, our evaluations often depend on what packages of goods and evils we would choose from an epistemically ideal and impartial point of view. In some cases, it is reasonably clear which of two opposing views better approaches this. In other cases it is not, and here reasonable persons are free to disagree. In the following chapter I will present a general theory of goods and evils intended to ground and to better clarify this picture.

Notes

1. Redefining is a matter of degree, and at a certain point on the continuum we might want to say that a role has not been redefined but eliminated (e.g., the role of the investment banker under socialism or the role of the parent among Plato's Guardians in the *Republic*). But one may make significant changes in each of these areas without reaching that point. The move from private medicine to socialized medicine involves significant changes in all of these areas without eliminating the roles of doctor and patient.

2. A deontologist might deny this. If Marx's Labor Theory of Value is true, the worker is exploited under capitalism even if he does better in absolute terms than he would do under socialism. If Robert Nozick's account of entitlements is true, almost all restrictions on free market capitalism are unjust even if free market capitalism is far less efficient than its rivals (i.e., even if a person, selected at random, is likely to be significantly worse off). As we shall see in chapter 6, ESA asks which system best promotes the reasonable goals of economic life. This does not entail that considerations of economic justice or fairness play no role in our choice. As we shall see in chapter 6, a particular conception of economic justice may be among those goals for some cultures. But in our case, there is no shared conception.

Moreover, the conceptions of justice to which most people subscribe are not decisive for them. Few workers would complain of the enormous gap between their salaries and the salaries of top management if they thought that reducing the gap would also reduce their salaries. Few owners would complain of restrictions on trade and of redistributive taxation if they thought their income or standard of living would fall more under free market conditions. Very roughly, we evaluate an economy on the basis of how well it delivers the goods. As suggested, there is a distributive condition built into this. But roughly, since everyone prefers to be better off, that condition will be satisfied whenever one system does significantly better on average than its alternative. Issues of justice and fairness seem important in this area when a group believes it is not getting as much as it should. That is why these issues seem academic if one comes to believe one is getting more under the present arrangement than one would otherwise get.

3. In deciding this, we are free to determine the magnitude of a harm by taking the source into account. Thus, John Harris has argued that we prefer random harms from natural chance to the institutionalized harm of a lottery ("The Survival Lottery," *Philosophy*, 50, 1975, pp. 81–87). If this applies to the present case, we could build it into our calculations. But it is not at all clear that it applies. What we suffer when we are raped or robbed is not random harm from natural chance (e.g., it is not like contracting a virus). Moreover, if one understands it *that* way, Harris's thesis would not be plausible. For it is not at all clear that most people would prefer being harmed by a criminal to being harmed unjustly by the state. Other things being equal, it is not obvious to me that it better to be robbed of $75 than to be fined $75 for a traffic violation one did not commit, or that it is better to be kidnapped and held as someone's private prisoner than to be unjustly imprisoned by the state. It may be better to be a victim of natural chance than to be a victim of a person or an institution. But it is unclear that it is always better to be the victim of a private person than a victim of an institution.

4. Of course, it is not entirely empirical. We might think that the injustice of convicting the innocent is greater than the injustice of letting the guilty go free, but disagree on how much greater. The 10:1 ratio of the familiar cliché is not self-evidently correct. In any case, slogans like that obscure the important fact that many of the guilty set free are highly likely to steal, rape, murder, etc., again. Surely this should importantly influence our choice of target ratios.

5. Sufficient agreement need not be complete agreement. I might support mandatory reporting of HIV positive results for medical personnel because I believe it will prevent four cases of AIDS per year. You might believe it will prevent twenty cases, but you might support mandatory reporting even if you believed there were only four. In that case there is sufficient agreement between us. In general, we agree sufficiently if each of us holds that a certain standard is justified when a certain empirical measure reaches or exceeds a certain value and we believe it has reached or exceeded that value.

6. Of course, one could have separate categories for mammals, sentient beings, etc., but since this list is simply for our convenience, I see no point in this.

7. Plato's *Republic*, Book 9, 580d–583a; John Stuart Mill, *Utilitarianism*, chapter 2.

8. Both Mill and Plato believe that there are qualitative differences between categories of pleasure. And both believe that social policy should promote the higher pleasures at the expense of the lower ones. An ESA theorist can (though need not) accept the distinction between higher and lower pleasures, and he can also accept the test Plato and Mill propose for this (although that test is not committed to either). On this account, if A is preferred to B from an epistemically advantaged standpoint, A is superior to B. But it does not follow from this that A is to be maximized. For A might be accessible to relatively few people and at the expense of relatively many. In that case, the social pursuit of A would not be justified from an impartial point of view.

9. R. I. Sikora, "Free Will." The manuscript is not yet in print.

10. It is misleading because so much thinking about virtues is influenced by Aristotle and these traits do not neatly fit an Aristotelian account. For one thing, Aristotle's moral virtues are supposed to be expressions of reason in social life. As such they are supposed to be open to any person of sound moral upbringing. Ex hypothesi, the traits in question are not. In addition, it is hard to represent the traits in question as a mean between an excess and a deficiency. What could be the excess in relation to never feeling jealousy, competitiveness, and so forth? This problem may also arise in relation to candidate virtues, but it is convenient to reserve "virtue" for characteristics we can reasonably expect of normal people (or of normal occupants of various roles).

11. Of course, someone might prefer them. One might hold that it is better to belong to a society of beautiful losers, that is, losers with lofty goals, than to belong to a society content with the ordinary comforts. But unless this sort of ambition is widely valued for its own sake, it is difficult to imagine how to defend it from an impartial point of view.

12. In *Brentano and Intrinsic Value*, Roderick Chisholm presents an interesting account of Brentano's discussion of the goodness and badness of various kinds of pleasure and displeasure in relation to their intentional object (Cambridge University Press, Cambridge, 1986, chapter 6, pp. 59–67). According to Chisholm's interpretation, Brentano is best understood to hold that "pleasure in the bad" is a "mixed evil"; it is bad, but it involves some good. This is compatible with what I have claimed here. Since the pleasure is predominantly bad, it does not reduce the evil of the total situation. Nonetheless, since I think that nothing is intrinsically valuable (but only reasonably intrinsically valued), I would argue for a more Aristotelian position. It is unreasonable to intrinsically value this sort of pleasure.

13. Strictly speaking, this is compatible with constancy. One could explain the overall change of value in these cases in relation to the effects of

pleasure and pain on other values relevant to dimensions of the situation. Thus, in the first case, it is not pleasure itself that reduces the value of the whole but the terrible state of character that pleasure entails. In the latter case it is not the pain that is important but the heroism. But other arguments against constancy in relation to the good can easily be constructed on the model of arguments against constancy in relation to the right. Just how much good is pleasure per se, heroism per se, and so forth? How is the good of pleasure weighted in relation to the evil of lying? And how are these rankings justified, if not by appeal to intuition?

14. Of course, we do not value social equality completely. In a wide range of contexts, it is widely thought fitting that certain people receive special treatment. Much of this is based on position and achievement rather than social class. In a variety of contexts, leading scientists, Supreme Court justices, and major writers are treated with more deference and respect than ordinary people, and it is widely supposed that they deserve it. Whether this can be justified depends on the sorts of benefits it provides. This is a complicated question. One argument in favor of special treatment is that it is an inevitable or necessary feature of any meritocracy, and meritocracies benefit everyone. One argument against it is that it helps to perpetuate false meritocracies, i.e., systems in which respect is absurdly grounded. Thus, status in American society is often a matter of celebrity (and celebrity itself is a matter of celebrity; as some comedian recently observed, people are now famous for being famous).

15. For an interesting account of the difference see Anthony Trollope's *Travels in America*, an account of his visit to the United States in 1861. He was enormously impressed with the energy and vigor of the people, and he attributed this partly to an absence of strong class divisions.

16. Of course, a rule utilitarian can attend to the details. See chapter 4, note 19.

6

Goods and Evils

In chapter 5 I argued that we can make many effective criticisms of moral standards without appealing to an abstract theory of the good. But I also acknowledged that our evaluation of some criticisms will depend on our choice between competing packages of goods and evils (or, more accurately, a/distributions of them). In at least some cases these choices will be controversial, and to discover the degree to which these controversies are subject to reason we need an abstract theory of the good. This chapter develops such a theory and explores its implications for evaluating moral standards. It concludes with an illustration of the power of ESA at the domain level by showing how that approach enables us to think systematically about business ethics.

Goods and Evils: The Relational View

The account defended here, relationalism, attempts to synthesize the strong elements of the subjectivist and the standard objectivist accounts of goods and evils. Subjectivists hold that something is valuable because and only because it is desired or valued by some subject. The relationalist argues that something's being valuable depends partly on the nature of the subject for whom it is valuable, but the relationalist denies that it is *entirely* dependent on the nature of that subject. The argument against the most popular form of subjectivism, the desire satisfaction version, was made in chapter 3. With minor adjustments this argument works against other subjectivist accounts as well.

The standard objectivist holds that value resides entirely in the object, that is, it is entirely independent of a subject. No matter what any subject wants, no matter what any subject's nature, certain states of affairs are just plain good and others just plain bad (e.g., knowledge or beauty). The relationalist agrees that value depends in part on the nature of the object. But, as suggested, he holds that it depends on the nature of the subject as well.

The relationalist has two objections to the standard objectivist view. To begin with, different objectivists compile different lists of absolute goods and rank them in different ways.[1] Some include knowledge, beauty, and virtue and rank them higher than health and pleasure. Others fail to include all of the above or offer different rankings. These lists are typically justified by appeals to intuition. The arguments against such appeals in relation to the right in chapter 1 apply in relation to the good as well.[2]

Second, there is something strange about the claim that the same things would be goods and evils no matter what sorts of subjects populate the universe. Typically, we think that if x is good or evil, it is good or evil for someone or something. And we realize that x may be good for someone or something without being good for everyone or everything. So the goodness of x would seem to have something to do with the nature of the subject for whom x is good. If x's goodness is entirely independent of any subject at all, then either (1) x is good for every possible subject or (2) x is not good for every possible subject, but is somehow good from the standpoint of the universe as a whole. It is hard to know what could qualify as (1), and it is hard to know what (2) could mean. I will say more about this later.

A more moderate objectivist view might allow that candidate goods and evils depend on subjects in the sense that their existence presupposes the existence of subjects of a certain kind. But he might deny that x's being good or evil depends on the nature of the subject in which x is realized. Thus, for example, the existence of pleasure and pain presupposes the existence of sentient beings. But pleasure and pain are good or evil by virtue of what they are, not by virtue of the nature of the subject that experiences them. Their existence is dependent on the subject, but their value is not.

Relationalism rejects this account but embodies certain objectivist elements. As suggested, according to the relationalist view something is good because it is good for some subject, but it is good for a subject in part by virtue of the sort of thing it is. Relationalists might differ on what count as subjects, or more particularly, on which subjects have moral standing. But whatever we say about this, relationalists hold that both the existence and the value of anything good or evil depend on the nature of the subject for whom it is good or evil and on its own nature as well. More specifically, a subject's good consists of an appropriate fit between some feature of its nature (innate or developed) and some state of the world. Goods and evils are like secondary qualities. Their existence depends partly on the nature of the subject and partly on the nature of the object. But it is a matter of objective fact that this fit occurs or fails to occur.

As we shall see, the test of this fit is (roughly) what the agent would choose with full knowledge, vividly appreciating the alternatives. Accordingly, if we were verificationists, the distinction between relationalism and certain versions of subjectivism (e.g., Harsanyi's hypothetical preference account) would collapse.[3] But verificationism is highly implausible. In any case, the relationalist denies that states of affairs are good for us *because* we desire them under epistemically perfect conditions. Rather, we desire them under epistemically perfect conditions because they are good for us (the war cry of relationalism might be "Remember the *Euthyphro!*"). As we saw in chapter 3, the requirement of perfect epistemic conditions and vivid appreciation is motivated by our concern that desires be properly aimed, that is, aimed at the right states of affairs (or objects).

The relationalist account is strongest in relation to the non-hedonic items on the moderate objectivist's list. Consider knowledge. The moderate objectivist with respect to knowledge holds that although knowledge can be realized only in beings of a certain kind, knowledge is valuable in and of itself (independently of the nature of that being).

It is hard to know exactly what this means. Although it is widely said that knowledge is valuable in and of itself, this view has rarely if ever been clarified, and it needs to be. Choose your favorite account of knowledge, for example, justified true belief caused in the right way. Presumably *that* is realized in the brain, and could be realized in anything capable of performing certain brain functions. According to many, this includes computers. But it seems arbitrary to hold that any bit of knowledge at all, realized in anything capable of realizing it, adds intrinsic value to the universe.

Typically, objectivists have in mind only certain kinds of knowledge realized in certain kinds of beings, namely, knowledge of higher, deeper, and nobler truths realized in beings like us (as opposed to knowledge of maze designs realized in beings like mice). These include truths about the nature and origins of the universe, and deep truths about human relationships and human aspirations.

Do these kinds of knowledge, in and of themselves, add value to the universe? They are obviously important to us. But then, we are the sorts of beings who seek meaning in our lives, demand justifications for our actions, and wonder about our origins and about distant future states of ourselves and our world. Thus, we are interested in questions about space and time (mind and matter, etc.) partly because they are related to questions about life after death, free will and determinism, and so forth. These in turn are related to questions about what will become of us when we die, and to questions about how we ought to live. Some of us are also just plain curious about these matters. But it is doubtful that we would attach such importance to this kind of curiosity (as opposed to a cat's) if we were not the sorts of beings I described. Knowledge is good for *that* sort of being because it is *that* sort of being.

Suppose we were different. Suppose we had as little need of meaning and justification in our lives as cats do, and were as little disposed to reflect about death. Imagine also that we live in an Eden-like environment that is entirely supportive and contains no enemies. Our brains are capable of knowledge about space, time, and infinity, but these topics are entirely unrelated to anything we care about and completely bore us. We much prefer lounging in the sun emersed in floral fragrances, grooming and petting each other, playing various games, and contemplating maps of the astonishing fruits and (non-sentient) animals we dine upon. Would the universe be a better place if we had knowledge of space, time, and infinity? Imagine that occasionally some errant bit of knowledge about space or time wafts dreamlike across our consciousness on a lazy summer day (or simply embeds itself, uninvited and unwelcomed, in our brain). We couldn't care less. Indeed, we experience it as an unwelcome intrusion, an irritating disturbance. Does it nonetheless add to the goodness of the universe?

Or consider another favorite of the objectivists: beauty. The case of beauty is more complicated than that of knowledge since beauty is almost certainly a dispositional property and since it may contain an ineliminable experiential element. Indeed, to say an object is beautiful is arguably to say only that it has a disposition to produce a certain kind of experience in beings like us. If this is so, it is hard to see how the goodness of beauty is something more than the goodness of that experience (and its subsequent effects on us). And if this is so, the moderate objectivist's case in relation to beauty will be the same as his case in relation to experiences in general (e.g., the pleasures of filling an empty stomach). We will discuss such cases presently.

However, objectivists may deny that beauty is a mere disposition to produce feelings of a certain kind in beings like us. They might hold that it is some other kind of property. Suppose they are right. And suppose we have an aesthetic sense that enables us to identify that property (given proper training). But suppose we (and every other being with this sense) are built such that we are incapable of enjoying beauty. In that case we recognize the same objects as beautiful that we now identify as beautiful. But our encounters with such objects might no more improve the quality of our experience than our encounters with rectangular shapes do. It might even be terribly unpleasant to us. In the former case, beauty could be a matter of complete indifference to us. In the latter it might be a complete horror. In either case, why should it be important from any other point of view? If the property of beauty, or the properties on which beauty supervene (e.g., harmony, balance, proportion, etc.), did not improve the quality of anyone's experience, why would anyone hold that the universe is a better place for it?

The most difficult cases for the relationalist account are hedonic goods and evils themselves, for example, pleasure, pain, anxiety, depression, exuberance, and so forth. Hedonic goods presuppose the existence of sentient beings. But a moderate objectivist holds that its goodness or badness is not dependent on the nature of those beings. A relationalist holds that it is. Thus, for example, a relationalist holds that there could conceivably be a sentient being for whom pain is good (or if this is a contradiction, for whom a sensation that feels exactly like one I now identify as painful is good). If this is false — if pain must be an evil for any sentient being, however constituted — relationalism is false, at least in relation to certain categories of sensation. In that case there are small islands of moderate objectivism in the wide relationalist sea. (As we shall see, such islands would not threaten anything important to the ESA account.)

We need to be careful about what we are asking here. Arguably, it is a fact about our language that to call a sensation a pain is to imply that one dislikes how it feels, and to call an experience a pleasure is to imply that one likes how it feels. If so, then it is tautologically true that pain is disliked for how it feels (by every sentient being). In that case, we can't deny that it is intrinsically bad.

But this is just to say that what is bad for a sentient being, qua sentient being, is a qualia (state of consciousness) that it happens to dislike because of what it is like to experience it. A relationalist grants this. That is just what it is for there to be a fit or misfit with respect to qualia. But the relationalist insists that the specific qualia that fall into this category depends on the nature of the subject. The

important question is whether any member of a certain set of sensations, the set that is extensionally equivalent to the typical extension
of pain, must necessarily be disliked merely because it feels like *that*.
If not, the goodness or badness of that particular sensation will
depend on the nature of the experiencer. And, since this is the hardest
case, we might conclude that the relational view of the good will hold
in all cases. Can we make sense of this?

Imagine a particular sensation that most of us regard as painful,
for example, the sensation that typically accompanies a severe burn.
It is hard to imagine how any sentient being could enjoy this feeling.
Accordingly, we are tempted to say that if any being does welcome or
enjoy a purported severe burning sensation for its own sake, it must
feel different to him than it does to us, that is, it must be a different
sensation. If we insist on this *must*, we have a synthetic a priori truth
about this qualia, namely, necessarily, no being can enjoy anything
that feels like *that*. Another possibility is that liking or disliking is a
response to a sensation and that it is a contingent psychological fact
about a subject that he likes or dislikes it, a fact that may differ from
experiencer to experiencer.

Consider taste, for example, the taste of beer. Some people love it,
some people hate it. *Must* we conclude from this that they have
different taste sensations? Imagine a taste you find repulsive (e.g.,
sickeningly sweet) but that other people like. It is hard to believe that
if they really had your sensation, if they tasted *that*, they could like it.
On the other hand, some people say they do not like the taste of
anything sweet (or salty, or bitter, etc.). And it is hard to imagine that
they can be so constituted psychologically or physiologically that *all*
of the experiences they identify as sweet are different from *all* of the
relevant experiences of someone who likes most or all sweet things.
We can easily imagine, for example, that the sensation of sweetness
derived from a certain ice cream is somewhat different for two people.
Still, each of them will have a range of sweetness sensations, and it is
hard to imagine that there can be absolutely no overlap (though the
sensations that overlap may be derived from different objects). Still,
one of them may dislike the taste of anything sweet, and the other
may like something sweet in the area of overlap.

What holds for taste seems also to hold for colors and sounds. A
color or sound sensation that pleases me may not please you. The fact
that I like a shade of green or a combination of notes that leaves you
cold does not entail that they look or sound different to us (though they
might). In general, it seems rather much to assume that—in the realm
of visual, auditory, olfactory, and gustatory sensations—everyone

necessarily has the same likes and dislikes. Why then should we say this of bodily sensations?

It might be argued that sensations are complex. In some cases, enjoyment and repugnance are not merely attitudes, but parts of the experience itself. There is a specific and important experiential difference between any taste we find repulsive and any taste we enjoy. The same holds for pain. Thus, victims of chronic pain sometimes report that although the intensity of the pain remains constant, the unpleasantness diminishes and sometimes disappears entirely (a process called "making friends" with one's pain).[4] So it might be said against relationalism that although it is possible for certain experiencers to enjoy sensations that others find repugnant, no one experiencer can like the experience of disliking or of repugnance itself, whatever her nature.

However, the analysis of repugnance — construed as an experience or a complex of qualia — works just the same way as the analysis of pain. A feeling of repugnance is, as a matter of linguistic fact, necessarily unpleasant. But it does not follow that the sensations that typically constitute the experience must be disliked by any experiencer, regardless of that experiencer's nature. If the sensations are liked they cannot be called "feelings of repugnance," but they may be qualitatively identical to feelings that typically bear that description. Consider the most palpable case. You smell or taste something disgusting, for example, a rotten egg. You are sickened (you are queasy, the room spins, etc.). Those sensations constitute your feeling of repugnance. By calling this a feeling of repugnance we imply that they are unpleasant to you. But again, it makes sense to ask whether these particular sensations are necessarily unpleasant for every possible experiencer (i.e., whether it is possible for some experiencer to enjoy the sensations of queasiness, dizziness, etc.).

These considerations suggest that even the good or evil of experiencing various sensations is in part a function of the nature of the subject. Again, if this inference is wrong, there will be a few islands of nonrelational good and evil in a sea of relational value. But these will not necessarily be more important than relational goods or evils. For as we shall see, we might be willing to suffer a good deal of pain for the sake of some merely relational good (under epistemically ideal conditions).

Virtues, Ideals, Enjoyments, and the Pleasure Machine

Applying this account to human circumstances, we can explain why most of us are not complete hedonists. The emphasis here is on complete." For almost everyone recognizes that enjoyment and the absence of suffering are important features of a good life. Those who deny it (or seem to deny it) for this life generally do so for the sake of a better hedonic situation in the next. Indeed, the goodness of pleasure and the evil of pain are built into even the grimmest of Calvinist theologies. On all accounts, God in His *wisdom* blesses the saved with enjoyment and torments the damned with pain. So, even from the most (apparently) antihedonic fundamentalist point of view, there must be something good about the former and something bad about the latter.

But most of us do not regard enjoyments and suffering as the only goods and evils. Moreover, as we have seen, we do not regard them as good and evil *unconditionally*. Again, most of us would not regard it as good that we enjoyed watching some barbarian torture our spouse or child. That is, we would not calculate the evil of the entire state of affairs by subtracting the good of our enjoyment from the evil of their suffering. We would think it better, on the whole, that we suffered. And this is not just to save ourselves guilt pangs in the future. At least some of us would think it better even if we knew we would die when the torture ended. We would not want to spend our last moments taking delight in the agonized screams of our loved one. Similarly, we would rather be sickened than delighted by witnessing injustice, treachery, and betrayal, especially in relation to people we love.

This shows that although most of us want to enjoy life, we do not want to enjoy life *promiscuously*. We want to enjoy the right things, and we want to suffer at the right times too. Some things are more important to us than feeling good.[5] And there is no reason to assume that this would be otherwise under ideal epistemic conditions. In any case, it is up to the complete hedonist to show that these nonhedonic preferences are grounded on some epistemic or imaginative defect. But why are we like this? What explains why we are not complete hedonists?

The answer is that every normal member of a human society has some conception of what it is to be an admirable and less than admirable person. Moreover, we value living up to that conception for its own sake. This is central to our nature as social beings. Arguably, if we were not like this, human societies could not function. In any case, we respect ourselves to the extent that we succeed in living up to such conceptions, and we are disappointed or ashamed of ourselves to the extent that we fail to live up to them. Or rather, this is so with respect to traits we believe that people in general or people in our position should have. I will call these traits personal virtues. We may also admire traits that require unusual natural capacities, fortunate upbringing, or enormous efforts to acquire. I will call these traits personal ideals.

To the extent that they are admired by others, personal virtues and ideals are also social virtues and ideals. A trait qualifies as a reasonable social virtue or ideal to the extent that it is desirable from an impartial point of view. In our society (at least) these include traditional moral virtues like honesty, fairness, and loyalty. But they also include nonmoral virtues like personal warmth, eloquence, the capacity to remain calm under pressure, and a sense of humor. Obviously, people may also value traits that are not reasonable in this sense. Some people in our society value the capacity to remain indifferent to suffering and the disposition to dominate others whenever possible. They judge themselves and others in relation to these capacities and try to inculcate these capacities in their children.

As this suggests, it is very important what traits of character we encourage in one another and cultivate in our young. Moral disapproval of actions, even moral disapproval backed by legal sanction, provides very inadequate protection against narcissists, sadists, and rational egoists with Hobbesian desires.[6] Moreover, to the extent that people are empathetic, compassionate, and fair-minded, our dependence on the deterrent role of moral disapproval and legal sanctions diminishes (although they still play an important educational role).[7] What protects us against abuse by others is that, by and large, others do not want to abuse us. They would rather be good and decent people. In ESA terms, that means that they want traits of character that are reasonably valued from an impartial point of view. To the extent that people evaluate themselves and others on the basis of other characteristics, we are all worse off.

This does not mean that we are all required fully to dedicate our lives to others. Any ESA account must consider the impact of P's honoring a set of standards on P's life as well. In particular, we want people to have room to enjoy life and to pursue enriching and fulfilling projects. We do not want people miserably devoting themselves to improving the condition of others who are miserably devoting themselves to improving the condition of still others, and so forth. The proper mix of self-directed and other-directed desires may vary with culture and circumstances and may also vary from domain to domain within a given culture. And there may be upper limits on the range of reasonable other-directed desires based on biological limits to our capacity for altruism.

In general, the most important traits we reasonably desire in others are those that protect us against murder, assault, betrayal, theft, and other forms of injury and abuse. People disposed to do such things are likely to do more damage than people who simply lack eloquence or a sense of humor, and the damage they do will almost certainly outweigh any good they accomplish by making speeches or good jokes. This is why it is reasonable for a society to give pride of place to virtues that promote conformity to reasonable action-regulating moral standards.

It does not follow, however, that virtues like a sense of humor, eloquence, personal warmth, and creativity are not reasonably valued.[8] Not only do they enhance the lives of those who have them, but they enhance the lives of others as well. Indeed, it does not follow that we ought to admire P rather than R because P has traits that promote conformity to action-regulating standards to a greater degree than R does. A scrupulously honest and fair individual who conscientiously respects the rights of others may do this to a greater degree than someone who is sometimes inappropriately partisan, occasionally tells minor lies, and sometimes misses unpleasant social gatherings she has promised to attend. But the former may be dour, unimaginative, cold, and devoid of humor while the latter is warm, gregarious, enthusiastic about living, and full of mirth. ESA allows us to say that persons of the latter sort are more worthy of our collective admiration than persons of the former sort.

When I say that traits that promote conformity to reasonable action regulating moral standards have pride of place, I do not mean that someone who does better with respect to them is necessarily a more admirable person. We want more from one another than mere conformity to action-regulating standards. Within limits, one can compensate for failings here with successes elsewhere. However, we must avoid the temptations of pseudorigor here. There are no scales, and the appropriate relationships cannot plausibly be expressed as a set of ratios. We cannot say, for example, that n units of honesty are equivalent to m units of eloquence. Indeed, our assessment of any given trait in a given person will depend on the cluster of traits with which it is combined. To the extent that one's thinking is partisan to begin with (as opposed to fair-minded), we might prefer that one's sense of loyalty is proportionately weaker. To the extent that one is cruel, we might reasonably prefer that one lack eloquence and a sense of humor.

As Plato and Aristotle emphasized, character traits have a great deal to do with desires, intentions, motives, and feelings. We do not encourage or discourage people to act in certain ways by Pavlovian or Skinnerian conditioning in relation to the actions themselves. We encourage or discourage actions by encouraging or discouraging feelings and desires. Moreover, if we did not do this, our moral code could not be agent-centered in the appropriate way. By educating feelings and desires—by raising children so that they want to be compassionate, to protect the weak, and so on—we narrow the gap between morality and self-interest. It is arguable that we sometimes suffer a net loss by narrowing this gap in certain ways (e.g., that by instilling too much compassion, we blunt the competitive edge and lose the benefits of competition). But unless one can *show* that this is so, and that the losses outweigh the gains, it seems reasonable to narrow the gap.

A hedonist might argue that although virtues and ideals often require individual hedonic sacrifices, they make collective hedonic sense. Communities with rational beliefs about virtues and ideals do better hedonically than they would do without any ideals at all. This is no doubt true, but it does not fully explain the importance of virtues and ideals. They are valuable not only because they regulate collective behavior in advantageous ways, but also because they provide individual lives with much of their drama and meaning. Indeed, they define the stage on which a primary drama of human life, the quest for worthiness, is played out. That is not the only drama. If we had no beliefs about virtues or ideals, we would still be interested in what happens to us, and we would continue to brave hazards and endure hardships to get what we want. But much would be missing as well. Indeed, most great drama and literature focuses on quests or conflicts involving virtues and ideals. And it is up to the hedonist to show that it is irrational for beings like us to be willing to endure hedonic deficits for the sake of greater meaning and drama.[9]

I need to make one further point to fill out the picture. According to ESA, our standards governing virtues and ideals are domain sensitive in the way our standards governing actions are. Clearly, we value a different mix of characteristics in military drill instructors than in mothers of small children. Indeed, what counts as a virtue in one domain may not count as a virtue in another. The capacity to make quick, action-related decisions in the face of uncertainty is a virtue in a police officer (on patrol) but not necessarily a virtue in a professor (as his word processor).

At a certain level of description, certain characteristics are virtues and vices in every domain. But like core moral standards, their importance and even their criteria of application are domain sensitive as well. Consider courage. Although there is a level of abstraction at which courage is everywhere the same, the more specific criteria for identifying instances of it differ from domain to domain. Thus, writers and soldiers are expected to exhibit courage in relation to different sorts of dangers. A soldier is cowardly (qua soldier) if he is too frightened to face bullets, bombs, and so forth to do his duty. But he is not cowardly (qua soldier) if he is too frightened of social disapproval to express unpopular views in writing. On the other hand, an editorial writer is not cowardly if he is too frightened to face bullets or bombs to get to his office (or even to publish his views), but he is cowardly if he is too frightened of social disapproval to publish unpopular opinions. Both are cowardly if they are too frightened to do what their vocations require of them. But their vocations require taking different risks on different occasions. The explanation obviously has to do with the goods and evils at issue in the respective domains. The corresponding point holds for parents, doctors, police officers, athletes, and so forth. And, of course, the case of courage is not unique. The analysis can easily be extended to honesty, compassion, loyalty, fairness, and so forth.

Other Intrinsic Valuings

The rejection of objectivism entails that nothing is intrinsically valuable (aside, perhaps, from fits). This does not mean that it is irrational to value something intrinsically. It makes sense to do that as long as there is a fit between the state of affairs we value and our nature. On this account, to value something intrinsically is not necessarily to believe that it has intrinsic value in any objectivist sense.

As we have seen, we value character traits intrinsically. But we may value other things intrinsically as well, both for ourselves and for others. In general, to the extent that we value x intrinsically, (1) we would be willing to sacrifice something to realize x for ourselves or for others; or (2) if we are unwilling to sacrifice anything to realize x for ourselves or for others, we regard ourselves as weak or irrational.[10] Thus, we may value friendship, artistic achievement, athletic excellence, status, power, or intellectual ability for their own sake. The more we value them, of course, the more we are willing to sacrifice.

As suggested, we may value these things for ourselves and/or for others. We value them for others if there is a fit between our nature and the state of affairs in which, for example, others get what we value for them. Thus, we may intrinsically value an end to poverty or the survival of endangered species.

Very roughly, the best virtues, ideals, and intrinsic valuings from an impartial point of view are those which, at expected levels of subscription, maximize the quality of life for all beings affected (including the subject, of course).[11] To estimate expected levels of subscription we need a rich picture of the society for which a package is proposed. The best package, moreover, may not be realizable without staggering transformation costs (e.g., revolution). To evaluate packages, then, it is best to begin with intrinsic valuings already in place and to ask whether we can move to superior alternatives with acceptable costs. Still, our goal is to choose a package that maximizes the quality of life for everyone affected.

As this suggests, other things being equal, we want people to intrinsically value things that move them to do socially useful things and to take pleasure or pride in doing them. Accordingly, other things being equal, a pattern of virtues, ideals, and other intrinsic valuings is rational to the extent that it reduces the conflict between self-interested and socially useful action. We may not be able to eliminate this conflict entirely. Again, there may be biological or cultural limits to what we can enjoy or wholeheartedly endure for the sake of others. But, other things being equal, we want a society in which one lives virtuously, satisfies one's ideals, and realizes other intrinsic values by doing socially useful things.

Choosing Packages

We are now in a position to address the question of choosing packages. Suppose that we must choose between competing packages of goods and evils to evaluate a moral standard. And suppose that the choices are controversial. To what extent can our choices be defended rationally?

According to the relational theory, we cannot defend our choices by appealing to some list of objective (agent independent) goods. Instead we must appeal to a/distributions of fits between the collectivity of agents and the world. Roughly, one package is better than another if it embodies a superior a/distribution of fits, where comparisons are made from an impartial point of view. As before, the proper understanding of impartiality is Rawlsean in spirit. One decides what would be the best package of fits not knowing how the alternative packages will affect his own prospects. One recognizes that different people have different fits by virtue of having different natures, and he chooses with everyone's interest at heart. He wants to choose the package that promotes the best pattern of fits for all concerned.

What counts as "best"? Sometimes we simply can't say. There are three problems here. First, we lack the resources to determine what others (or even ourselves) would choose from an epistemically ideal position. Second, all the problems surrounding the individuation, ranking, and weighing of preferences or desires arise here as well.

Third, there is no rationally compelling abstract principle for identifying the optimal a/distribution of fits to begin with.

In some cases, this leaves us with intractable problems. For example, what moral attitude should we adopt toward risk-taking by parents of young children (e.g., serious mountain climbing, race car driving, etc.)? That is, when is an activity so risky that we should morally criticize a parent for doing it? Assuming that we know how risky an activity is, our answer depends on (1) the importance of the relevant activities in the lives of the parents (from an epistemically ideal point of view); (2) the damage done to children whose parents are killed, paralyzed, or seriously injured; and (3) the various benefits and hazards of producing people who are willing to accept the relevant risks (and more generally, who live relatively fearlessly).

We have some idea of how to assess (2). So, if we know how risky an activity is, we have some idea of the likely costs to children. But we have more trouble with (1) and (3). Some people claim that doing risky things is of fundamental importance to them. They say that overcoming their fear of death much improves the quality of their lives, and they want to pass this on to their children (even if they must subject their children to hazards to do so). Within certain risk-taking limits, there will be many more beneficiaries than victims. And within these limits, they claim that the benefits to the relatively many survivors will outweigh the damage to the relatively fewer orphans, children of invalid parents, etc.

The critic wonders whether the risk-takers would say this from an epistemically advantaged point of view, for example, vividly imagining the plight of orphaned children. But how can we know? Perhaps some risk takers would say this and some would not, depending on their psychological profiles. We should not pretend that we can order their preferences here or that we can discover a rationally compelling principle of a/distribution that tells us what is best for the collectivity. And we should acknowledge our predicament.

There is an ongoing discussion of this issue, and it is possible that someone will eventually make a compelling case for one side or the other. We can contribute to this discussion by articulating our beliefs and suspicions, but we should represent them as such. We should not parade our intuitions as if they had evidential weight. In the absence of compelling argument, we should hold that no one is in a position to make compelling criticisms of our current standards. In such cases, we should retain what we have. We have limited energies for working for change, and we should direct them toward areas in which we have confidence.

But as some of the examples in chapters 4 and 5 illustrate, matters are not always so difficult. One advantage of ESA is that it provides us with a method of settling many disputes before they reach intractably high levels of abstraction. Another is that it provides us with a method for isolating the empirical issues on which many other disputes turn. We begin with the concrete, subject it to rational reflection, and move toward the abstract only when we are compelled to by disagreement or doubt born of reflection. These advantages are connected. By isolating the empirical issues, we can rationally settle many disputes before matters become too abstract.

It might be objected that the point of ethical inquiry is not to settle disputes but to reach the right conclusion. We might settle some disputes by agreeing on false empirical claims. Or if we have the same irrational fears, we might settle them because we make the same mistakes when we try to determine what people would want from an epistemically advantaged point of view. ESA acknowledges this. Obviously, we never occupy an epistemically ideal position. So our agreements may in fact be based on widely shared errors. But ESA asks us to strive to eliminate such errors. The point is to evaluate existing standards in the light of accurate information and understanding. The assumption is that we can thereby improve our beliefs. Accordingly, the mere fact that we agree should never be taken to be conclusive. The agreements in question must be rational, that is, able to withstand critical scrutiny. Of course, this process of critical examination may be influenced by cultural biases, ideology, and the like. But ESA holds that we can rise above many such distortions by rational examination. The critic must show that we cannot do this. For example, he must show either that the pictures of African Americans and women in relation to which we now condemn earlier practices are no more accurate than their nineteenth-century ancestors, or that rational inquiry has not helped us to see this.[12]

Still, some disputes cannot be settled before they reach a very abstract level. Yet even at very high levels of abstraction, our choices between standards are not always entirely arbitrary. Most of us intrinsically value justice and fairness, and believe that certain principles of a/distribution produce fairer results than others. At the very least, then, one could not choose a principle that most other people would regard as unfair or unjust from an impartial point of view. Of course, the problem of a/distribution arises at this level as well. But, depending on the pattern of fits at this level, certain choices may now be excluded.

But in the end we arc left with some issues that we cannot settle. This is what one should expect from ESA. On this view, we justify moral standards in much the same way we justify social policies. And few of us believe that there are rationally compelling answers to every question of social policy (even where there is complete empirical agreement). The most we can do is show how the discussion goes when it goes rationally. Fully rational discussion does not necessarily culminate in agreement between fully rational people. Again, there is no *guarantee* that employing the method of ESA will always improve one's assessments of moral standards. Given inaccurate empirical beliefs, ESA might lead one to support moral standards that are inferior to those one learned at one's mother's knee. But this is no more an objection to ESA than it is to the rules of logic. Good reasoning from inaccurate premisses sometimes leaves one worse off.

Were moral standards like the theorems of Euclidean geometry, understood Platonically, no successful account of the justification of moral standards could leave room for disagreement. The standards would be there to be discovered, and reason would be capable of discovering them. But once we abandon accounts according to which moral standards are discovered in favor of a picture according to which they are decided upon, there is no reason to expect such agreement. Reason has an important role in evaluating and designing standards, but there are not always unique solutions. In *this* limited respect, moral standards are indeed like rules of games. Baseball, basketball, and bridge all have been improved over their original versions by new rules. And it's easy to imagine further rule changes that would ruin them entirely. But there are changes on which reasonable people may disagree as well.

Application: How to Think Systematically about the Economic Domain

I have already provided numerous examples of how ESA explains variations in the weights of core moral standards and how it can be used to evaluate domain-specific ones. I now want to show how ESA enables us to think systematically about the ethics of a domain as a whole. This should help us assess the degree to which the "competing package" problem limits the use of the method. I have chosen the economic domain because our thinking about this domain is in such disarray.

Reflections on the ethics of the economic domain typically occur under two headings: political economy and business ethics. Political economy proceeds at the macro level. To the extent that it is normative, it asks, what set of basic economic institutions serves us best?

Here the most basic institution is property. And the question is, what forms or rules of property ownership and exchange serve us best? The traditional candidates are laissez-faire capitalism (unregulated private ownership and exchange), regulated capitalism (private ownership with restrictions on ownership and exchange), and various forms of socialism (public ownership, with varying degrees of central planning or control).

Business ethics is a relatively new area in philosophy, and its boundaries are not precise. For the most part it addresses questions that arise within the context of capitalism. Many of these questions are wholly or partly about the degree to which private ownership and exchange should be regulated (i.e., about the form of capitalism we should adopt). At a certain point these questions become questions of political economy (the difference is one of degree). But many questions are considerably more specific than that (e.g., whistle-blowing, affirmative action, and corporate responsibility). In any case, however we answer the questions of political economy—even if we are socialists—those of us who live under capitalism will also need to answer the more specific questions of business ethics. This suggests an important theme that will be developed in chapter 7, namely, the fact that a set of basic institutions is flawed does not by itself entail that those institutions impose no obligations.

ESA employs the same basic strategy for questions of both political economy and business ethics. The difference is that in addressing questions of business ethics it takes capitalist institutions as background conditions. In relation to political economy, the question is, roughly, what general set of economic institutions best promotes the goals of the economic domain? In relation to business ethics the questions are, roughly, (a) what form of capitalist institutions best promotes these goals (i.e., to what degree should private ownership and use of property be regulated)?; and (b) given the institutions currently in place, what more specific distribution of rights, duties, virtues, vices, and so forth best promotes these goals? These formulations are rough since we also need to take into account the ways in which various answers affect the a/distribution of goods in other domains. (Some of the most interesting socialist arguments against capitalism contend that capitalism by its nature is corrosive of them.) In any case, ESA holds that disputes about political economy and business ethics are disputes about what the ends of economic life are and how they are best promoted.

I now want to illustrate how this strategy helps to think systematically about business ethics.

The familiar cliché that "business ethics" is an oxymoron may express a low opinion of the character of business people: they are greedy, crass, sleazy, and so forth. Or it may express an accurate understanding of how business is characterized by many of its theorists. According to Milton Friedman, Albert Carr, and others, the ethics of business are and should be quite minimal.[13] There are prohibitions against killing, stealing, extortion, breaking contracts, and perhaps breaking the law. But within this narrow set of constraints, anything goes. In general, the strong may bully the weak, the well-positioned may take advantage of the desperate, and the credulous may be led as far down the garden path as their credulity allows. In particular, under appropriate market and legal conditions, workers may be paid starvation wages, poisons may be pumped into the air and water, and poor people may be reduced to homelessness to make way for corporate office space. In short, many familiar moral standards may be completely ignored, and principles central to our moral and religious tradition may be violated without a second thought.

Not surprisingly, this barely constrained egoism, this moral minimalism, appalls most moral philosophers. And the discipline of business ethics has emerged largely as a result of their insistence on higher standards. Business practices are condemned by invoking precepts or principles that obtain in other domains of life or that are central to our moral tradition. But those who take this line rarely if ever attempt to *argue* that the principles they cite are relevant to the business domain. Nor do they attempt to determine what weight they should carry there. This is unfortunate. *If* we are permitted *unconditionally* to apply standards from outside business to the business domain, the moral minimalism of Milton Friedman is replaced by a kind of moral maximalism. No one endorses maximalism. But those who import moral precepts that are at home in other areas to the domain of business need to provide some principled basis for stopping short of it. ESA provides a principled basis for establishing limits.

As suggested, the strategy is to assess the wisdom of candidate principles in relation to the goods and evils at stake in the economic domain (and as appropriate, a more general class of goods and evils as well). What are these goods and evils? That is, what goods do we, collectively and impartially, want from an economy? I will propose a vague but reasonable answer and show that, vague as it is, it enables us to settle certain important points of difference between theorists.

To begin with, other things being equal, we want as much prosperity as we can get given our resources and technology. Prosperity, of course, is not reducible to the aggregate volume or value of goods and services (e.g., to the GNP). A society that produces an enormous volume of goods that very few people want or need, for example, pyramids or jet-powered snowmobiles, is not prosperous in the relevant sense. A society is prosperous to the extent that its members enjoy the material basis for a good life (I will call goods that meet this description "life-enhancing" goods). Very roughly, life-enhancing goods promote "fits." To provide prosperity, then, an economy must produce the right kinds of goods and distribute them to the appropriate people. The variety and magnitude of these goods will vary with cultural values and environmental conditions. What enhances life in New York may ruin life in Eden. I will ignore these complexities here.

Prosperity also has a distributive dimension. A society that produces an enormous volume of goods but makes them available to very few people is not a prosperous one. Here, as above, I am stipulating a sense of "prosperity." But it is the sense that captures what interests us when we are giving an account of the reasonable goals of the economic domain from an impartial point of view. We want the best overall pattern of fits, impartially considered. Although there is no one rationally compelling abstract principle for deciding this, certain distributions can be excluded. And this includes most historically actual ones.

Production and distribution are not the only dimensions of prosperity. We also need to consider certain externalities. For example, an economy does less to provide the material basis for a good life to the extent that it poisons its air, food, and water and destroys the beauty of the land. Accordingly, these evils must be subtracted from the goods of productive activity in estimating the life-enhancing value of the whole. This is another reason that the GNP is a bad measure of social prosperity. Ironically, the damages in question may lead to increases in the GNP. When water and air are poisoned, pure water becomes a commodity, and industries devoted to water and air filtration flourish.

The second goal of the economic domain, maximizing the quality of working life, also has several dimensions. Most of us spend more than half our waking time working, so we have a considerable stake in the quality of our job experience. Other things being equal, we want our jobs to be safe, socially useful, secure, and interesting. We also want them to preserve our dignity, that is, we want to eliminate demeaning occupational statuses and demeaning work relationships. In addition, we want our jobs to leave us with sufficient time and energy to enjoy our home life and to develop other interests. Of course, there will be tradeoffs among these goals and between them and the goal of prosperity. But we do not need to worry about that now.[14]

Suppose one accepts these as basic economic goods. In that case ESA holds that we can decide basic questions of political economy and business ethics primarily in relation to them. According to ESA, the best set of basic economic institutions is (roughly) the one that advances these goals best while doing the least damage to the goals of other domains. And the best business ethic is the one that satisfies this description within a framework of capitalist institutions. Vague as this is, this is enough to show why minimalism demands too little and those who import principles may demand too much.

Let's begin with the imported principles approach. Moral criticisms of business practices take at least three forms. Practices are said to violate human rights, to violate some principle of commonsense morality, or to violate some abstract principle central to our tradition (e.g., that persons should be treated as ends in themselves, or that practices must satisfy rules that promote utility). According to ESA, these criticisms are valid only if the precepts on which they are based can be shown to be relevant to the business domain. And they are only as powerful as those precepts are in that domain. Both issues are decided by determining to what extent adopting these precepts promotes the social goals of business activity (and prevents business activity from undermining other goods). Let's apply this to the kinds of criticisms just sketched.

Consider human rights. According to business ethicist Patricia Werhane, free expression and due process are human rights.[15] Accordingly, businesses violate human rights if they penalize their employees for exercising their right to free expression or if they penalize employees without due process.[16] Unfortunately, however, Werhane does not provide us with a principled basis for fixing the scope or importance of these rights in the domain of business. Clearly they do not have the same scope or force there as they do, for example, in the political realm. What scope and importance should we grant them?

Consider free expression. The American courts have ruled that our right to free expression *against the state* includes the right to dress more or less as we please. Should we have this right against businesses? If we did we could dress as we pleased on the job; that is, there could be no dress codes or uniforms at all. However, there are obvious economic arguments in favor of dress codes and uniforms in a wide range of occupations, and there are no domain-related arguments against them (although, of course, they should not be stronger than they need to be to realize their objectives). Moreover, restrictions on dress very rarely undermine the goods at issue in other domains, and exceptions can be made when these harms are sufficiently strong (as, for example, where religious values are at stake).[17]

Political expression works differently. The political domain is undermined if employers are allowed to prevent employees from making public speeches, participating in political demonstrations, and so forth. Particular companies may have economic reasons for imposing such restrictions; for example, they might lose customers if highly visible employees take politically controversial stands. But it is not clear that this sort of thing will undermine the goods of the economic domain *as a whole.* And it is clear that such restrictions on political expression directly and seriously undermine the political domain (e.g., the goods of democracy). According to the minimalist, employees have no rights to free expression against businesses (e.g., one can be fired for expressing political views on or off the job). According to the maximalist, they have the same right to free expression against businesses as they have against the state. On Werhane's account, it is not clear on what principled basis the right to free expression against businesses should be delimited. ESA approach explains how to draw the line.[18]

The same holds for due process. According to the minimalist account, employers have no obligation to provide workers with opportunities to appeal dismissals, demotions, and so forth. According to the maximalist, they are obligated to provide them with the same safeguards we enjoy against the state. Again, ESA allows us to take a principled middle position. There are good job-quality reasons for grievance procedures. Workers are protected against the exercise of arbitrary power, job security is enhanced, and so forth. However, we can achieve these without instituting the elaborate range of safeguards maximalism would require (e.g., lawyers, juries, etc.). So, as Werhane in fact recommends (but without a principled basis), some compromise is in order.

Moreover, there are good reasons for varying both the grounds and the procedures for grievance from one kind of enterprise to another. Thus, for example, other things being equal, corporate managers should not be allowed to make personnel decisions on the basis of personal relationships or likes and dislikes. This is inefficient and creates a low-quality working environment. But personal considerations might be a reasonable basis for hirings, firings and so forth in small, owner-operated businesses or family businesses. In small businesses, the quality of the work environment and everyone's job performance may depend heavily on goodwill among the employees and between the owner and her work force. And, of course, its hard to know how one could have a family business if one could not hire family members preferentially. Obviously, moreover, small businesses cannot afford the time and energy for elaborate courtroom-like grievance procedures that might be appropriate to a large corporation.

We turn now to the second form of importation, namely, criticisms that proceed from some standard of commonsense morality. Such criticisms are common. They appear in sermons, in editorials, and in speeches by business leaders themselves. In his ground-breaking book, *The Moral Foundations of Professional Ethics*, Alan Goldman attempts to provide a theoretical defense of this approach in relation to business (and the professions in general).[19] On Goldman's view business people (and professionals in general) are sometimes exempt from ordinary moral constraints. But they are exempt only if granting exemptions can be justified in terms of more important *moral* consideration (or for him, rights). That is, professionals and business people are exempt from a commonsense, prima facie duty D in their domains if and only if honoring that precept in that domain violates D', a more important prima facie duty. Since Goldman believes that we can make this judgment on a domain-by-domain basis, his view is domain sensitive. But since he holds that we make these judgments by making tradeoffs between a set of (presumably) constantly weighted duties and obligations, it is not domain sensitive enough.

Consider this account in relation to lying. Goldman would condemn lying in business except in contexts where there is an important moral reason to lie (a reason that outweighs the wrong of lying). But consider lying in business bargaining ("That's my last offer"; "If you don't, I'll take all my business elsewhere," etc.). There seems to be no *moral* reasons favoring such lies. But they seem harmless enough. One's "last offer" can always be sweetened if rejected. And the seller can always accept an offer he had (falsely) described as utterly out of the question. Nothing is lost when business people engage in this commonplace strategy. Indeed, the game dimension adds interest to the negotiator's job.[20]

Other lies in business are far more serious, for example, lying about the characteristics of one's products or lying about the terms agreed to in verbal contracts. This can be explained in ESA terms. The former lies obviously interfere with getting the right goods to the right people. The latter lies undermine trust in verbal agreements and destroy a useful economic resource. These lies are more serious precisely because they interfere with the goals of economic life.

We now turn to the third form of criticism, namely, criticism made on the basis of higher level principles. Consider Kant's principle that we should never treat another person as a means only. Although it is not entirely clear what this means, at the very least it forbids us to disregard the good or interests of those affected by our actions. Yet business life abounds with cases in which we disregard the interests of others. It is difficult to see how a market economy could function otherwise. If we had to treat everyone as an end in himself, we could not win business from a competitor without considering the impact of our decisions on that competitor's life (will she be driven out of business? Will her income be so reduced that she cannot send her children to college? etc.). Nor could we reject offers from prospective house buyers or renters *merely* because we could get a better price elsewhere (where will they end up living or how much benefit would they get from one's house? etc.). In areas in which a market economy is justified, people must be free to meet as buyers and sellers, considering one another merely as means to each other's financial ends. Of course, charity is permitted. But it cannot be obligatory. Markets could not survive routinized charity-driven decision making. *If* there are good economic arguments for a market economy, then, we cannot be required to treat others as ends in themselves in bargaining contexts.[21]

There are also business contexts where we should take the interests of others into account. It is wrong to use high-pressure sales techniques to sell people what they neither need nor want, to underproduce some necessary good in order to keep the prices high, to pay starvation wages to people who are desperate for work if one can afford more, etc.[22] These particular ways of treating others as means retard prosperity as I have described it.[23] In one way or another they prevent us from getting the right goods to people on a sufficiently wide basis. The problem with Kant's principle is vagueness. We need to know *when* and how we are required to take the good of others into account in our actions. ESA provides us with a principled basis for answering that question.

In sum, many well-motivated responses to the minimalism of Milton Friedman and his followers involve importing principles from other areas into the business domain. But no one has yet provided an adequate principled basis for doing this. ESA does. Nonetheless, Minimalists will argue that ESA requires too much, so we should also review the ESA case against minimalism.

One theoretical foundation of minimalism is libertarian. Property rights are said to be natural rights. And the exercise of those rights is said to be limited only by a very narrow range of moral side constraints (viz., those mentioned earlier). Any transaction, exchange, or strategy that falls outside the range of these constraints is simply the exercise of a right, and is therefore beyond moral criticism.

The main argument against this natural rights approach was developed in chapters 1 and 2. Appeals to natural rights are based on appeals to intuition about principles or cases, or on appeals to the nature of persons, and they have no sound theoretical basis. According to ESA, the rules governing acquisition, use, and exchange may differ reasonably from culture to culture, and from historical period to historical period. These rules delimit recognized property rights (and hence define "property"). And there is no set of "real" or "true" property rights in relation to which they can be evaluated. Rather, other things being equal, they are justified by how well they satisfy the purposes of economic life.

Even if there were natural property rights, miminalism would not follow. Natural rights provide us with protections against certain sorts of interferences by other persons or the state, but they do not provide us with moral carte blanche. Within those protected boundaries, there are plenty of chances to act immorally. Thus, the right to free association does not morally entitle us socially to exclude someone for petty or malicious reasons. The right to free speech does not morally entitle us to gossip maliciously or say hurtful and insulting things for our own entertainment. And the right to property does not morally entitle us to pay our workers starvation wages whenever the market allows.

There is a second defense of minimalism as well, a defense in the spirit of Adam Smith. According to this defense, private selfishness in the economic realm best promotes the goals of the economic domain. This defense is consistent with the general methodology of ESA. I object to it because I think it is based on an excessively narrow view of the goals of the economic domain and because I disagree with its assessment of the capacity of the free market to realize those goals.

As indicated, I take these goals to include the quality of working life. A minimalist might reject this goal, or he might believe that the Invisible Hand assures it. If the latter, our dispute is empirical. If the former, he surely needs an argument. Although people are often willing to sacrifice certain dimensions of job quality for higher wages, the quality of working life is obviously important to almost everyone. According to ESA, it is a presumptive good of the economic domain. And the minimalist needs an argument against it.[24]

The minimalist might respond that minimalist business practices so far outstrip morally constrained practices in producing wealth that they provide everyone with a better prosperity/job-quality package even if some job quality is lost. Again, this argument may be empirical, axiological, or some combination of the two. To the degree that it is empirical, the minimalist accepts my account of "prosperity" (and uses "wealth" as a synonym for it). To the extent this is so, we differ on whether minimalist practices do a better job than morally constrained practices at producing and distributing life-enhancing goods, where externalities are taken into account. The arguments are economic, but the burden of proof is surely on the minimalist. For the straightforward examples are on the other side. Every time a corporation refuses to produce assault rifles, pollute the air, or lower wages to the minimum, it refuses to reduce prosperity as I understand it. The minimalist needs to show that the collective positive impact of unconstrained profit maximization on prosperity is sufficient to compensate for such obvious losses.

Of course, the Adam Smith minimalist might reject my account of prosperity as a goal of economic life.[25] But to reject prosperity from an impartial point of view is (roughly) to oppose getting the right goods to the right people on a wide scale with the least destruction to the environment. Clearly one needs a powerful argument for rejecting this.

It may also be that the minimalist accepts an additional goal, namely, the opportunity to become fabulously rich by hard work and intelligence (or simply the opportunity to become fabulously rich). Perhaps he takes this to be more important than one or more of the dimensions of prosperity (or job quality). He acknowledges the value of these presumptive goods, but he believes that they are subordinate to promoting the opportunity for great riches. And he believes that minimalism is necessary to promote that opportunity. Accordingly, he rejects all but the most minimal ethical constraints on property acquisition and use (i.e., all but those required for there to be any orderly system at all).

In evaluating this view we need to consider how much *more* opportunity of this kind there would be in a minimalist economy (if any) and how important these opportunities are (or would be) to how many people (under epistemically ideal conditions). We then need to consider how much prosperity and job quality we would have to give up on average to secure these additional opportunities. In the last analysis, we are faced with a choice between packages. The contents of these packages will depend on the economic beliefs we hold. On some factual scenarios, for example, my own, the choice between packages will be easy. The switch to a minimalist ethic (and minimalist legal regulations) will provide very little new opportunity for individuals to become fabulously wealthy and will be very costly in other ways. Like the lottery, it is a bad risk (considered impartially). But some will dispute my version of the facts.

In this section, I have illustrated the use of ESA in the economic domain. The discussion has been highly general. The main point has not been to settle issues, but to show how ESA enables us to stake out a principled middle ground between minimalism and maximalism. Obviously, to defend specific positions on the issues requires additional empirical argument and a further specification of the goals of economic life (e.g., we may disagree on the best distributive patterns, on tradeoffs between job quality and life-enhancing goods, on the relative importance of wilderness areas, etc.). Some of these differences might be overcome by further argument. Others may not.[26]

Notes

1. For some examples, see chapter 3, note 3.

2. It is strange that many deontologists, especially rights theorists, trust their intuitions about the right but not the good. If intuitions are evidence of universal moral truths in the former case, why are they not evidence in the latter as well?

3. See John Harsanyi, "Morality and the Theory of Rational Behavior," in Bernard Williams and Amartya Sen, eds., *Utilitarianism and Beyond*, Cambridge University Press, Cambridge, 1982.

4. As this suggests, the evil of painful sensations is generally increased considerably by the complex of other disagreeable feelings that accompany it (e.g., tension, fear, despair, etc.). Often when we think of pain we have elements of this complex in mind.

5. Most of us are also willing to sacrifice some net lifetime enjoyment to achieve something we regard as worthwhile. Anyone who believes that sitting at a word processor struggling with philosophical arguments eight hours a day maximizes enjoyment suffers from an acute poverty of imagination.

6. Any reasonably nimble and intelligent person could make a decent living as a thief in many American cities these days. In 1991 the police department in Portland, Oregon, announced that it was no longer even investigating most household burglaries. If we had to rely on the police to protect us against our neighbors, we would be in very serious trouble.

7. Moral disapproval, especially moral disapproval backed by legal sanction, is an expression of our moral code. It reminds us of what we stand for and teaches this to our children.

8. Its not clear whether we should call these "moral virtues," but the issue does not sem an important one. The problem of distinguishing between moral virtues and nonmoral virtues is like the problem of distinguishing between moral rules and other desirable social rules. ESA tells us how to justify rules and virtues of each kind. As I suggested in the Introduction, as

long as our account tells us how to justify moral ones, we should not worry that it tells us how to justify the other ones as well. That should be regarded as a merit of the theory, not a defect. The main thing is that we know how to determine whether a certain trait is or is not desirable.

As in the case of rules, it is difficult to arrive at a clean, noncontroversial distinction between moral virtues and nonmoral virtues partly because it is not clear what we should take as data. Aristotle includes pride among the ethical virtues. At least certain Christian traditions include humility as a fundamental virtue. The Puritans include thrift, diligence, and prudence. The Yanomamo admire ferocity, cold-bloodedness, and guile. The Buddhists admire compassion. Does all of this count as data? Or could one say that the Yanomamo, the Buddhists, or even Aristotle lacks the concept of a specifically moral virtue? We have the same choices here that I outlined in the Introduction in relation to rules. The account I have proposed there seems as reasonable a way as any to make the distinction. In any case, it serves the purposes of a theory of justification by isolating a particularly important class of traits. But not everyone need make the distinction in this way. For other purposes, there might be better ways to do it.

9. The hedonist might try to explain the value of meaning hedonically. Meaningless lives, he might claim, are quite unpleasant. But this is not promising. Meaningless lives are unpleasant only to those who care about meaning to begin with. Cats and dogs don't seem to care. Meaning may redeem suffering; it may even diminish it. But there is no reason to believe that meaningful suffering yields net hedonic benefits. Moreover, as many Buddhists argue, the desire for meaning may itself be a significant cause of suffering.

10. Paralleling what R. M. Hare says about the moral "ought," some philosophers think the test of believing that x is intrinsically valuable is being disposed to choose x under appropriate circumstances. One might take this to be the view that actions speak louder than words. What both Hare and others do not seem to realize is that we need not choose between actions and words. Affect is also an important part of the picture. If I say that A is right and I don't do A, but I feel guilty about not doing A, one cannot conclude that my words were insincere or self-deceiving. The corresponding point holds with respect to value choices.

11. The effects on the subject of acting on a morality have often been disregarded by moral theorists. However, other things being equal, it is surely a virtue of a morality that people want to act in accordance with what it requires.

12. This is not the place to argue against the forms of skepticism associated with the latest French fashions in philosophy. But I cannot resist the following observations. To begin with, much of the attack on scientific reasoning and our capacities for critical reflection are based on sociologies of knowledge that have empirical premisses as their starting points. Thus, e.g., it is said that women and colonized peoples have been oppressed and mar-

ginalized and that their vision of the world has been unfairly ignored. I agree. But I don't see how one could justify such claims except by the standard forms of observation and argument, i.e., the very sorts of processes it is supposed to help us to undermine. If the varieties of skepticism in question are to earn credibility, they must be able to survive their own criticisms.

A more serious challenge is posed by traditional Marxian explanations of moral change. Roughly, changing economic circumstances produce changing social relations and new moral structures to support them. The new morality is declared the progeny of universal reason by the victors. If this is true, of course, it challenges not only ESA but also any attempts to justify moral codes. All justification becomes the mere rationalization of class interests (or whatever). Although I cannot do justice to the issues here, I think this picture is false. As a matter of empirical fact, class interests have played and do play a key role in determining what standards a society adopts. But rational argument also plays a role. It is worth mentioning in this regard that universalist theories that appeal directly to reason or intuition are much more easily manipulated for ideological purposes than moral codes justified in relation to ESA. In the latter case, empirical facts play a large role. And although ideological manipulation is capable of promoting distorted factual beliefs, it is harder to do this than to distort intuitions. A person whose intuitions are under attack has no recourse. A person whose factual beliefs are under attack can defend himself. Given enough time, these defenses can prevail (though there is no guarantee that they will).

13. Milton Friedman, "The Social Responsibility of Business Is to Increase Profits," *New York Times Magazine*, September 13, 1970; Albert Carr, "Is Business Bluffing Ethical?" *Harvard Business Review*, January-February 1968.

14. Of course we also want our jobs to be high paying, but that falls under the heading of prosperity. To get goods to the right people on a wide enough basis, we must supply people with buying power.

15. Patricia Werhane, "Individual Rights in Business," in Tom Regan, ed., *Just Business: New Introductory Essays in Business Ethics*, Random House, New York, 1984, pp. 100–126.

16. Werhane, "Individual Rights in Business," pp. 107–20.

17. In 1990 the Canadian Sikh community complained that the Royal Canadian Mounted Police (RCMP) violated their rights by requiring that RCMP officers wear the familiar Mountie hat. Sikhs, who often work in law enforcement, are required by their religion to wear turbans. So the RCMP's dress code does undermine an important good. But clearly, "the" right to free expression does not entitle one to express himself anyway he wants in any circumstance. It is not just that one cannot cry "Fire!" in a crowded theater, but one is rightly evicted for talking loudly during a performance as well. Similarly, employers may rightly fire workers who carry on in loud, obnoxious ways that interfere with work, and teachers may penalize students for doing the same. The right to free expression does not trump our competing concerns in these cases, nor should it.

18. Werhane's actual policy suggestions are domain sensitive and intelligent. But she tries to settle the matter by appealing to general human rights, and her account of these rights is universalist and not domain sensitive at all. She says, e.g., that if anyone has them everyone has them and has them equally (even if they are members of different societies with different structures). "Individual Rights in Business," especially pp. 104–5.

19. Published by Rowman and Littlefield, New York, 1980.

20. The fact that people expect lies here does not change the fact that they are lies. One still speaks falsely with the intent to deceive.

21. We can require that people are treated with respect in various ways. We should be polite, we should not lie about our product, and so forth. But when it comes to accepting or rejecting offers from prospective buyers, or offering a competitor's client a better deal, we cannot be required to take as our first priority the impact our decision will have on the lives of those affected. A Kantian might hold that this is sufficient for respect in these circumstances, and argue that respect itself is domain specific. But short of appealing to intuitions I don't see how he could do that without appealing to domain-specific goods and evils. If one appeals to domain-specific goods and evils to fix the requirements of respectful treatment, I don't see how one gets anything from respect alone. In that case, respect functions as a kind of summary term for the ways in which people ought to be treated, where that is determined in ESA terms.

22. It is harder to decide whether there should be laws against some or all of these activities, and if so, how strong these laws should be. It is clear that there should be a strong moral feeling against them.

23. It might be objected that harsh business practices were necessary to fuel rapid economic development and that rapid economic development benefits generations to come. Our assessment of this argument depends in part on the degree to which we think the rate of economic development depends on harsh practices. Once we establish the rate, we compare various kinder practice/slower rate scenarios to various crueler practice/faster rate scenarios and see which do the best for all concerned. To do this we need to know to what degree we should discount the interests of future generations.

24. The extent to which we should rely on legislation to protect job quality is a separate question. One could consistently argue that our moral standards should require that employers sustain a certain level of job quality without arguing that they should be legally required to sustain it. However, given the ineffectiveness of merely moral criticism with respect to this matter in the past, this seems an implausible position. Unless it is expressed in law, moral opinion will not do much to protect job quality.

25. The libertarian minimalist, of course, rejects the view that economic life should have goals. Or in any case, she holds that the ethics of economic life are entirely independent of them. The Adam Smith minimalist, on the other hand, agrees that the ethics of economic activity are instrumental. So

she could consistently accept the general ESA picture. My difference with her in part concerns the goals in relation to which the instrument is judged.

26. Some disputes that now appear unresolvable may later turn out to have powerful arguments in their favor. There is a developing body of argument to the effect that almost everyone would be better off were people taught to be more appreciative of nature or more connected to living things in general. It is perfectly conceivable that this line of argument will be developed to the point that it becomes compelling. One can imagine studies of various kinds that would greatly strengthen the case.

7

Ethics and Agents

ESA is a theory about how to evaluate moral standards. It tells us how to decide whether prevailing moral standards are justified. And, if they are not justified, it tells us how to evaluate proposed revisions or substitutions. But it remains unclear at this point what ESA entails for individuals. More specifically, we want to know (1) what does morality require of *me*? and (2) how ought I to judge the actions (and character) of others?

As I will treat them here, these questions raise three different problems. The first, the problem of principled moral nonconformity, arises from a recognition that there is a gap between the claim that some set of standards S is justified for group G and the claim that an individual i is obligated to act on S, where i is a member of G. This will surprise many moral philosophers. There seems to be a widespread assumption that once we determine what morality is best for a society, we have thereby determined how its members should act and judge one another. Thus, rule utilitarianism is standardly described as the view that we ought to act on those rules which, at expected levels of compliance, would maximize utility.[1] Both sympathizers and opponents of utilitarianism accept this as a reasonable formulation of the spirit of that view. And, more generally, no one to my knowledge has developed a general critique of the inference from

(I) S_b is the best possible morality for group G; to
(II) Every member of G ought now act on S_b.

But I will argue that this inference is invalid. The premiss entails *something* about what we should do and how we should judge others.

But it does not entail the conclusion. Moreover, and perhaps more importantly, this way of formulating the issue obscures the problem we face as agents. That problem is to determine when our *belief* that an alternative set of standards S_b is superior to an existing set of standards S_e obligates or permits us to violate S_e in order to act on S_b. Notice that this category includes cases in which we are wrong about the superiority of S_b as well as cases in which we are right about it. The first part of this chapter attempts to clarify the problem of principled nonconformity and to describe the resources ESA has for addressing them.

The second problem raised by (1) and (2) is the problem of moral motivation. Why should we care about morality to begin with? This problem arises in a particularly urgent way for ESA and other instrumental accounts of morality. Indeed, some might charge that by robbing morality of its dignity and grandeur such accounts entirely undermine moral motivation. If morality is simply an instrument for promoting the interest of some collectivity of individuals, why should any particular individual care about being moral? After all, there might be a better way for him to promote *his* good. The second part of this chapter will discuss this problem. In the course of doing so it will also address the third problem raised by (1) and (2), namely, how much is one required to sacrifice of oneself for the sake of morality?

The Problem of Principled Moral Nonconformity

An agent may believe that the moral code of his society is defective and that there is a superior alternative. Under what conditions should he act on what he takes to be the superior alternative? We need standards that direct us as agents in these cases. We also need standards for those who advise agents and judge *their* acts. As we shall see, these two sets of standards are not necessarily symmetrical.

The importance of formulating standards directed at agents is not generally appreciated. Indeed, discussions of this issue tend to reduce the first-person problem to a third-person problem. Thus, for example, as Richard Brandt understands the issue of principled moral nonconformity in *A Theory of the Good and the Right*, the problem is to determine whether a fully rational person should *advise* a member of a society S to act on the standards of an ideally rational morality for S even if that morality is not currently in place. Brandt believes that he should so advise and that this determines the agent's obligation. That is, Brandt holds that because an ideally rational adviser should advise a member of S to act on an ideally rational morality for

S, every member of S is obligated to do so. He acknowledges that certain members of S may not recognize the superiority of S_b. But he claims that they are nonetheless obligated to act on it. That is the right thing for them to do (although, if their ignorance is nonculpable, they are not blameworthy for failing to do so).

But as suggested, this formulation fails adequately to address the problem we face as agents. As agents we must decide whether, or in what range of cases, our *belief* that there is a superior alternative to conventional morality justifies forsaking conventional morality for the sake of that alternative. This is a problem because, unlike Brandt's fully rational, fully informed observer, actual agents may be mistaken in their belief that an alternative standard is superior. They need to know in what range of cases they are entitled to trust their judgment about this, and when they are entitled to violate conventional morality for the sake of that judgment. Clearly, we don't want everyone to trust his judgment and act on it in every case. To encourage agents always to trust and act on their judgment, whatever its basis, is to encourage moral anarchy.

It is important to keep in mind that the judgment in question concerns the superiority of a standard; it is not a judgment about what act is right in the agent's situation. These questions are related but not identical. Before an agent is in a position to believe that an act dictated by an alternative standard is right, he must trust his judgment that that standard is superior to the conventional standard. But it does not follow *directly* from the fact that he is entitled to trust his judgment, that he should be encouraged to act on the alternative standard. One could also hold that there is a range of cases in which we should encourage agents to trust their judgments about the superiority of an alternative but not encourage them to violate conventional morality in its favor. Rather, we might encourage them to advocate their alternative while abiding by conventional morality. That is, we should encourage agents to adopt the attitude toward morality that many people argue they should adopt toward the law.

It is not obvious what limitations on trust and action are called for. Clearly, we want to encourage agents to trust and to act on their own judgment only if their own judgment is informed and considered. But it is not clear what we should count as informed and considered here. How much time and effort and what forms of reflection should we, as a society, require of someone before we encourage him to trust his judgment? To demand the type and quality of reflection required to get an A on a paper in a beginning ethics class is to withhold this right from 95 percent of the population. To demand significantly less could invite disaster. Moreover, it is not clear that agents who meet the requirement for trusting their judgments should be encouraged *always* to act on them. Certain categories of action may be prohibited no matter what an agent believes or what he has done to arrive at his beliefs. Suppose that after years of reflection a philosopher comes to believe that it is morally acceptable to torture intellectually inferior persons for his personal pleasure. Our moral code might encourage him to trust this judgment, arrived at after years of thought and effort. It might even encourage him to advocate it. But it may nonetheless discourage him from acting on it. With respect to certain areas of morality, we might say, no one is entitled to act on his personal judgment if it conflicts with conventional standards.

I will call standards that direct agents in these circumstances "first-person standards." First-person standards provide answers to (1) above in the cases of principled moral nonconformity. I will call standards by which the rest of us judge agents and their actions "third-person standards." Third-person standards provide answers to (2) above in this range of cases. It is tempting to assume that first-person standards and third-person standards will be symmetrical. In that case, if first-person standards direct an agent to trust his own judgment and violate conventional morality on their behalf, the rest of us should advise him to do the same and should approve of the act that expresses his judgment. But as we shall see, there is no necessity about this. Indeed, certain asymmetries may better promote the values at stake here.

Principled Moral Nonconformity: Limiting the Cases

Brandt's account of principled nonconformity is not only incomplete but also mistaken in an important range of cases. For there are conditions in which a fully rational informed adviser would not advise a member of S to act on the ideal morality for S, where that morality is not in place. If an agent believes that such conditions obtain, he is not obligated to act on the superior standard even if he believes it is superior. If an observer believes such conditions obtain, he ought not to advise an agent to do so or to condemn his failure to do so. Before we get to the hard cases, we need to narrow the field.

Suppose that we believe our criticism of some set of moral standards has succeeded. That is, suppose we have convinced ourselves that some alternative set S_b is superior to an existing set S_e (where S_b is either an entire morality or some portion of one). Why shouldn't our first-person standard require that we act on the standards of S_b and our third-person standard require us to approve of those who do so?

There are a number of reasons. To begin with, as we have seen, many moral standards are role specific, and role-specific standards presuppose certain institutional structures. The standards of S_e both define and are defined in relation to existing institutions. But the standards of S_b may presuppose institutional structures that are not currently in place. In that case it may be logically impossible to act in accordance with them, and the claim that one ought to do so will be empty. The preconditions for such actions will not arise. Suppose we live under a dictatorship, but we believe that dictatorships are immoral. That is, we believe that democratic institutions are the only morally defensible ones. It does not follow from this that we ought now to act on standards that would be in place were we living in a democracy. We cannot. It is the obligation of a citizen of a democracy not to sell his vote and to report any offer to buy it. But unless one lives in a democracy, the opportunity to do or refrain from doing such things cannot (logically) arise. So it is pointless to claim that we ought morally to do them or refrain from doing them. Similarly, we may believe that nonadversarial legal systems are morally superior to adversarial ones. Judges in nonadversarial legal systems are permitted to interrogate witnesses and defendants, and are morally required to do so in ways that help establish the truth. Judges in adversarial systems are not permitted to question witnesses or defendants (if they do, they invalidate the proceeding). So it is pointless to tell judges in adversarial systems that they are morally obligated to question witnesses fairly and impartially.[2]

This point presupposes that there is no difference in kind between evaluating moral standards and evaluating certain aspects of institutional design. This, of course, is a central tenet of ESA. Institutions are, among other things, sets of roles and positions. And questions of institutional design are, to a considerable extent, questions about distributions of rights and duties. The fact that the application of certain moral standards presupposes the existence of certain institutional structures simply means that certain moral options exist only because other more basic moral options have been chosen.

In any case, there are further problems. In some cases, it may be logically possible for someone to act on S_b but psychologically impossible for most people to do so. Accordingly, if "ought" implies "can," it is not necessarily the case that everyone convinced of the superiority of S_b is obligated to act on it. Moreover, whether we agreed with them or not, it would be foolish to condemn them morally for failing to do so. Suppose Jones believes that open marriages are morally superior to monogamous ones, which are standard in his society, but he realizes that it is psychologically impossible for him to conform to the requirements of an open marriage (e.g., to overcome sexual jealousy and possessiveness in himself and to regard them as a terrible vices in others). In that case, no reasonable standard would require him to do so, and no one with the relevant knowledge should condemn him for not doing so. The corresponding point holds if it is possible for Jones to change but only with considerable work, effort, or suffering. The price may be too high. Of course, the price of change must always be considered in relation to the importance of change. And to the extent that the changes are beneficial and affect greater numbers of people, we should expect people to pay a higher price.[3]

Another problem with requiring unconditional conformity to S_b is that if S_b is not in place, acting in accordance with it might make things worse with respect to the very values S_b is supposed to promote. Suppose that the condition of children in our society would be much improved if adults were required to take a significantly greater interest in their neighbor's children. Suppose further that a superior morality assigns us roughly the same rights and obligations toward our neighbor's children as we now have toward our nieces and nephews. We give them birthday presents, they make themselves at home in our houses, we give them advice about how to run their lives, we discuss their problems with their parents, and so forth. Were the relevant S_b in place, children would be happier and more open, parents would have more help and more free time, and relations between neighbors would be closer and more familial.

But the relevant S_b is not in place, and if we act as if it were, we risk creating many evils. We may deprive our own children of time, attention, and money that other children comparably situated receive from *their* parents. We thereby make them jealous and unhappy. Our unusual attention to neighbor children (under present conditions) may arouse the distrust of their parents and hence of the children themselves. Their parents, moreover, may regard our advice to their children as interference. In short, our relationships with our children, our neighbors, and our neighbors' children may deteriorate as a result of all this. Accordingly, we may undermine the very values S_b is supposed to promote. So it is foolish to act on it (although, barring the success of other arguments, we should act on it if we can do so without generating these consequences).

In other cases, acting on S_b instead of S_e is likely to interfere with the eventual adoption of S_b itself. Consider education. Suppose that S_b

requires grading according to the principles of cooperative learning, but that this system is prohibited by the rules of one's institution.[4] Were everyone who supported S_b to act on it, no one who supported the wider vision of education in which it is situated would retain her job (or, anyway, would advance in the system). In that case, there would be no chance of introducing acceptable elements of that vision now and little chance of *eventually* implementing it. Accordingly, we should not require that one act on it. (The fact that this form of argument is open to abuse does not mean there are no legitimate uses.)[5] Indeed, depending on the potentials of the situation, it is not clear that one should be permitted to act on it. Surrendering a post for the sake of principle but without gain can be a form of moral self-indulgence (if such acts inspire others, of course, the surrender is not without gain).

Principled Moral Nonconformity: The Harder Cases

The considerations we have just examined apply only to some S_b standards. In these cases the question of principled nonconformity is easily resolved. Either it is impossible to act on S_b or acting on it undermines the very goals that S_b is supposed to promote. Where this is the case one should be willing to do something to promote those goals, but one is not required to violate S_e for the sake of S_b. But there is a significant range of cases in which these considerations do not apply. What do our first-person standards require of us there? And what do our third-person standards tell us about advising and judging the actions of agents in this position?

If we were ideally rational and informed, there would be no problem. Obviously, we should then trust our judgment, and we should act on the standards of the superior morality in these cases. After all, if a standard is superior, and the conditions discussed in the last section do not apply, that standard would better promote and protect a rationally valued way of life. The problem arises because we are epistemically imperfect.

According to ESA, we establish the boundaries by considering the harms and benefits of the various alternatives. At one extreme, we might require people to distrust their unconventional judgments and to conform to prevailing standards in every area of life. Less radically, we might encourage them to trust those judgments that originate in certain ways but insist that they to conform to prevailing standards no matter what they themselves believe. Or, at the other extreme, we might require people to trust their own moral judgment in all cases, no matter how they arrive at their views, and to act on these conclusions no matter what others say or think.

It is useful to characterize third-person alternatives in relation to first-person options. At one extreme, we might encourage third parties always to advise agents to do what first-person standards would allow or require and to approve of all actions that satisfy first-person standards. At the other extreme, we might encourage third parties to advise agents against acting on standards that third parties reject and morally to disapprove all such actions. In this case we must decide what judgments should be made about the agents themselves. Here we might follow Brandt's suggestion that we condemn the action but exempt the agent from blame.[6] On the other hand, there may be cases in which we want to blame the agent as well. It is not blindingly obvious that our moral code should require us to withhold blame from people who advocate Nazi beliefs even if they arrive at these beliefs in a manner that satisfies first-person standards.[7]

I cannot here attempt to defend a set of first- and third-person standards that are specific enough to settle a significant range of cases. That is a highly complex question of application. What is reasonable for one society and set of historical circumstances may not be reasonable for another. And, to add to the complexity, our standards may turn out to be domain sensitive as well; for example, it may be harder to justify principled moral nonconformity in relation to the duties of public office than to justify principled nonconformity in sexual matters between consenting adults. What I can do here is illustrate how ESA approaches this issue.

Principled Moral Nonconformity: The ESA Approach

As should be clear by now, the ESA strategy is to consider the harms and benefits of the various alternatives and to design standards that achieve the most favorable balance. We might begin by considering the harms of nonconformist action.

To begin with, violations of existing standards can be very disturbing to some people. Most of us learn these standards as children, and we develop an allegiance to them. That others conform to them contributes importantly to our sense that the world is a good and decent place. And this feeling is very important. It is very depressing to believe one lives in a world of wickedness or barbarism, and these beliefs also undermine one's moral resolve. In addition, violation of S_e threatens our sense of stability and order. We plan our lives, or want to be able to plan our lives, with the expectation that there will be widespread conformity to certain standards. Violations of these standards make the world seem less predictable and other people seem less trustworthy. This lack of trust is a psychological and a material burden. It restricts the range of psychologically rewarding human relationships, and it restricts the scope and raises the costs of cooperative activity.[8]

But these considerations are not terribly weighty. To begin with, little such damage is done by acts that are performed discretely. Further, to the extent that a society is pluralistic, it must encourage its members to be relaxed about differences. This does not mean that we should regard nothing as wicked or barbarous. But we should reserve these responses to acts that violate moral sensibilities because they do significant damage of other kinds. Indeed, to the extent that people are distressed by nonconformity per se they will be perpetually distressed. Technological changes and economic changes create social change, and moral change is an inevitable and welcome consequence of social change. But moral change is never instantaneous. Societies with a rapid rate of change do well to develop tolerant attitudes to nonconformity per se.

A second set of worries is more significant. All manner of evil may be justified in the name of a superior morality. Leopold and Loeb believed it was permissible to murder an innocent young boy because they believed ordinary moral standards did not apply to superior people like themselves. Some members of the KKK kill, intimidate, and promote hatred because they believe that it is morally required of them. By encouraging principled nonconformist action, we also risk principled nonconformity on the side of evil. Conservatives since Edmund Burke have stressed the potential harms of radical breaks with our moral traditions, and history has too often vindicated their fears.

These deficits must be balanced against the benefits of principled nonconformity. Perhaps most importantly, principled moral nonconformity provides us with a safeguard against socially sanctioned injustice, oppression, and madness. The grim history of our species abounds with social moralities that promote hideous suffering and other evils on a grand scale. The moralities of Stalinism, Nazism, and apartheid are just the most recent and dramatic examples. Principled moral nonconformists helped save some people from the horrors of Nazism, and at least accelerated the fall of Soviet communism and South African apartheid. In America, they were also instrumental in winning civil rights for women and minorities. In general, the more we encourage and train people to think for themselves and act on their conclusions, the more resistance there will be to the mass hysteria and mass indoctrination on which socially sanctioned evil often depends.

By discouraging nonconformity, moreover, not only do we discourage resistance to socially sanctioned evil, but we also discourage perhaps useful forms of social experimentation, relatively harmless forms of self-expression, and criticism of our basic institutions and practices. People engage in such criticism in part because they hope to find a better way to live. If we had to abide by prevailing standards no matter how absurd we took them to be, we would have less incentive to reflect.[9] Discouraging critical reflection is particularly dangerous in times of rapid social change. The faster the change, the faster prevailing standards become obsolete.

As suggested, we do not have to make a blanket decision in favor of or against principled nonconformity. Instead, we can devise standards that tend on the whole to encourage useful instances and discourage harmful ones. As we have also seen, two strategies are available to us. First, we can assign epistemic burdens to nonconformist beliefs. And second, we can exclude certain categories of action *completely* (e.g., torture and cold-blooded murder). In relation to these acts, no one is permitted to act on nonconformist standards, no matter how much time and energy he has spent arriving at them. One might be free to advocate an alternative, but not to act on it.

Roughly, the greater the impact that switching to an alternative standard is likely to have, the more work one must do before trusting one's judgment that his alternative is superior. The higher the stakes, the more one is required to check one's facts, review one's reasoning, seriously consider objections, and so forth. We should not regard it as a basic moral right to form beliefs about important issues without having thought seriously about them.

As suggested, there may be justifiable asymmetries between first-person standards and third-person standards. Since first-person standards are directed at agents, the epistemic burdens attached to them are process-related. One is entitled to trust one's judgment if one arrives at it in the right way. But third-person standards ought not to require us to advise or to judge on the basis of the agent's process. To do so would be to discourage important forms of moral discussion and to insist that observers abandon their own moral perspective. Assuming that judgment is improved when disagreements are aired, this is a foolish policy. Rather, if we are called upon to advise or to judge, we should require that an agent make a good case for his standard. In most cases, if he cannot make a good case for his alternative standard, our job is to advise him to abandon it and, if he does not, to disapprove of acts that express it (unless we have reasons to trust his judgment at least as much as our own). We may, however, want to acknowledge certain classes of exceptions. In certain contexts, we might encourage advisers to respect certain standards even if they are not convinced by them. Contemporary American morality treats religiously generated standards this way. In certain contexts, we do not advise people against acting on these standards even if we reject the standards themselves (especially in cases where acting on these standards mainly affects the agent).

These considerations tell us how to evaluate actions, not agents. In particular, they do not tell us when we have a right to blame. As the enormous literature on responsibility, blame, and moral luck indicates, this is a difficult and complicated problem. Here as elsewhere, however, ESA directs us to adopt the policy that promotes the most good.[10] To decide this we must decide what useful functions, if any, blaming serves in our moral life. The answer to this question is not obvious. If it is in fact possible and most beneficial to hate the sin but not the sinner in these cases, we should encourage that policy. But arguably, that is not possible.[11]

Thus far we have been considering first- and third-person standards in relation to principled nonconformity. It is worth mentioning that comparable considerations may arise in relation to conformity. To the extent that we reasonably value critical reflection, we cannot hold that agents must conform to prevailing standards merely because they prevail. At the very least, our first-person standards should require that agents reflect on the standards on which they act and that they consider opposing viewpoints. The question is whether our first-person standards here should be any less demanding than our first-person standards in the nonconformist case. In fact, we do give the benefit of the doubt to prevailing standards. We need to decide whether, or in what range of cases, this makes good sense.

A corresponding question arises in relation to third-person standards. Opponents of conventional standards may be called upon to advise and to judge the acts of those who favor them. Again, if we reasonably value moral dialogue, we should encourage them to advise others against conforming to conventional standards and to criticize the relevant conformist acts. However, here, as in the first-person case, we must decide whether to favor conventional standards as such, that is, whether to make it a consideration in favor of a standard that it is generally accepted. If we do, critics of conventional standards will need stronger arguments in favor of their alternatives than supporters of conventional standards will need in favor of theirs.

Moral Motivation

I turn now to the second problem generated by the questions "What does morality require of me?" and "How shall I judge the actions and character of others?," namely, the question of moral motivation. As it is usually understood, to solve this problem is to answer the question "Why be moral?"

If we believe that moral worth is the supreme measure of human worth, this problem is easily handled. In that case we might echo Kant's pronouncement that the only thing unconditionally good is the good will or insist with Socrates in the *Crito* that wrong doing "mutilates the best part of us." But it is difficult to see how we can hold that moral worth is the supreme measure of human worth unless one holds that morality is somehow constitutive of an independent and supreme realm of values. And if we subscribe to an instrumental theory of ethics we must deny these claims. On instrumental views, moral standards are implements to promote and protect values of other kinds. Moreover, they are not supreme in any interesting sense. On an instrumental account, there will be cases in which moral standards are properly overridden by considerations of other kinds (for example, in which one is permitted to break a promise to produce great music, or perfect some important talent, etc.).[12]

ESA, and other instrumental accounts, do allow us to speak of good persons and bad persons. But we can do so only in a (roughly) Humean way. Good people are people who have qualities that are desirable from an impartial point of view. Bad people have qualities that are undesirable. In a rational society, there will be advantages to being a good person. Indeed, the reward system of a rational society encourages goodness and discourages badness. It also encourages people to value goodness intrinsically. In this way it will narrow the gap between morality and self-interest. But it is doubtful that any actual human society can educate its members to value moral goodness intrinsically to such an extent that it can close that gap completely. In any actual society, there will be times when almost anyone might better promote his own good by acting immorally. So given a Humean account, the question "Why be moral?" remains for them.

In this section I will present the most promising answer to this question available to an instrumentalist. If this answer is sound, all instrumentalist theories (including ESA) have a solution to the standard problem of moral motivation. But, for reasons that will be familiar enough, I do not think it is sound.[13] On the other hand, I do not think that this matters much. Here I will defend Bernard Williams's view that the consequences of our inability to convince the amoralist by reasons are much exaggerated. Nothing important is threatened by our failure to do it.[14]

Let us simplify matters by considering the strongest argument in relation to the hardest case. The hardest case is the Hobbesian egoist. The Hobbesian egoist takes no interest at all in the good of others. He is interested only in maximizing the satisfaction of his own desires, and his own desires are entirely egocentric (i.e., they are desires for his own sensual pleasure, wealth, power, etc.). What reason has such a person to be moral?

Our attitudes toward him are clear enough. He is a kind of monster. But what argument can we use to get him to change? We might tell him that we are the same sort of creature he is, so that if his good matters, so does ours. Surely the burden of proof is on him to describe a difference between him and us such that his pain matters and ours does not. If he cannot do this he is simply making a distinction without a difference.

But the Hobbesian egoist is not convinced. His familiar response to this argument is that there is a difference between our pain and his pain, namely, that he feels his pain. This gives him a reason to care about his pain that he does not have in relation to ours. He acknowledges that we have a comparable reason in relation to our own pain. Our pain reasonably matters to us, and his pain reasonably matters to *him*. If his pain also matters to us, so much the better for him. However, he does not see why it should matter to us, and he doesn't see why our pain should matter to him.

We might reply in four familiar ways. First, we might say that our pain should matter to him because it is pain, and pain is an evil. Anyone who understands what pain is knows that. To deny that pain is an evil is simply irrational. If this is right, ESA has as sound an answer to the question of moral motivation as any other approach to ethics. That is certainly good enough.

But I am not convinced that this answer is right. The amoralist can deny that pain, in general, is an evil. He will certainly deny this if it is supposed to entail that everyone has a reason to care about every pain. He claims he has a reason to care only about *his* pain. That is because only his pain matters to him, and he claims he has a reason to care about something only if it matters to him (or, better, only if it would matter to him from an epistemically ideal point of view). It is not clear that this involves a logical error.

We might say that other people's pain would matter to him from an epistemically ideal position. This is our second response. We might put this by saying that the actual amoralist simply lacks a capacity, the capacity to vividly imagine another's pain. We claim that if he had that capacity he would realize that another person's pain should matter. But he may plausibly reply that we are merely projecting contingent features of our own psychology onto him. He *can* in fact vividly imagine the suffering of others. Sometimes it is a matter of indifference to him. Sometimes it gives him pleasure. The fact that we respond otherwise is a contingent fact about how we are built. This may give us a reason to care, but it does not give him one. He has no more reason to care about us than a rational shark would.

Third, we might object that the egoist's perspective is partisan. If he considered the question from an impartial point of view, he would see he has a reason to care. But the familiar rejoinder to this has merit. Why is the egoist rationally required to adopt that point of view? He believes in partiality. That is the very essence of his position. And he is challenging us to tell him why he should change. To insist without argument that he should look at things impartially is to beg the question. Finally, we might try to convince him that he would be better off in his own terms were he a constrained maximizer. Again, if this is right, ESA has a solid answer to the problem of moral motivation. But again, I do not think it is right. The general reason for my dissatisfaction is familiar enough. Simply put, in a wide variety of cases, the clever phoney does better than the constrained maximizer in Hobbesian terms. Even if this is wrong, the constrained maximizer approach provides only a partial solution to the traditional problem. As David Gauthier and other supporters acknowledge, the constrained maximizer does better than the unconstrained maximizer only under a carefully delineated range of conditions. Moreover, even given those conditions, the upper limits of sacrifice it is rational for him to make for the sake of morality may be far below what morality requires of him.

In sum, I think we can offer no reasons to be moral that are logically compelling for amoralists in general. But what is so terrible about that? Why are we so worried about convincing the amoralist by arguments to begin with? Bernard Williams is among the few philosophers to recognize that there is not much worth worrying about here, but his treatment of the issue is too heavily rhetorical.[15] In what follows, I will defend this minority position.

Of course, it is desirable to convince the amoralist to be moral by reasons. If we could convince him to be moral, he would behave better because he believed in behaving better. In that case, we would not need to threaten him with reprisals or manipulate him by psychological conditioning to get him to do so. Also, if we must judge him badly or punish him for his failures he will know what he did wrong, and he will acknowledge the justice of his punishment.

However, we can (and do) live without these advantages. Moreover, our failure to achieve them in no way undermines the ESA account of the nature and justification of moral standards. It remains rational for groups to adopt moralities. It remains rational for groups to justify and criticize moralities in relation to how well they promote reasonably valued ways of life. And it remains rational for groups to enforce their moralities. Thus, our judgments about the amoralist remain valid. We can continue to say that he violates other people's rights. And we can continue to complain with vehemence and indignation that he is a cruel, self-centered, untrustworthy, sleazy, slimy, poor excuse for a human being. It may not matter to him that he is that way, but it certainly matters to us. And the fact that it does not matter to him should not change that at all.

Indeed, the amoralist himself cannot plausibly deny that we can legitimately make these judgments of him. If ESA is correct, he must admit that moralities can be more or less rational for a group. He must also admit that there is such a thing as applying moral standards to particular cases and that our standards warrant the ascription of unflattering adjectives to people who act as he does. He simply denies that any of this should matter to *him*. Although he wants to appear virtuous for strategic reasons, it does not matter to him that he is not genuinely so. This is unfortunate for us. It creates serious practical problems. But it threatens nothing important philosophically, and it calls for no changes in our conduct or attitude.

Why then are philosophers so threatened by the fact that they cannot convince the amoralist with reasons? I suspect there are two sorts of explanations. First, if we cannot convince *him* with reasons, we might think that we do not have reasons either. After all, the amoralist is rational, and reasons should be reasons for all rational agents. His resistance challenges our complacency. Perhaps we should rid ourselves of our unreasonable and self-limiting attachment to morality. Perhaps we should become as *he* is.

But the fact that he is not rationally compelled to care about others does not entail that it is irrational for us to. What counts as a reason for one rational agent need not count as a reason for every other. One can acknowledge this without being an internalist. One need only hold that having a certain desire or ideal is a sufficient condition of having a reason. Thus, we may have a reason to be moral because we subscribe to a certain specific ideal (e.g., justice). Or, we may be so constituted psychologically that we do not want to be villains, knaves, or rotten human beings. Or, other people's pain may matter to us. Or, we may want to see ourselves as part of a wider whole or identify our good with the good of others. Characteristics like these give us reasons to be moral. The fact that we cannot convince the amoralist to be like us by reasons does not mean that he can convince us to be like him.

The amoralist might insist that it is irrational for us to have the characteristics in question to begin with. But almost every member of a normal human community has them. And it is not obvious that we would be better off as individuals were we to try to transform ourselves into Hobbesian egoists. The transformation costs would be high. And, more importantly, we would be surrendering a good deal of satisfaction and fulfillment. It is certainly arguable that we are happier by virtue of our sympathetic connections with other individuals. In any case, the burden is now on the Hobbesian egoist to show that we are not. And it is hard to see how he can carry that burden.

There is another reason that some philosophers are threatened by our inability to convince the amoralist by reasons. They want to condemn the amoralist, but they are worried that we cannot reasonably condemn or punish someone merely for acting rationally. But we do not condemn the amoralist merely for acting rationally. We condemn him for being selfish, unjust, deceitful, cruel, etc. We do not accept "I acted rationally" (in the relevant sense) as a justification for or an exoneration from that sort of conduct. Why should the fact that someone acted intelligently from a tactical or strategic point of view undermine these judgments? Clearly there is no necessary connection between being a good person and being a good planner. Had the Nazis been somewhat better planners, they would not have been somewhat better people. As I argued in chapter 2, it is entirely unclear why anything noble or great should attach to the capacity for strategic and tactical planning. To regard this as a general excuse for evil is disastrous from the standpoint of ESA (or any remotely plausible moral theory).

In sum, nothing catastrophic follows from the fact that we cannot convince a Hobbesian egoist to be moral by rational argument. There is also something decidedly academic about our concern to do so. The idea that we could convince any actual Hobbesian egoist in this way is foolish and arrogant. Egoistic rapists, murderers, and torturers already know that their victims are people very much like themselves and that their victims feel pain. The suffering of others just does not matter to them. We are not going to change this by argument. Most philosophers recognize this. They are not looking for arguments that will convince actual egoists, but arguments that *should* convince them. But what do we gain by that? As I have argued, we do not need such arguments to condemn cruelty, treachery, selfishness, and so forth and to condemn the people disposed to them.

On the other hand, there is a very real and pressing problem of moral motivation, namely, how best to promote moral motives and ideals in a population. To the extent that we can do this, we can reduce the conflict between morality and self-interest, and to the extent that we can do *that*, we achieve the authentic advantages that some hope to achieve by convincing the amoralist with reasons. People will more often behave morally, they will do so for the right reasons, and they will accept criticism or punishment for immoral actions without resentment.

Not surprisingly, the real problem of moral motivation is motivational. The problem is to change what people want and feel. It is unclear how best to do this. But it is a mistake to focus on the hardest case: the authentic, full-grown, hardened Hobbesian egoists. It is unclear what will work with them. At this point, we do not know how to change a sociopath.

Barring unlikely genetic explanations, the existence of authentic Hobbesian egoists represents a social failure. In a well-ordered society, normal people develop strong attachments to other people, and a certain measure of general sympathy or compassion. They also have a reasonably strong desire to be good people (i.e., to live up to certain ideals). The real problem of moral motivation is to develop these traits on a wide scale, that is, to convert our society into a well-ordered one. To discover how to do this we need to focus as much on our successes as on our failures.

The problem of moral motivation is sometimes confused with a related problem: how much is one required to sacrifice for morality? In practice, this question arises when people face hard choices. If one blows the whistle on the company, one may lose one's job and never work in one's field again. If one tells the truth to prevent the conviction of an innocent man, one goes to jail. As ESA suggests, we should not expect a general answer to the sacrifice question. Like almost everything else about morality, degree of sacrifice questions are domain sensitive. In some domains, people are expected to risk their lives to do their duty (e.g., soldiers, police officers, firemen, and medical personnel). In other domains such serious sacrifice is rarely called for. In general, then, standards of sacrifice are domain sensitive and are justified in just the same way other standards are.

Notes

1. Actually, this is a slight improvement. The more familiar formulation is "which, if generally adopted, would maximize utility." But this is much less plausible than the current suggestion. We are interested in the utility generated by making a set of rules a part of a social morality. This is not the same as the utility generated by everyone's following those rules. In the former case compliance will always be partial. And in some cases rules which would generate great utility if universally adopted would be disastrous if violated by just 5 percent of the population. Consider the pair "Always speak truthfully to strangers" and "Always trust what strangers say." If 5 percent were unscrupulously dishonest, the remaining 95 percent would be thoroughly and consistently victimized.

2. Since Brandt denies that role obligations are moral obligations, he will not be moved by such examples.

3. Moral attitudes in relation to race and gender are a good example. These attitudes obviously affect large numbers of people in very fundamental ways. Over the last thirty years, they have changed considerably. One reason for this is that those who saw the evils of the old system were committed to acting on new and superior standards (and insisting that others do the same). They felt this way in part because our first-person standard insists on principled nonconformity when the stakes are this high. When so much is at stake, we are required to make the difficult changes demanded by the superior morality and to insist that others do the same. Those who recognized the evils of the old system but refused to try to change in this way were rightly condemned as hypocrites.

Many people sincerely opposed these changes and condemned people who favored them for violating existing standards. Had existing standards been justified, this would have been reasonable. The higher the stakes, the less room third-person standards leave for principled nonconformity. Those of us who supported these changes condemned these people as racists, sexists, and reactionaries. We applied a third-person standard to their acts just as they applied a third-person standard to ours. In neither case did the fact that someone acted from conscience excuse or justify his acts in the eyes of the other.

4. Here students are graded in part by how well other students perform. Typically, a class is divided into groups of mixed skill levels. The brighter students in each group are instructed to help the slower students. And everyone's grade depends in part on how much everyone else improves over the term. This technique has apparently turned out to be effective in a wide range of cases.

5. Some people who held positions under the Nazis probably excused themselves by saying that by acting on the superior alternative they would impede the wider realization of that alternative. But like any reasoning open to abuse, the question of abuse is decided by the facts of the case. We need to determine how bad the prevailing morality is, what chance we have to

implement aspects of the alternative, just how important *those* aspects are, and so forth. Moreover, our prospects of implementing the alternative will depend in part on our prospects of remaining uncorrupted. Often, those prospects are slim. Most people are importantly influenced by the people they work among. And most people are tempted to adopt the going "justifications" for the evils with which they will be complicit if they work within a corrupt institutional setting.

6. Brandt says that we should do this when the agent is ignorant of the ideally rational standard but is not culpable for his ignorance. Agents who arrive at their beliefs in a manner that satisfies first person requirements should not be culpable (Brandt, *Theory of the Good and the Right*, pp. 300–305).

7. It is ridiculously optimistic to assume that one could not arrive at morally distasteful beliefs in this way. First-person standards are process-related. They place restrictions on the process one must undergo in arriving at and sustaining his belief. But process restrictions do not guarantee rational conclusions. People are obviously vulnerable to all manner of error in reasoning, interpretation, and evaluation. Often, there is a strong tendency toward partiality in one's own favor or in favor of one's group. One may also be strongly attracted to certain positions by virtue of certain personality traits.

8. It is commonly said that we also have a promissory obligation to others with respect to existing standards. I have never seen the force of this. The promising in question is quite strange. On one version, it is supposed to be tacit, not explicit. By conforming to existing standards we are supposed to tacitly signal our consent to them. But there are many familiar problems with tacit consent, especially in associations that are not fully voluntary. And it is arguable that membership in a society is not fully voluntary (many people do not enter it by choice and do not have the resources to leave without enormous sacrifice). In any case, on tacit consent accounts the amoralist can escape the force of moral rules by simply announcing that his conformity to them should not be regarded as a promise to continue to conform.

Perhaps to escape objections of this kind, some consequentialists have moved from tacit to hypothetical consent. We consent hypothetically to a system if we would consent to it were we fully informed and fully rational. But given what is usually meant by "fully informed and fully rational," the class of standards to which we would consent hypothetically would very rarely if ever be the class of existing standards. Moreover, even if one could make sense of the claim that hypothetical consent generates an obligation, it is hard to understand how that obligation is promissory.

9. We would, of course, complain a lot. At least some of the current chaos in Eastern Europe is present because people under communism were not allowed to act in a manner consistent with their alternative visions of society or human relations. Because there appeared to be no possibility of changing existing institutions and practices, there was little incentive for serious thinking about alternatives (and no institutional support for this).

10. Thus, as I argued in "Blame and Bad Wills" (a address to the Society for Philosophy and Social Affairs, Pacific Division, APA, March 1988), we should not adopt standards that require us to identify certain internal conditions of a person (e.g., could he have resisted his impulse, did he try hard enough?). Nor should we base our judgments on certain inner states we can identify. Although a failed attempt at murder may be characterized by the same inner state as a successful attempt, there may be good instrumental reasons for regarding successes as more seriously wrong than attempts. But I cannot pursue this here.

11. Blame, I would argue, goes beyond merely judging that someone is responsible for doing something wrong. It also involves a negative attitude toward that person (roughly, one holds it against the person that he did what he did). Blame is eradicated by forgiveness. But one may forgive someone without surrendering the judgment that he did something wrong. Questions about the usefulness of blame, therefore, are questions about the usefulness of this attitude. That is, if you will, they are questions about the usefulness of holding moral grudges. I argue for this in "Rationality, Responsibility and Blame," *Canadian Journal of Philosophy*, 17, Spring 1987.

12. Of course, one can defend the supremacy of the moral by simply defining the morally right thing to do as the best thing to do, all things considered. But in that case the claim that morality is supreme is uninteresting. When we wonder about the supremacy of the moral, we have in mind cases in which moral considerations (or standards) favor one course of action, and considerations of another sort favor another course of action. These other considerations are usually identified as prudential, but that is not the only important case. Moral considerations can also conflict with aesthetic considerations, religious considerations, educational considerations, etc. When this occurs, it is not a foregone conclusion that moral considerations should prevail. For a discussion of this question see Michael Philips, "Moralism and the Good," *Philosophical Studies*, 52, no. 1, July 1987.

13. The question "Why be moral?" is among the most often discussed questions in ethics during the last fifty years. The literature is enormous and highly repetitive. To get to my thesis, I must make familiar objections to familiar arguments. It would be tedious and difficult to trace these arguments to their original sources in the literature, and I hope I will be excused from that responsibility. But I obviously owe much to Kai Nielsen's work on this topic.

14. Bernard Williams, *Ethics and the Limits of Philosophy*, Harvard University Press, Cambridge, Mass., 1985, chapter 10.

15. Williams, *Ethics and the Limits of Philosophy*.

Index

a/distribution: choosing between
patterns, 141–48; critique of
Rawslean and utilitarian views,
97–98; as domain sensitive, 141; ESA
approach, 97–99; example of
educational goods, 144–48; no
uniquely rational principle for,
97–98; and problem of ignorance,
98–99; summary of ESA position, 8;
absolute good: *See* goods (and evils);
objectivist theories
act utilitarianism: possibility of
metaphysical and instrumental
versions, 121 n9; *see also* hedonic
goods; rule utilitarianism
affirmative action: and group-related
standards, 93
amoralism: absence of logically
compelling reason for amoralist to
be moral, 194–95; judging the
amoralist's acts and character,
196–97; summary of ESA position, 9
animals (nonhuman): moral capacities
of, 65 n11; as practical agents, 55–56
applied ethics: and constancy
assumption, 100; and domain
specific standards, 94; engineering
model, 94; *see also* business ethics;
family ethics; medical ethics; police
ethics
Aristotelian ethics: account of virtues
compared to ESA, 150 n10; and
character traits, 161; as teleolgical

competitor to ESA 70, 120 n2; *see
also* character traits; virtues (and
vices)
autonomy: autonomous choice, 66
n18; Dworkin's account, 66 n14; and
ESA 61; as instrumental value for
FPR moralities, 57–58; in medicine,
111; and preference satisfaction
accounts of the good, 72, 77–79; and
supportive lies, 126 n36; as
supposedly protected by moralities
grounded in formal practical reason,
52–53; *see also* formal conception of
practical reason; paternalism
axiological arguments: argument
against constancy in relation to
goods, 140; distinguished from
consequential arguments, 128;
estimating costs and benefits,
138–41; possibility of rational
disagreement, 134; strategies
discussed, 132–41; *see also* illusory
values; poor prospects

background theories: and defense of
intuitionism, 29–32; and wide
reflective equilibrium, 37–42
Baier, Kurt: and rules of superiority for
weighing moral reasons 22, 43 n4,
123 n20
bare difference (in weight of moral
considerations): *See* constancy
assumptions